PAKISTAN

This book is part of a series, Comparative Politics
and International Studies

Series editor, Christophe Jaffrelot

This series focuses on the transformation of politics and societies by international and domestic factors, including culture and religion. Analysing these changes in a sociological and historical perspective, it pays attention to trends from below as much as state interventions and the interaction of both.

MARIAM ABOU ZAHAB

Pakistan

A Kaleidoscope of Islam

HURST & COMPANY, LONDON

First published in the United Kingdom in 2020 by
C. Hurst & Co. (Publishers) Ltd.,
41 Great Russell Street, London, WC1B 3PL
© Mariam Abou Zahab and the Contributors, 2020
All rights reserved.
Printed in India

The right of Mariam Abou Zahab and the Contributors to be
identified as the authors of this publication is asserted by them
in accordance with the Copyright, Designs and Patents Act, 1988.

A Cataloguing-in-Publication data record for this book
is available from the British Library.

ISBN: 9781787383227

A version of the Preface was originally published as an obituary in the *Herald*'s
December 2017 issue and has been adapted here by Laurent Gayer, with
kind permission of his original co-authors and the *Herald*. Chapter 2 was first
published in 2007 in *The Other Shiites* (eds Monsutti, Naef & Sabahi), and is
reproduced here with the kind permission of Peter Lang Publishing. Chapter
3 was first published in 2002 in *Pakistan: The Contours of State and Society* (eds
Mumtaz, Racine & Ali), and is reproduced here with the kind permission of
Oxford University Press (Karachi). Chapter 4 was published in 2004 in *Lived
Islam in South Asia* (eds Ahmad & Reifeld) and is reproduced here with the
kind permission of Oxford University Press (Karachi). Chapters 1 and 10 are
reproduced with the kind permission of their co-author, Olivier Roy.

This book is printed using paper from registered sustainable
and managed sources.

www.hurstpublishers.com

PUBLISHER'S NOTE

Chapters 1 and 5–10 of the present volume were first published by Hurst in the following works:

Chapter 1—Mariam Abou Zahab & Olivier Roy, *Islamist Networks*, 2004.

Chapter 5—Laurent Gayer & Christophe Jaffrelot (eds), *Armed Militias of South Asia: Fundamentalists, Maoists and Separatists*, 2009.

Chapter 6—Roel Meijer (ed.), *Global Salafism: Islam's New Religious Movement*, 2009.

Chapter 7—Magnus Marsden & Benjamin D. Hopkins (eds), *Beyond Swat: History, Society and Economy along the Afghanistan-Pakistan Frontier*, 2013.

Chapter 8—Jeevan Deol & Zaheer Kazmi (eds), *Contextualising Jihadi Thought*, 2012.

Chapter 9—Brigitte Maréchal & Sami Zemni (eds), *The Dynamics of Sunni-Shia Relationships: Doctrine, Transnationalism, Intellectuals and the Media*, 2013.

Chapter 10—Mariam Abou Zahab & Olivier Roy, *Islamist Networks: The Afghan-Pakistan Connection*, 2004.

CONTENTS

CONTENTS

PART FOUR
TRANSNATIONAL JIHADI-SUNNI SECTARIAN CONVERGENCES

PREFACE

SCHOLAR WITH A CAUSE

Laurent Gayer, with additional contributions by
Amélie Blom, Aminah Mohammad-Arif, Zia ur Rehman, and Paul Rollier

In 2008, French scholar Mariam Abou Zahab met with Abdullah Anas, a known Algerian Islamist and veteran of the Afghan Jihad, over dinner on the sidelines of a conference in London. At some point, the conversation turned to Afghanistan, and Abou Zahab—who was conversing with him in Arabic—mentioned how dear the country was to her heart. Anas's interest was piqued, and he asked her if she had travelled to the war-torn country during the 1980s. She replied that she had indeed spent a considerable amount of time there. 'But what were you doing in Afghanistan? Were you a journalist?' asked Anas, only to see his interlocutor shake her head in denial. A few more questions followed as he tried to probe this enigmatic French woman further. Was she an aid worker there, or a scholar? he asked. She was visibly amused and continued to answer in the negative. 'So, what were you doing in Afghanistan?', Anas asked in desperation. 'Jihad' replied Abou Zahab with a smile.

According to a witness of this exchange, her laconic answer petrified Anas, who was still struggling with the stigma of his militant past. 'He was so shocked that he did not dare ask for precise details. He just

ix

clung to his chair and waited for the conversation to move on,' the witness recalls. Those present were left wondering what she could have meant by her ambiguous statement.

This was not the first time that Mariam Jan, as her Afghan friends affectionately called her, had left her audience high and dry after arousing its curiosity; not to say that she was secretive—she merely had a gift for dissuading others from enquiring further about her past lives. For like a cat, she lived several lives, until cancer took her away on 1 November 2017 in Paris.

Longing for new horizons

Mariam Abou Zahab was born Marie-Pierre Walquemanne in 1952 in Hon-Hergie, a village in northern France. She hailed from a family of small-scale industrialists and grew up in a Catholic environment. Feeling somewhat restricted in this milieu, her desire for new horizons manifested itself early on. Moving to Paris was a first step in this direction. At the age of seventeen, she passed the entrance examination for the prestigious Institute of Political Studies (better known as Sciences Po) and graduated three years later.

At age twenty, she showed an inclination for travelling on the cheap. In 1972, she bought an inter-Europe train ticket and accompanied her elder brother on a tour of European capitals. As she later confided to one of her closest friends, Marie-France Mourrégot, the two siblings were briefly detained by the Italian police after they were found sleeping in a park. After their release they went back home, but the train ticket was still valid, so she decided to hit the road again, returning to Warsaw on her own.

The following year, she travelled overland to India. It was during those years (1973–4) that she discovered Afghanistan and Pakistan, as well as the Indian city of Lucknow—to which she would remain particularly attached. Her remarkable linguistic skills—alongside political science, she studied Hindi/Urdu and Arabic at the National Institute of Oriental Languages and Civilisations (INALCO) and would later learn Persian, Pashto and Punjabi as well—allowed her to engage deeper with these societies than other travellers. Her conversion to Islam, made official at the Great Mosque of Paris in 1975, also contributed to her acculturation. After becoming a self-declared Shia, Marie-Pierre gave way to Mariam.

Her conversion was rather unusual in mid-1970s France, although some prominent intellectuals and artists of the time were attracted to the mystic traditions of Shiism, starting with the famed choreographer Maurice Béjart, who was initiated into Islam by the Iranian Sufi master Nur Ali Elahi in 1973.

If her conversion estranged her from her original milieu, it was also a matter of concern for her husband. Nazem Abou Zahab, a young Syrian whom she had met in Damascus and whom she married in 1976, came from a Sunni middle-class family with a secular orientation and, as he told us, he found his spouse's turn to religion rather disturbing. In those days of political upheaval throughout the Middle East, spiritual matters were not the only thing on her mind, however.

Activism without borders

When Mariam Abou Zahab settled in Damascus in the mid-1970s, she was no stranger to political activism. Five years earlier, she had responded to the call of French novelist and former minister of cultural affairs, André Malraux, to form an 'international brigade' in support of Bengali nationalists in East Pakistan. And when this project failed to materialise, she did spend some time in the war-torn eastern wing of Pakistan alongside several French intellectuals influenced by Maoism. Although she did not share these young men's infatuation with Mao's Little Red Book, she remained a defender of the oppressed throughout her adult life—a 'revolutionary' commitment that, far from working against her religious devotion, went along with it. Her fascination with Shia Islam had a strong mystical component as well as an aesthetic and a scholastic one. It also fuelled her public interventions and was nurtured by them in return. She was, after all, a child of May 1968—as attested by a number of books in her library devoted to the social movement of the era that changed the face of French politics and society.

After having taken the side of the Bengalis in 1971, she became an active sympathiser of the Palestinian liberation struggle. In 1975, before settling in Damascus, she made her first trip to Beirut where she met Issam Sartawi, an early supporter of peace negotiations with Israel. It is unclear if she shared his political views, but she remained close to him until his assassination by Abu Nidal Organisation militants in Portugal in April 1983.

She was not an armchair activist and she faced up to the violence that was engulfing her world. During the spring of 1983, after separating from her husband, she briefly took up arms in the ranks of the pro-Arafat faction of the PLO. For a couple of weeks or so, she took part in combat in the Bekaa Valley, opposing the pro-Syrian faction of Fatah led by Abu Musa—an episode which she related to one of her former comrades at Sciences Po, Elizabeth Picard, who at that time was completing her PhD on Hafiz El Assad's 'corrective movement' in Syria.

Mariam Abou Zahab's close proximity to notorious Palestinian militants attracted the attention of French intelligence agencies. (Between 1980 and 1982, several attacks against Jewish restaurants and religious places were recorded in Paris; Palestinian terrorism remained a source of concern throughout Europe in the following years). She was even interrogated by France's leading anti-terrorist judge, Jean-Louis Bruguière. She would later claim that she was denied entry to the French ministry of foreign affairs because of her Palestinian acquaintances.

The making of Sheenogai

Mariam Abou Zahab was a participant observer of most of the crises that affected the Middle East and West Asia from the early 1970s onwards. She also made a transition from supporting secular freedom struggles to aiding holy wars—as the region at large did. In the early 1980s, she was more involved than ever in the Palestinian movement even though she had already started spending more time alongside the Afghan mujahidin.

Persistent rumours over the decades have suggested that she could have been involved in military activities against the Soviets on the behalf of the mujahidin. In the mid-1980s, an article in the French magazine *Actuel* even suggested that she was heading a band of Afghan fighters in southern Afghanistan. While fuelling her legend, these rumours remain unsubstantiated. If she did fight with and for the Afghans, it was essentially by distributing financial aid to villagers affected by the war and occasionally to local mujahidin commanders so as to legitimise her presence and that of her organisation among them. As a volunteer for Afrane, a French non-government organisation she had been associated with from 1982 onwards, she also provided medical care to the sick and the wounded, spread awareness among women about health issues and visited local schools to assess their needs. According to Eric Lavertu, another volunteer for Afrane who later joined the French ministry of foreign affairs, her affection for children and her concern for women's issues were defining traits of her personality. More than her alleged radicalism, it is her 'romantic side' (*son côté fleur bleue*) that veterans of Afrane now remember her for.

She travelled extensively across the provinces of Ghazni, Zabol and Kandahar whereas most French volunteers worked in the north of Afghanistan or around Herat in the west. In order to gain acceptance from the populations to whom she distributed help, she insisted that the funds for her work did not come from the French government. They were gifts, similar to donations made under *zakat* and *sadaqa*.

Her mission reports for Afrane are a unique and often poignant testimony on the socio-economic dynamics of Afghanistan at war, even if they are focussed on practical concerns and tend to over-simplify her relations with local populations (which, she would later admit, were often more conflictive than she could acknowledge at the time). She recorded in great detail the disruption of the agrarian economy and also documented the transformations of the education sector, conveying the desire for change among her informants (a significant number of whom seemed favourable to education among girls). She also underlined the positive role of madrasas in a country where secular education had virtually disappeared.

She acquired an intimate knowledge of Afghanistan through strenuous and perilous travels, under the cover of a shuttlecock burka that limited her movements and made the summer heat even more unbearable. Jean-Pierre Perrin, a former reporter for *Libération* who accompanied her on a particularly challenging journey along the fringes of the Registan desert during the summer of 1983, was impressed by her courage and endurance: 'It was a very painful trip. We had to ride motorbikes, trot on camels, and walk long distances. But she tolerated all this, often better than me,' he recalls. She was not invincible, however: as Perrin remembers, long walks on rocky paths took their toll on her and she sometimes collapsed from the heat.

These activities pertain to a now bygone era of humanitarian aid, predating its professionalisation. The clandestine nature of their work and the absence of telecommunications only reinforced the isolation of volunteers (Afrane generally covered the travel costs of its aid workers but they were not paid). Etienne Gille, one of the co-founders of Afrane, recalls, 'Once our volunteers had crossed into Afghanistan, we had no way to communicate with them for two to three months.' This complete immersion only reinforced Mariam Abou Zahab's bonds with Afghans, in particular with Pashtuns. Her fondness for them was reciprocated—sometimes beyond her expectations. Mariam Jan was also known as Sheenogai, or 'green-eyed beauty' in Pashto, and she would often joke about the number of marriage proposals she had received from Pashtun commanders during the Jihad.

For her critics, her romance with the Pashtuns and her proximity with some mujahidin commanders in eastern and southern Afghanistan often blinded her. Many French journalists, aid workers and diplomats eulogised Ahmed Shah Massoud, a celebrated mujahidin commander who died in bomb blasts in 2001. Known as the lion of Panjshir, he was widely perceived in France as an enlightened figure with the soul of a poet, if not as an Afghan Che Guevara. Mariam Abou Zahab, for her part, always considered the myth surrounding him a fable for Western consumption. Her views on the Afghan Taliban also caused controversy in France after she argued that they were a social movement, largely autonomous from Pakistani intelligence agencies. Instead of projecting the Taliban as an archaic formation, she depicted them as a reaction of the poorer and younger strata of Afghan society against traditional elites (Khans and Maliks). She also saw their rise as a revolt of the countryside against the cities that were perceived as dens of iniquity.

Her earlier texts on the origin of the Taliban—published in 1996 in the journal of Afrane—do not make an explicit mention of class as a sociological category but it featured prominently in her analysis. This approach anchors her writings into critical, if not Marxist currents of sociology. The centrality of class to her work only became clearer as the years passed by, especially featuring in her later works on sectarian conflicts in Pakistan.

PREFACE

Making sense of Pakistan's religious politics

While Afghanistan had a special place in Abou Zahab's heart, she also developed a vibrant relationship with Pakistan early on. This set her apart from most other French aid workers active in the region during the 1980s. According to Gilles Dorronsoro, who worked for Afrane before becoming an internationally acclaimed scholar of Afghanistan, 'We were utterly ignorant about Pakistani society and, to be honest, even a bit contemptuous of it. While in Peshawar, we were just longing to cross over to Afghanistan. On the contrary, she [Abou Zahab] was fluent in Urdu and Pashto and she could talk extensively about Pakistan—not only about Peshawar but about many other parts of the country as well, which in those days was truly original.'

Her first contacts with Pakistanis dated back to her days as a young student on an exchange programme in the United Kingdom. From 1968 onwards, she spent three successive summers in Kent where her curiosity led her to accompany Pakistani migrants harvesting strawberries. Her mischievous sense of adventure, her insatiable curiosity and her unflinching sympathy for those on the wrong end of domination continued to inform her relationship with Pakistan even as it matured into an intellectual and personal engagement in later years. So did her love for Urdu and its literature, which reveals itself in her marvellous French translation of Naiyer Masud's collection of short stories, *Itr-e-Kafoor*.

Her contribution to Pakistan studies is impressive, especially considering that she published all of her scholarly works in the last fifteen years of her life. Following her intellectual journey is not always an easy task because her academic publications often took the shape of chapters in edited volumes. One precious exception is the book she wrote along with French scholar Olivier Roy, *Islamist Networks: The Afghan-Pakistan connection*. Published in 2002, it revealed her unparalleled knowledge of Islamist political groups and militant outfits active throughout Pakistan, Afghanistan and Kashmir.

Located at the crossroads of political science, sociology and Islamic studies, her academic work encompasses a vast array of topics. The Pakistan Peoples Party (PPP) was one of the first political organisations to engage her interest. She dedicated her master's thesis to the party—

yet another indication of her progressive inclinations. In later years, however, she turned to the place of Islam in Pakistan's public sphere. Although not explicit, the one thread running throughout her multi-faceted work is her class-based analytical perspective. She primarily understood Pakistani religious politics through the grid of social cleavages, structures of domination, status conflicts, power struggles over scarce resources and phenomena of 'frustration'—an emotional variable that she used in many of her works to explain the motivations of the 'dominated'—be they Sunni '*ajnabi*', or strangers contesting the domination of Shia landlords in Jhang, or the 'rural poor' challenging the authority of *malik*s in the Federally Administered Tribal Areas (FATA).

Her fieldwork in Punjab mainly focused on Sunni supremacist groups, such as the Sipah-e-Sahaba (SSP). She was the first scholar to study the organisation's socio-genesis in southern Punjab. Her papers on this topic, especially her ethnographic study of socio-economic status conflict and sectarian violence in Jhang, have become classics. Besides their intrinsic academic value, these studies underline the originality of her approach towards her research objects: a convert to Shiism, she did not try to show the adherents of her own sect as victims; instead, she documented a relation of domination where Shia landlords oppressed Sunni tenants. And, like in her earlier writings on the Afghan Taliban, she argued that the rise of Sunni militancy in southern Punjab was the reaction of an emerging social group (in this case, the urban lower-middle-class) against traditional elites (mostly comprising Shia landowners). Her intellectual honesty—as well as her courage—was also attested by her visits to prominent figures of Sunni sectarian movement. She would remember her meeting with Azam Tariq, the now slain leader of the SSP, as one of her most challenging experiences in her life.

In the mid-2000s, she turned her attention to another Sunni supremacist organisation, the Lashkar-e-Taiba (LeT). In a preliminary paper, she retraced the evolution of the Ahl-e-Hadith sect in Pakistan, its involvement in proselytising and education (through the establishment of *madrasa*s) and its jihadist activities through the LeT, which she described as the 'largest private jihadi army in South Asia'. In the process, she unravelled the Arab connection of the Ahl-e-Hadith movement and unearthed its internal dissensions (between pietist, political and jihadi elements) based on differences over rituals and strategies. This article is an excellent illustration of her methodological approach. Always mobilising an impressive amount of documentary evidence, she explored not only contemporary (geo-)political developments but also historical contexts, ideological and religious doctrines as well as individual trajectories of the leaders and foot soldiers of the movement under study.

Best known for her work on Islamist movements, Mariam Abou Zahab was also a keen observer of Twelver Shia religious life in Pakistan. Her contribution in this field has brought attention to the role of women in the transmission of religious knowledge and to the richness and vitality of Muharram rituals in the country. Though home to the second largest Shia population in the world, Pakistan has long been overlooked in the study of lived Shiism. Her cross-provincial and longitudinal perspective of 40 years made her uniquely equipped to detect subtle variations and innovations in Shia piety. In turn, her familiarity with Iraqi and Iranian forms of Muharram rituals, and with the networks of learning connecting these countries, allowed her to offer rare comparative insights.

The performance of Muharram rituals in Punjab was the focus of some of her latest seminars, as well as a 2008 article subtitled *How Could This Matam Ever Cease?* In this article, she examines how variations in the performance of processions and self-flagellation are revealing of changing attitudes among Pakistani Shias towards transnational Shia networks and the adherents of the sect in the Middle East. Paying attention to these processions, she writes, can help us situate the singularity of Pakistani Twelver Shiism. If they once denoted a composite interreligious culture, since the 1980s the *julus* have increasingly become a means for the community to assert a distinct, sectarian Shia identity. Increasingly more ostentatious yet always vulnerable to attacks, Shia public rituals are now part of an inter-sectarian tussle over the use of public space and, by extension, over the community's right to exist. She demonstrates that, paradoxically, the modernising and purifying impulse of the Iranian revolution and later the Shia revival in Iraq have led to a revival of local heterodox practices in Pakistan. Elaborate processions and the self-infliction of ritual wounds, she argues, have become cardinal to the way ordinary Pakistani Shias mark themselves as distinct from local Sunnis and as more intrepid lovers of the *ahl-e-bait* than Shias abroad.

PREFACE

Her work on Pashtun society also built on her prolonged and multifarious experience in 'the field', in particular on her familiarity with regions such as FATA, which have become inaccessible to foreign or even Pakistani scholars over the past two decades. In the last few years of her life, she had started reflecting upon the social and political changes brought to FATA by religious militancy, state repression and economic disruptions. As the tribal areas were no longer accessible to her, she proceeded to study these transformations from the outside, in particular through the Pashtun diaspora in the Gulf. Her fieldwork in the United Arab Emirates with migrants from FATA was central to her comprehension of emerging social dynamics in their home regions. It was also in consonance with her long-term interest in Pakistani diasporic communities and transnational relations—be they economic or religious in nature—between overseas Pakistanis and their homeland. Indeed, her interest in Pakistan did not stop at the country's borders. She was in personal contact with numerous members of the diaspora in France and elsewhere, and kept a close eye on their activities. These experiences, together with her immense erudition, greatly enriched the people she taught about Pakistani migration for more than fifteen years at the Paris-based INALCO.

If Pashtun expatriates in the Gulf were the primary focus for her latest work, she was also concerned with the fate of the populations forcibly displaced from FATA by military operations. This took her back to Karachi—a city of which she was not particularly fond, but where she had nonetheless built strong ties over the years. Many local Deobandi and Shia clerics knew her personally and respected her due to both the in-depth and impartial character of her work. In Sohrab Goth, she conducted interviews with Mehsud tribesmen displaced from South Waziristan by military operations against the Pakistani Taliban. Her ability to converse with them in Pashto was truly impressive. So was her familiarity with a little-known movement from South Waziristan, the Teeman Tehreek Force (TTF), which was launched in the late 1990s by a gangster-turned-social bandit, Gokhan Mehsud, who attracted a number of Mehsud youths. By 1999, the acronym TTF started appearing on the windshields of buses and trucks often run by Mehsud tribesmen in Karachi. Despite its influence at the time, the TTF did not attract much attention from non-Mehsuds, which made her interest in this group all the more intriguing. By returning to this long-forgotten group, she was trying to shed new light on the genealogy of the Pakistani Taliban movement.

Although far from being central to her work, the social and political transformations of Karachi did not evade her attention. She was the first scholar to write on the development of a Pashtun middle-class—a development of considerable importance for the city at large and not just the Pashtuns living there.

Her new research was scheduled to be published in a comprehensive monograph on social and political changes in FATA (or, possibly, among Pakistani Pashtuns at large). She had been working on it for several years when illness took her away.

A generous pedagogue

Mariam Abou Zahab was a gifted and generous pedagogue who never tired of guiding policy makers, journalists and students through the maze of Pakistani and Afghan politics. She delivered lectures—which were often highly critical of Western interventions in the region—in front of institutions as diverse as the French ministry of foreign affairs, the Carnegie Endowment For International Peace and the United States Central Command (US CENTCOM). For many years, she also worked as a translator for the public institution in charge of assessing requests for asylum in France, the Office Français de Protection des Réfugiés et Apatrides (OFPRA). One of her contacts there remembers that 'ion officers would get annoyed because she often delivered a whole lecture during the auditions of Pakistani asylum seekers. She really had a gift for understanding individual trajectories and replacing them in their context.'

It was in the classroom that Mariam truly shared her intimate knowledge of South Asia and the Middle East. At the INALCO, where she taught classes on subjects as varied as Pashto literature, Pakistan's history, South Asian Sufism and diasporic communities, she trained a new generation of French scholars on Pakistan. At Sciences Po, where she taught with various specialists of the Middle East (such as Gilles Kepel and Elise Massicard), she inspired many young scholars specialising on the Arab world or Turkey.

Her students marvelled at her ability to mobilise first-hand ethnographic knowledge. A lecture on *qawwali* traditions would thus end with her recollection of being Nusrat Fateh Ali Khan's interpreter in Paris and a class on *dargah* culture would culminate with her sharing *tabarruk* (offerings) that she would have brought back from a recent visit to Pakistan.

Abou Zahab was an unconventional teacher. As Stéphane Lacroix, a former student of hers at Sciences Po who would become a renowned specialist of political Islam in Saudi Arabia, says: 'Her classes were not the usual university seminar. She spoke passionately and often didn't care much about structure. As far as I'm concerned, she fuelled my desire to do fieldwork. She had gone so far that she had fused with the field.'

Even as her health deteriorated, she continued to teach. Now unable to travel to Pakistan, she would ask her friends there to film religious rituals—especially those of Muharram in Pakki Shah Mardan, for which she developed a growing fascination during the last years of her life—so as to discuss them with her students. This was her last jihad—a struggle to hold back the tide and fulfil her educational mission just a bit longer.

When she realised that this battle was coming to an end, she prepared meticulously for her last journey. She organised her own funeral in the Iraqi city of Najaf and told her friends with a smile that she hoped Shia militias would turn up and escort her to her last abode. She also set up a foundation that will provide funding to promising scholars working on her favourite region and she made donations to a number of welfare projects that will perpetuate her lifelong engagement with Pakistan and Afghanistan. In Pakistan, these donations will go to the Acid Survivor Foundation.

It really takes more than death to disarm fighters of this calibre.

INTRODUCTION

MARIAM ABOU ZAHAB'S MULTISCALAR APPROACH TO ISLAMISM: THE SOCIAL AND LOCAL ROOTS OF SECTARIANISM AND JIHADISM IN PAKISTAN

Christophe Jaffrelot

This book was devised in conjunction with Mariam Abou Zahab a few years before she died. We compiled it together when I was Senior Editor of Hurst's now-concluded CERI series in collaboration with Miriam Périer, who served as the series' Editorial Manager. Mariam did not have time to write the introduction, but she selected the articles and book chapters that have been reproduced in this volume.

These texts reveal Mariam's intimate knowledge of South Asia—especially Afghanistan and Pakistan—a region she had explored extensively throughout her life, beginning her travels there as early as 1973, which Laurent Gayer and his co-authors recall in the preface of this book. She not only spoke Urdu, but also the languages of the regions where she did field work, including the Pashtun belt. This book reflects her anthropological erudition, which was particularly exceptional in respect to different facets of the Twelver Shia community and the Sunni schools of thought in South Asia—the two main facets of Islam in this region to which the first part of this volume is devoted. Her expertise, which was enhanced by her first-hand knowledge of the way Shiism was evolving in the Gulf (especially in Iran and Iraq), is richly illus-

1

trated through her pedagogical accounts of the transformation of conservative Sunni groups, including the Deobandis, into Islamist and neo-fundamentalist movements ('Pakistan: from Religious Conservatism to Political Radicalism'), and her study of the 'neo-islamisation of Pakistani Shias' ('The Politicisation of the Shia Community of Pakistan'),[1] which have been reproduced within these pages.

This combination of an ethno-historical and regional approach was the first trademark of Mariam Abou Zahab. The fact that she commanded an in-depth knowledge of history is evident from the manner in which she reconstituted the genealogy of Salafism in South Asia from the seventeenth century onwards in 'Salafism in Pakistan: The Ahl-e Hadith Movement'. Also, the way in which she factored in transnational interactions is exemplified by her account of the interactions between Osama Bin Laden (as well as other 'Arabs') and Pakistani Sunni militant groups ('Connections and Dynamics').[2]

Because of her erudition and avidity for details—and in spite of her legendary sense of synthesis—Mariam's perspective may seem rather descriptive, but she was not only interested in ethnographic descriptions and historical narratives; she offered interpretations in a way that appeared understated and nuanced when compared to the more prominent voices of her scholarly peers. In fact, her reading of any given situation flowed naturally from the story she was telling the reader, elegantly problematising these narratives and patterns. While she did not refer to methodological debates, as is evident from her footnotes, wherein few theoreticians are mentioned, she had a method and a theory as well as a clear idea of what social scientists should focus on when analysing major developments within the region.

This book focuses on two of these major developments: the Shia-Sunni conflict, known as 'sectarianism', and Islamism (including Afghan, Taliban and Pakistan-based jihadi groups). Accounting for these phenomena, Mariam hardly mentions religion. In fact, the word itself is conspicuously absent, perhaps in spite of, or even because of, her personal spiritual commitment.

She assumed that there only exist culturally specific strains of Islam informed by their respective social contexts, rather than a single, universal Islam. This is a notion she applied to Shiism in particular when sharing one of the stimulating theses of Olivier Roy[3] (with whom she co-authored a remarkable book).[4] Mariam contended that Shiism can only exist if it is rooted in a particular culture'[5]—and not as a religious global ideology, as some reformists have claimed. Therefore, she attributed more importance to cultural codes and symbols than to theological discourses. For instance, she explained some of the motivations of young jihadis by factoring in the 'codes of honour' which varied among different ethnic communities.[6] She also distinguished denominational nuances among Islamists, and thereby, on occasion, illuminated the contrast between the Deobandi repertoire and the Ahl-e-Hadith modi operandi.

But these notations are never the most decisive ones. They are listed among others, which finally appear to be more important: Mariam acknowledged the cultures and belief systems as well as the customs and rituals she knew so well without ever being culturalist, instead establishing a hierarchy of explanatory variables wherein religion and culture never prevail.

Why (and what) sectarianism?

For Mariam, sectarianism and Islamism are not religious repertoires; they are ideologies that make use of religion as 'a tool [...] rather than a faith' ('Sectarianism as a Substitute Identity'). In these 'isms', religion is a mere 'pretext' ('The Sunni-Shia Conflict in Jhang'). But this rather commonplace, anti-primordial stance does not mean that Mariam was an instrumentalist—she was too sophisticated for that and very much aware of the role of social imaginaries in identity politics. (We'll return to this dimension below).

Her rejection of instrumentalism is evident from the moderate attention she paid to state actors, particularly those who are usually considered responsible for the creation of sectarianism and Islamism in Pakistan: the army and the Inter-Services Intelligence, especially when the country was ruled by Zia-ul-Haq. Undoubtedly, Mariam partially attributes the crystallisation of a separate Shia identity to Zia's policy, as the 1980 *zakat* ordinance made the Shia community 'realize that, in an Islamic State, their political and religious interests were different from those of the majority' ('The Politicisation of the Shia Community in Pakistan'). Moreover, Mariam does not overlook the fact that the 'radicalisation of the Deobandi movements can be traced to the policy of conservative re-Islamisation instituted by General Zia ul-Haq' ('Pakistan: from Religious Conservatism to Political Radicalism'), especially the manner in which Zia and his army sponsored Sunni militant organisations in order to suppress Shia movements.[7] She also mentioned the way in which mainstream parties, including the PML(N), patronised these movements, but did not consider that these strategies played a decisive role in the rise of sectarianism in Pakistan. Mariam constantly tried to balance the impact of state actors with those of two others in a multi-scalar approach: the foreign powers and the local players.

The influence of Iran in the creation of a Shia sectarian identity in Pakistan is a case in point for documenting one of the faces of this Janus-like configuration. In 'The Regional Dimension of Sectarian Conflict in Pakistan', a text not reproduced in this volume, Mariam dwells on the fact that the 'Iranian revolution inspired Pakistani Shias and contributed to their politicisation'.[8] She also emphasises the support—financially or otherwise—that Tehran gave to the Shia movements. Furthermore, in several of the texts reprinted below she recognises that this Iranian attitude had a spill-over effect—Saudi Arabia and other Sunni countries were starting to patronise Salafi groups in Pakistan, transforming the country into a playground of proxy wars.

However, Mariam looked at the input of these external forces—like others including the Iran-Iraq war and the Afghan jihad—merely as 'enabling factors' ('Sectarianism as a Substitute Identity'). Moreover, whenever she valorised international aspects, she focused more on the transnational ones. For instance, she analysed in detail the outflow of Shia students who met Khomeini in Najaf or who were trained in Qom after 1979 because they gave birth to 'a new generation of clerics' who amplified the reception of the Iranian revolution in Pakistan—and even made it possible. She offers here a sociological explanation of a trans/international phenomenon that harks back to her inclination that people—and not just as a collective—matter more than anything else.

The sociological overtone of Mariam's approach is linked to her valorisation of local factors, which mattered the most to her. Indeed, the local factors accounting for the rise of sectarianism in Pakistan, according to her, are mostly sociological, as the 'Jhang paradigm' testifies. According to this paradigm, named after a district of South Punjab where Mariam did extensive field work, the roots of sectarianism have to be found in social relations of domination and exclusion. Her socio-logical approach, although she never explicitly refers to Marxist authors like Hamza Alavi lest she should become a prisoner of ideologi-cal dogma and jargon, derives here from the commitments she embraced in the 1970s (as evident from her personal trajectory, which is summarised in the preface of this book). The 'Jhang paradigm' is based on several empirical findings. First, 'madrasas proliferated in South Punjab', not for religious reasons, but because 'the landlords did not allow the establishment of schools' and peasants' children 'were forced by poverty' to go to these boarding institutions which took care of them fully ('Sectarianism as a Substitute Identity'). Second, the Green Revolution, if it 'has increased the prosperity of some ... has impoverished many in the rural areas' of Punjab, forcing peasants to migrate in large numbers to cities. Third, in a place like Jhang, the main fault line divided Shia landlords and the Sunni urban middle class, who largely emerged from the milieu of East Punjab refugees (*mohajir*), asserting their position gradually and harbouring resentment for the socio-economic and political domination of the Shia landlords. These Sunnis 'found allies in the ideologically motivated madrasa graduates', which suggests that ideology was an important variable but a latent one, activated by socio-economic triggers. In 'Sectarianism as a Substitute Identity', Mariam argues: 'Sectarianism can thus be described as a phenomenon of collective outburst against structures of power which must be pressurised or done away with'. Even sectarian violence is interpreted along these lines; undoubtedly, the Sunni mili-tants 'are persuaded that they have a religious mission', but 'they are often conscious of their low status in society, so they seek to compen-sate by serving the cause of religion'.

This analysis validates what she calls 'micro-level' sociology in 'The Shia-Sunni Conflict in Jhang'. In addition, Mariam did not hesitate to consider that 'the Jhang paradigm' applies elsewhere, and that religion is therefore 'not the main reason for the [sectarian] conflict, but only a pretext which proved to be a powerful means of mobilisation in the 1980s'. This perspective echoes some of the instrumentalists' oversim-plifications, especially when she considers that 'sect has become an identity marker, a temporary refuge and a platform to articulate grievances *and get access to power*' (my emphasis). However, she is more a constructivist than an instrumentalist when she shows that sectarianism has endowed militant groups with a new identity. For instance, Mariam analyses the Sunni activists of the Sipah-e-Sahaba Pakistan (SSP) from a sociological point of view in her chapter 'The SSP: Herald of militant Sunni Islam in Pakistan', in which she articulates that their leaders were 'peripheral' and indeed *lumpen* rather than traditional *ulema*. She posits that 'many belonged to the Arain caste which, while occupying a fairly low ranking in the Punjabi hierarchy, had become economically dominant in the province after Partition'. Their followers among the young, urban, 'resented graduates of the English-medium private schools'. However, besides its 'class struggle rhetoric', Mariam writes in 'The Sunni-Shia conflict in Jhang', 'The SSP wants to convert Sunnis to a rationalised Islam, to replace customary practices by the Islam of urban *ulemas* and *madrasas*, their struggle is directed as much against local rituals seen as Shiism as against the influence of *pirs* [sufi saints], both Sunni and Shia'.

Certainly, these sectarian repertoires are invented and imagined, but this is how ideologies manufacture a sense of collective belonging and create new 'selves', as Geertz, Hobsbawm and Anderson, among others, have shown. These new identities become sustainable and even permanent when groups make them their own. In this light, the key question for Mariam is: why would people, and not only militants, shift from their version of Islam to sectarian identities that have been shaped by ideologues? She evaluated this question in the same way that she had assessed the reception of the Iranian revolution in Pakistan, judging that this is because of social factors. Among these social factors, she focused on inequalities fostering social antagonisms, similar to the situation in Jhang. Such immersion in the 'micro-local' implies a very complex assessment of a multifaceted reality. Considering caste in addition to class and creed, Mariam states that in Jhang

> The social conflict has thus several levels: feudals versus the emergent middle class, Shias versus Sunnis, local Shias versus Mohajir Shias, local Sunnis versus Mohajir Sunnis, Syed (local and Muhajir Shias) versus *julhahas* and *kammis* (Sunni Muhajirs), Sheikh *biradari* (local Sunnis) versus Arain *baradari* (Muhajir Sunnis) and also competition for power inside the local Sheikh *baradari*.

However, a major quality of Mariam's work comes from her capacity to combine anthropological erudition and local complexities with an inherent urge—which she always displayed—to rank explanatory factors in a hierarchical system.

Ergo, Mariam's assessment of sectarianism in Pakistan offers an interpretative framework wherein this 'ism', invented by ideologues, transforms into popular identities. And this is not because of religion and culture (even though they incorporate Islamic and cultural references), or even because of domestic politics (including state interventions) or external influences (although they form 'enabling factors')—but rather, due to social conditions. The frustration of aspiring groups which resent the domination of elites belonging to another ethno-religious community explains their shift towards a new, sectarian identity. This 'Jhang paradigm' would be the blueprint for larger patterns, wherein Mariam used the same approach to make sense of the rise of the Taliban in the Federally Administered Tribal Areas (FATA), particularly in South Warizistan.

Islamism as a social issue, from the Pashtun belt to Punjab

In Parts Three and Four of this book, which handle the subject of jihadi groups, Mariam again relativises the role of state actors—including the army, which has notoriously helped key regional players detailed above, including the Haqqani networks. She acknowledges the role of the army, and specifically the military intelligence, known as the ISI, an institution which decided to use jihadi groups against India in a more systematic manner in the 1990s, which Mariam explains in 'Connections and Dynamics'. Yet, she does not consider that the army instrumentalised the jihadis. Firstly, because some of the officers shared ideological affinities with them, and secondly, because the jihadi groups enjoyed a lot of autonomy and even sometimes dictated their terms to the army. In 'Pakistan: From Religious Conservatism to Political Radicalism', Mariam points out that 'the "militants", in due course, turned to autonomous action and, while conserving their close connection with the services of the ISI, *imposed their own strategy*' (my emphasis). In order to regain its influence over the jihadi groups which had spiralled out of control, the ISI had to orchestrate a split in their ranks—or create new, rival groups.

Mariam distanced herself from another standard explanation of the rise of Islamism in Pakistan in playing down the international factors. Certainly, she acknowledged the role of Saudi Arabia not only in the financing of Salafi groups like Lashkar-e-Taiba (LeT), but also in the shaping of their ideology (via madrasas and even universities).[9] But she held that external factors, such as the state's strategy, would not have made any significant difference in the 1990s–2000s, when Islamism surged in Pakistan, if local youngsters had not been interested in joining the Taliban or parts of jihadi groups. For Mariam, 'such movement arose from the initiative of young militants who had personally experienced *jihad* while fighting in Kashmir and Afghanistan' ('Pakistan: From Religious Conservatism to Political Radicalism'). The question then is: what motivated these young men whose agency is the key factor in explaining the rise of Islamism in twenty-first century Pakistan?

Again, religion is not the main explanation for the rise of Islamism in Pakistan, and external factors, including anti-Americanism, are mentioned only as 'enabling factors'. In fact, the international dimension matters less than the transnational connections which have been responsible for facilitating the travel of these young radicals to different war zones, including Bosnia. But again, the question of their motivation remains. To answer this question, Mariam retained the biographical approach she had already adopted to analyse sectarianism in the same way in which she had accounted for Azam Tariq's itinerary. She focused on the life stories of Masood Azhar, Mufti Nizamuddin Shamzai or Sheikh Omar Saeed—but again, studying these individuals from a sociological perspective.

In the second chapter of Part Three of this book, '*Kashars* against *Mashars*', Mariam argues that the Taliban of the FATA were primarily the products of 'local dynamics', which harks back to the 1970s. The protagonists in this chapter are the *kashars*, 'the young, the poor and those belonging to minor lineages or powerless tribes', and the *mashars*, the 'tribal elders'. The latter, known as 'Maliks', who were already economically dominant as landlords, had risen to political dominance under the umbrella of an increasingly powerful Pashtun, secular nationalist movement. For Mariam, the *kashars* had adopted an alternative ideology—Islamism—in the context of the anti-Soviet jihad, which enabled some of them to become warriors and heroes with the intention of removing the ruling groups from power.

In Afghanistan, this 'led in the 1990s to the emergence of the Taliban as a social movement'. Similarly, the young Pakistani jihadis who had crossed over to Afghanistan in the 1980s when they were back in the FATA (or elsewhere in the Pashtun belt) decided to compete with the Maliks in the name of their new, Islamic legitimacy. They reiterated the same strategy after the next Afghan war, which occurred in direct reaction to 9/11. Mariam does not ignore the role of transnational actors—including Al-Qaeda, which helped the *kashars*-turned-jihadis—but she insists that these youngsters joined the ranks of the Taliban because of the social conditions in which they lived. Al-Qaeda operatives only facilitated their integration into the organisation by means of training and finance. Looking at this situation from a sociological viewpoint in this manner retains the cultural dimension of this examination—because the Taliban are described as using 'reinvented Pashtun values'—however, this approach also emphasises the malleability of culture under the influence of material interest. For instance, to explain the way Pashtuns welcomed Al-Qaeda leaders in the name of hospitality was irrelevant for Mariam: '*Melmasia* (hospitality) which is one of the strongest Pashtun traditions has lost its meaning, it is no more a free hospitality but a way of acquiring wealth and influence'.

In the same, rather materialistic vein, Mariam placed this political economy of Talibanism in a larger context. For her, one could only make sense of the motivations and ambitions of the *kashars* by taking into account the societal impact of post-1970 migrations to Karachi and the Gulf, when 'old inequalities based on Pashtun values of hospitality and manhood were replaced by new inequalities based on money, which transformed the character of tribal society'. These changes did not mean that old values had been systematically replaced by others; Mariam knew that there was never any tabula rasa, and she therefore tried to identify the values which, effectively, had been reinterpreted by the Taliban. For instance, those who played the role of Robin Hood exploited the Pashtun notion that 'standing by the weak reinforces one's honour'—but the main factors here have nothing to do with culture.

Mariam embraced a similar, predominantly sociological approach in seeking to make sense of the recruitment drives of LeT. After analysing 'about one hundred testaments (*wasiatnamah*) and life stories of martyrs',[10] she comes to the conclusion that 'Most of the LeT militants do not belong to higher castes, but rather to emergent or lower castes (*kammis*)' and come from the 'lower middle class' of towns, cities and 'semi-urban neighbouring villages' of Central and South Punjab. She considered that 'joining a jihadi movement gives young boys who cannot afford to migrate to the West or to the Gulf and are socially frustrated a substitute identity, [which] compensates for their frustrations'. In this respect, financial incentives should not be overlooked either—the militants engaged in *daawat* work receive a monthly salary from the LeT as well as fringe benefits, which are quite attractive to unemployed young boys. In addition, being a martyr is an opportunity for lower class boys to become famous, be remembered for their military actions, and gain a privileged status for themselves and their families through their deaths.[11]

In this introduction, I endeavour to capture Mariam's approach to the issues at hand, which can be described as socio-psychological or socio-cultural. Certainly, social factors come first, but they only make sense in a certain cultural context, the context of a jihadi culture. Without taking this milieu into account, no one can make sense of the psychological motivations of the jihadis. For them, to be a part of the LeT and fight—or, even better, die—for Islam was a way to improve their self-esteem and even to give their lives a sense of purpose. Indeed, Mariam does not explain the attraction of the LeT only on the basis of social factors: ideas, as belief systems, matter too. This is why she analyses the different phases of the jihadi training, both ideological and physical, so meticulously. Some of her finest work—based on long citations of testimonies (written and oral), peppered with the usual selection of meaningful details—is reproduced here. This field work-based study of jihadism enabled her to conclude that local considerations matter above all else, and that among these local factors, the social ones—which are analysed through a well-informed psycho-cultural lens—play a major role.

This social perspective delineates both the social work dimension of militant groups, and their criminalisation. Indeed, if money is a key variable, these groups can exploit it through the aforementioned means, which were already highlighted by Mariam in her study of the SSP, whose leader, Haq Nawaz, was 'involved in social work, [that] attempted to resolve the population's material difficulties, arbitrated in conflicts between neighbours and found jobs for the unemployed'. His successor, Azam Tariq—with whom she spent one full day while doing fieldwork—adopted a very similar attitude. At the same time, Mariam emphasised the criminal dimension of the SSP, which cultivated close relations with drug traffickers in particular. Similarly, she pointed out the affinities between Islamism and criminality in the FATA, as well as within many jihadi and sectarian groups that indulge in mafia-like activities. The predatory dimension of sectarian and jihadi groups partly explains the way in which they resorted to violence, luxuriate in riots and killings themselves, or rather, as in the case of the SSP, out-source such activities to specialised brigades, such as the Lashkar-e-Jhangvi (LeJ). But again, here Mariam combines material factors with ideological ones.

In fact, the manner in which Mariam analyses sectarian and jihadi violence offers a great illustration of her epistemological perspective. Violence is a reflection of social parameters, which has two sides to it: a material, socio-economic one, and a cultural, socio-psychological one. The following quotation from 'The SSP' concerning the violence of Sunni militants evidences this profusely:

> Having suffered rejection and humiliation when looking for work, they realized that the SSP, which blamed Shias for their predicament, offered them a way to defend their interests. These young people were eager to acquire social status and saw membership of the SSP as a means of inspiring respect, even if only through the fear the organisation aroused. In a society which regarded violence as a legitimate way to settle differences, considerable power accrued to those prepared to use it. Moreover, the militants regarded violence against the Shias as a per-fectly legitimate activity, since the aim was to purify their religion.

Towards the merging of jihadi and Sunni militant groups

The final part of this book deals with the convergence between the Sunni militants and the jihadis. This rapprochement, which was first initiated by the SSP, the LeJ and the Jaish-e-Mohammad (JeM), a jihadi group active in Kashmir, resulted from social similarities and ideological affinities. For Mariam, 'the SSP, JeM and LeJ appeared to be three wings of the same party: the members of the groups had the same profile and were mostly recruited from the rural and urban lower-middle classes of Central and South Punjab, as well as from Deobandi *madrasas*' ('Pashtun and Punjabi Taliban: The Jihadi-Sectarian Nexus').

However, the convergence of Sunni sectarians and jihadis gained momentum after the 2007 crackdown on the Red Mosque, which had been a stronghold of the SSP as well as the JeM. This precipitated a geographical shift, as Punjabi jihadis and Sunni sectarians found refuge in the safe haven that the FATA had become—where SSP militants had already settled down when they had been sporadically targeted. Both networks worked together under the aegis of a new organisation, the Tehrik-e-Taliban Pakistan (TTP), a movement which 'brought to light the Punjabi-Pashtun nexus'.

This collaboration found expression in two-way traffic, each group helping the other to maximise its strike force. The Pashtun-dominated TTP wanted to expand its activities beyond the Indus, as civilian and military elites based in Islamabad were not terribly sensitive to terrorist actions in the Pashtun belt or Baluchistan. However, Pashtun jihadis were not familiar with the Punjabi landscape. Mariam has shown that 'Punjabi militants started providing manpower for attacks outside the FATA and the NWFP...'—which sheds light on the circumstances around the spectacular attacks which took place in Lahore, and even in Islamabad, from the late 2000s until the early 2010s. The TTP could also expand its operations to Karachi where it could not only rely on the growing Pashtun community, but also on jihadi groups which had also had strong roots in this mega-city (where JeM was founded, for instance).

In line with this, Pashtun jihadis had helped Sunni sectarian groups to target large numbers of Shias who were gathered in once place. The Federally Administered Tribal Agency of Kurram, where Shias represented 40 per cent of the 500,000 inhabitants, was a case in point. In the penultimate chapter of this book, '"It's Just a Sunni-SHIA thing": Sectarianism and Talibanism in the FATA of Pakistan', Mariam demonstrates that 'rising sectarianism' is 'a direct offshoot of growing Talibanisation', which suggests that both schools of thought began to overlap more and more. This evolution, which translated into mass violence which spilled-over to the neighbouring region of Orakzai, was again fostered by socio-economic factors, as Shias were 'relatively affluent compared to Sunnis in the Tribal Areas':

They own huge properties—forests, mountains, fertile agricultural land. Sunnis prevent them [from] cut[ting down] their trees and selling them. The Taliban also expelled the Shia from fertile land and forced them to pay *jizya* (poll tax on non-Muslims). Shia had acquired contracts for developing coal mines, they were expelled from the area by the Taliban saying that infidels had no right to extract coal.

Once again, however, Mariam does not only focus on the socio-economic dimension of conflicts, but paid attention to socio-cultural ones. For instance, she emphasises the role of tribal identities—which have eroded but have not been erased altogether by forms of Islamisation. She points out that the tensions between Mehsuds and Wazirs formed the subtext of some intra-Taliban clashes in North and South Waziristan, for example.

* * *

The pages that follow deserve close attention, not only because of the erudition of Mariam Abou Zahab—whose style, free of jargon, makes them so pleasant to read—but also because her command of the history, the ethnography and the politics of the regions under discussion in this volume is systematically used for supporting a twofold thesis: sectarianism and Islamism are not religious phenomena, but ideologies which borrow from Islam and ethnic cultural codes, and are instead primarily overdetermined and shaped by social factors. Some of them are purely socio-economic and can be understood in terms of class conflicts. Others are more socio-psychological, and it is even more necessary to have Mariam's ethnographic expertise at one's disposal in order to make sense of them. This reading of some of the most important developments experienced by Pakistan since the 1970s implies a valorisation of local dynamics at the expense of state-national and inter/transnational variables, which were only 'enabling factors' in Mariam's eyes. In the conclusion of 'I Shall be Waiting at the Door of Paradise', reiterating the lesson she had learned in Jhang about sectarianism, she points out that 'as is the case with every jihadi movement in Pakistan or elsewhere in the region (Afghanistan, Central and South East Asia), local considerations always prevail over global ones'[12]—a point that she made very clear in the case of Pakistan.

PART ONE

MILITANT SUNNISM AND SHIISM IN PAKISTAN

1

PAKISTAN

FROM RELIGIOUS CONSERVATISM
TO POLITICAL RADICALISM

The situation in Pakistan is increasingly complex. Since the 1990s movements and acronyms have arisen in profusion. In the background there are two clear distinctions to be made. First, there is the division based on ethnicity, which is mainly between Sindhis, Baluchis and Muhajirs, on the one hand, and Punjabis and Pashtuns on the other. In the conflicts between individuals it is important not to overlook caste loyalties which, while not publicly acknowledged, play an important role. Second, and principally, there is the religious divide which places the Shias, who make up 15–20 per cent of the population, in opposition to the Sunnis. In addition, within the Sunni population, the Deobandis—reformists drawn mainly from the Muhajirs, the Punjabis and the Pashtuns—are opposed to the Barelvis, traditionalists who venerate saints and the Prophet. The latter are in the majority in the country. Meanwhile a third religious group characterised as 'wahhabi' is antagonistic to these other two.

The religious movements have undergone two different forms of radicalisation: Islamist and neo-fundamentalist. The prototype of the Islamist party is the Jamaat-i-Islami, founded by Maulana Maududi in the 1940s, and up till the 1980s it enjoyed a virtual monopoly on political Islam and served as the link between the Pakistani army and the pro-Pakistan Afghan mujahidin of Gulbuddin Hekmatyar's Hizb-i-Islami. This came about in particular as a result of the role played by Qazi Hussein Ahmad, the party's 'emir', who is himself a Pakistani Pashtun and in the early 1970s kept a tutelary eye on the young Afghan militants, including Hekmatyar and Massoud when these two were political refugees in Peshawar. Jamaat-i-Islami recruited mainly among intellectuals with a modern education, and maintained its distance from pre-existing clerical and religious movements. It has always respected the rule of law, in spite of its ideological radicalism which declared Pakistan's status as an Islamic state to be the sole reason for its existence. It was also élitist, advocating 'entryism' into the senior civil service and the army, and has never undertaken armed action. It lost impetus after 1991, and its former position is occupied today by a radical tendency which has arisen out of other movements which were initially more conservative.

Jamaat has never been included in the roster of terrorist parties drawn up by the United States government. On the other hand, it developed into an Islamo-nationalist party—for example, at the time of the campaign against the signature of the non-proliferation treaty in 2000. No doubt it was attracted by the idea of becoming the civil alternative to the military regime of Musharraf, who came to power in October 1999. However, the American campaign of 2001 placed it once more in the dissident camp, although it had not gone so far as to enter the armed conflict. Jamaat seems to have opted definitively for the political route.

The principal formative influence of this new radicalism, coming from a conservative background, has been the Deobandi school, named after Deoband, a great religious academy founded near Delhi in 1867. It is made up of religious figures of a traditional and conservative inclination, whose manifestation in the sphere of politics is the Jamiat-i-Ulema-i-Islam, the largest Deobandi-based party, established in 1945, of which the two principal factions today are led by Maulana Fazlur Rehman and Maulana Sami Ul-Haq. Also located in this neo-fundamentalist orbit is the Ahl-i-Hadith, founded in the nineteenth century, whose adherents distinguish themselves from the Deobandis by their refusal to accept theological and philosophical thinking which has accrued in the course of Muslim history. In this sense they are close to the Saudi Wahhabis, and are often so described by their enemies. In 1987 members of the Ahl-i-Hadith, in the course of a process of radicalisation similar to that of other groups, set up the group Da'wa wa'l-Irshad (Preaching and Guidance), which has become their militant branch.

The Barelvi movement—counterpart and rival of the Deobandi school—has developed a more popular Islam, strongly focused on the Prophet Muhammad, and is often viewed by the Salafi and Wahhabi tendencies as having deviated from the true faith. However, the Barelvis are scarcely involved in Afghanistan, and promote their international networks only in Europe among the migrants from the Indian sub-continent.

The various religious movements—Deobandism, Barelvism and Ahl-i-Hadith—have no tradition of political radicalism. Even though they are strongly sectarian when religion is at issue, this always relates to specific problems, for example the condemnation of the Ahmadi movement or the campaign against Shiism, which is regarded as a heresy, and they do not militate for some particular form of government. These are very conservative movements, even when like the Deobandis and the Ahl-i-Hadith, they profess their adherence to religious reformism. Their transition into politics dates from the 1980s, and has taken the form of a growing radicalism and the adoption of violent action. This radicalisation has been characterised by the formation of armed splinter groups, often organised within a clandestine framework. It is therefore difficult to discover to what extent such groups are wholly autonomous or whether, on the other hand, their links to their parent organisations persist, although the acts of violence in which they engage may drive them further into clandestinity, especially after being listed in the various registers of terrorist organisations maintained by the United States.

This radicalisation of religious conservatives may also be observed elsewhere besides Pakistan, as in the case of the Taliban in Afghanistan. In Pakistan it is promoted by the military intelligence service, the ISI, and relates to two defined objectives. These objectives are the struggle against Shiism, and the jihad, both in Kashmir and in Afghanistan. The objectives are not new but the means employed are novel. These include military training, the adoption of armed struggle, the assassination of individuals, and armed attacks on mosques of other persuasions. In addition there are strategic consequences. In Afghanistan, after the departure of the Soviets, jihad was waged against Massoud, both for the benefit of the Taliban and, with inexorable logic, also on behalf of al-Qaeda which at that time had rallied these movements both against the United States and, after 11 September, against General Musharraf himself and the Pakistan army. Anti-Shiism and jihadism eventually coalesced.

Deobandi movements and violent action

The radicalisation of the Deobandi movements can be traced to the policy of conservative re-Islamisation instituted by General Zia-ul Haq after his seizure of power in Pakistan in 1977. It was afterwards nurtured by the hardening stance of the Pakistani state and of the radical movements which shared the same enemies—namely India, the communists and, to a lesser extent, the Shias. However, the 'militants' in due course turned to autonomous action and, while conserving their close connection with the services of the ISI, imposed their own strategy. The jihad in Afghanistan was both their model and, during the 1980s while it was still encouraged by the Saudis and the United States, their cover. The radical Islamic movements were therefore instruments for the regional policy of the Pakistani authorities and in particular for the ISI. The concern of the government over the uncontrollable spread of violence between Sunnis and Shias led to the beginnings of a change of policy under the government of Nawaz Sharif in 1998, though without real results. In 1999 the new head of state General Musharraf embarked on the repression of the most sectarian movements while continuing to utilise some of them—for instance the Lashkar-i-Taiba— in Kashmir and Afghanistan. The impact of 'sectarian conflict', an expression used to designate Sunni-Shia tension, is frequently misunderstood and demands re-evaluation.[1]

Radicalisation in the internal sphere in Pakistan was undertaken as a stratagem against the Shias in 1985, at a time when the Pakistani authorities feared that the Shia community might be utilised by Iran's Islamic Revolution. Thus a number of movements of Deobandi sectarian character appeared, with the blessing of the authorities.

The Sipah-i-Sahaba Pakistan (SSP—the Army of the Companions of the Prophet) emerged from the Jami'at-i-Ulema-i-Islam, which professes to be in agreement with the SSP over ideology but not over methods. However, there has been no explicit break between these two parties, and hence their relationship is ambiguous. The SSP was founded in September 1985 at Jhang, with the backing of the military authorities, to counter the rise in the influence of Shiism, and apparently had the financial support of Saudi Arabia and Iraq. The principal objective of the SSP was to affirm the apostasy of the Shias and to transform Pakistan into a Sunni Muslim state applying the Sharia. The SSP was anti-Barelvi and strongly anti-Iranian, and accused the Pakistan government of conducting repression against the Sunnis with the aim of gratifying Iran. It demanded the enactment of a law imposing the death penalty for any slur on the honour of the *sahaba*, the companions of the Prophet, or of Aisha, the Prophet's wife. This specifically implied condemnation of the Shia ritual, which disapproves of both Aisha and the Caliph Omar. The assassination in February 1990 of the movement's founder Haq Nawaz Jhangvi unleashed a cycle of inter-communal violence which continued through December 1990 with the assassination in Lahore of the consulgeneral of Iran, Sadiq Ganji. The assassin, who had taken the name Haq Nawaz, was condemned to death and hanged in February 2001. The successors of Haq Nawaz Jhangvi were also murdered—Maulana Isar ul-Qasmi in 1991 and Zia ul-Rehman Farooqi in 1997.

The last leader of the SSP was Maulana Azam Tariq, a Punjabi whose family left the Indian Punjab for Pakistan in 1947. In addition to Jhang, the areas of the SSP's strength were in the centre of the country, around Faisalabad, and in the southern Punjab including Bahawalpur, Multan, Muzaffargarh and Rahimyar Khan. Its support came from the Sunni and Deobandi urban lower middle class, merchants and junior officials from the Punjabi and Muhajir communities. It continued to receive financial backing principally from private Saudi sources, as well as from the Punjabi diaspora, in Europe and even more in the Middle East, and from the Islamic *zakat* tax. It may well also have been supported by the (internal) transport cartels and drug-trafficking mafias.

The SSP, which claimed to be a religious rather than a political party, made an entry into electoral politics in its own right in 1992, its candidates having previously stood for election under the banner of the Jami'at-i-Ulema-i-Islam. It won seats in the National Assembly and in the Provincial Assembly of the Punjab. Under Benazir Bhutto's second government, from 1993 to 1996, Sipah-i-Sahaba entered an alliance with the Pakistan Peoples Party (PPP) in the Punjab and secured a ministerial post in the provincial government. The SSP claimed to have 300,000 members, and to be especially well represented in the Punjab and in Punjabi circles in Karachi. It recruited largely from the Deobandi madrasas of the Punjab. It has maintained offices abroad, in the United Arab Emirates, Saudi Arabia, Canada, Britain and Bangladesh among others. Its leader Azam Tariq visited France in January 2001, shortly before he was once again placed in detention on 27 February 2001 after the disturbances which followed the hanging of Haq Nawaz. At the end of the 1990s the SSP fought alongside the Taliban against Massoud and the Afghan Shia Hazaras, and is thought to have been responsible for the massacre of Hazaras and Iranian diplomats in northern Afghanistan in August 1998. It was banned on 12 January 2002.

Azam Tariq was first placed under house arrest, although the authorities granted him a monthly allowance of 10,000 rupees. He contested and won a parliamentary seat in the October 2002 election as an independent candidate, although he faced about sixty criminal cases including murder, inciting people to commit sectarian violence and making hate speeches. He challenged the ban on his group by filing a petition in the Supreme Court. The defunct SSP, which took the new name of Millat-e Islamia Party (MIP, Party of the Islamic Nation), spared no effort to become acceptable to the government. Azam Tariq insisted that his party was purely a religio-political one whose sole aim was the implementation of Sharia laws, and that it had no links to jihadi or sectarian groups. In April 2003 he appealed to the Lahore High Court to suspend the state orders freezing his party's bank accounts and imposing functional restrictions on it, claiming that these orders had brought its social and humanitarian work to a halt and affected its religious functions since hundreds of mosques drew funds for their maintenance from the party's coffers. Although Azam Tariq denied it, there is every reason to believe that his release and his election to the National Assembly were the result of a deal with the government which apparently wanted to use him to undermine the Muttahida Majlis-e

Amal (MMA, United Action Council), the alliance of six religious parties which has been at the forefront of the opposition to General Musharraf since its success in the October 2002 elections. Azam Tariq was assassinated in Islamabad on 6 October 2003. Meanwhile the SSP, which had been declared a terrorist organisation by Pakistan in December 2001, was placed on a terrorist watchlist by the United States in May 2003. Inside Pakistan itself, incidents of sectarian violence perpetrated by Sunnis have always tended more to be the work of the Lashkar-i-Jhangvi (LJ—Army of Jhangvi).

The latter, a terrorist group, split off in 1994 from the SSP, which it accused of having abandoned the agenda laid down by Haq Nawaz Jhangvi. It was led by Riaz Basra, an SSP veteran from Sarghoda, who is said to have lived in Kabul till October 2001 and was accused of implication in the assassination of Sadiq Ganji. Malik Ishaq, the ideologue of the LJ, has been in prison since 1998. This is a very decentralised and compartmentalised group, and until the autumn of 2001 it numbered several dozen dedicated assassins based in Afghanistan. It has claimed responsibility for numerous assassinations, the victims including Iranian diplomats and military personnel, high-ranking police officers, senior officials, lawyers, doctors and Shia preachers. The organisation has also carried out massacres at Shia mosques. It drew up a death-list of Shia personalities and even attempted to kill the Prime Minister, Nawaz Sharif, in January 1999 as a reprisal for the oppressive campaign carried out in the Punjab in 1998 by his brother Shahbaz, who was the provincial Chief Minister. The LJ was proscribed in August 2002. Riaz Basra was arrested in December 2001 on his return from Afghanistan and executed extra-judicially by the police on May 2002 in a false encounter, two days before the recovery of the dead body of Daniel Pearl was announced. He had always been suspected of collaborating with the agencies since his 'escape' from jail in Lahore in 1994, after which he created the Lashkar-e Jhangvi.

The active jihadist tendency in Kashmir and Afghanistan: from the Harakat ul-Ansar to the Jaish-i-Muhammad

The Soviet invasion of Afghanistan imparted a new dimension to the idea of jihad in Pakistan, which till then had only been employed by the

Pakistani state in the context of mobilising the population against India. However, from the beginning of the 1980s the concept of jihad was to become 'privatised'. Radical groups emerged out of the large traditional religious movements and embarked on armed operations.

There are three elements which serve to explain the complexity of the process of radicalisation, and in particular the multiplication of small groups of terrorists. The latter often occurs through a process of larger groups becoming subdivided. The first of these elements is that such movements arose from the initiative of young militants who had personally experienced jihad while fighting in Kashmir or Afghanistan. The second is that the development of these movements was supervised by the Pakistani secret services (ISI), which had two objectives in view—to take control of the jihad in Kashmir by marginalising their nationalist elements to the benefit of the 'Islamic internationalists', based in Pakistan and reporting directly to the ISI, and to intervene in internal Pakistani politics, in particular against the Shias who were suspected of serving as a fifth column for a hypothetical Iranian infiltration. And the third is that the rise of such movements was discreetly overseen by the great politico-religious organisations, which were thus able to furnish themselves with an armed branch while at the same time being able to deny all responsibility if a serious crisis had arisen.

The first genuine Pakistani jihadist movement is said to have been founded in 1980.[2] Three students from the large Deobandi madrasa (Jamiat ul Ulum ul Islamia) at Binori Town in Karachi left for Afghanistan in February 1980, without money and not knowing what they intended to do there. They gave their group the name Jami'at ul-Ansar of Afghanistan (Society of the Partisans), which in 1988 became Harakat ul-Jihad-i-Islami (HJI). When the three students arrived in Peshawar they joined the Harakat-i-Inqilab-e-Islami, the radical extremist faction of Maulvi Nasrullah Mansur, which was well established in the Afghan province of Paktia (close to the Pakistan border) and was run by traditional clergy educated in Pakistan. They were also connected to the Hizb-i-Islami of Yunus Khalis and to Jalaluddin Haqqani, who would become one of the senior local commanders of the Taliban.

The HJI was pan-Islamic, and its intention was, by means of a renewed jihad, to combat the worldwide oppression of Muslims by infidels. Its objective was to give the Muslims back their past glory, and it placed special emphasis on the liberation of occupied Muslim territory such as Kashmir and Palestine. It also aimed at launching a struggle for Muslim rights in non-Muslim countries, such as the Philippines and Burma. In due course its activists fought in Bosnia, where a first group arrived in 1992, and in Tajikistan, as well as in other places. However, from 1980 to 1988 it restricted its activities to Afghanistan. A split took place in 1991, resulting in the formation of a movement called the Harakat ul-Ansar (HUA), later known as the Harakat-ul-Mujahidin (HUM). The leading figure in this group, Fazlur Rehman Khalil, a Pashtun, had great influence, and numerous militants rallied to him. The HUM, led by Fazlur Rehman Khalil and Masood Azhar, featured on an early list of terrorist organisations drawn up by the US State Department in 1998. This movement devoted itself primarily to the struggle in Kashmir, where Masood Azhar was taken prisoner by India in 1994. In February 2000 a new split followed, apparently along ethnic lines. The Punjabi militants followed Masood Azhar into the Jaish-i-Mohammad (JM—the Army of Mohammed), as the new group was named, while the Pashtuns remained with Fazlur Rehman Khalil in the HUM, which henceforth became an essentially Pashtun movement allied to Bin Laden with camps in Afghanistan.

Here a pattern is observable which was to repeat itself with other movements, namely that religious and ethnic connections reinforced each other. Recruitment for the new group was conducted mainly among the veterans of Sipah-i-Sahaba Pakistan, the Punjabis of the Harakat-ul-Mujahidin, and the Kashmiri and Punjabi communities in Britain.

The founding of JM in Karachi in February 2000 followed the hijacking of an Indian Airlines plane at Kandahar airport in December 1999, which led to the release of Masood Azhar by the Indian authorities. He was subsequently re-arrested and released twice by Pakistan in February and April 2000 because of his over-vigorous criticism of the Musharraf government. However, he retained the backing of the Pakistani secret service (ISI) and continued to go about armed in public. Shortly after the launch of the Jaish-i-Muhammad he went back to Bahawalpur, where he married before setting off again for Afghanistan. JM and its founder merit close examination, since it undoubtedly became the most active jihadist movement and the closest to al-Qaeda.

Masood Azhar was born in 1968 at Bahawalpur into a religious family of six sons and six daughters. His father was an instructor in Islamic studies. He was intellectually able, so his father sent him to the major Deobandi madrasa at Binori Town in Karachi, where he studied from 1980 to 1989. He afterwards lectured in Arabic at Binori Town to foreign students for two years. A visit by a leader of the Harakat ul-Ansar prompted the principal of the madrasa there to suggest to Masood Azhar that he should follow a course of preparation for the jihad. He returned converted to the necessity for action. Appointed by the Harakat ul-Ansar in 1993 to be responsible for *da'wa*, he published the periodicals *Sada ul-Mujahidin* (Voice of the Mujahidin) in Urdu, and *Sawt ul-Kashmir* (Voice of Kashmir) in Arabic.

He went to Afghanistan with his brother Ibrahim Azhar, a madrasa graduate and former amir of the Bahawalpur chapter of the Harakat ul Ansar, who was one of the hijackers of the Indian Airlines plane in December 1999. Ibrahim lives in Karachi and runs the Idara Khairul Amin, an organisation based in Binori Town which prints jihadi literature. His younger brother, Abdul Rauf Asghar, also studied at Binori Town, and later joined the madrasa as a teacher. Two younger brothers are currently studying at Deobandi madrasas in Karachi. Masood Azhar entered India from Bangladesh on a forged Portuguese passport in 1994 and was captured by the Indians in Kashmir. During his detention in India, he wrote numerous articles and works on the jihad, often referring in these writings to Africa; he is said by some to have followed Bin Laden to Sudan in 1992, and to have fought in Somalia for the local warlord Aidid. He is also said to have been involved in the training of militants in Yemen.

After the seizure of power by General Musharraf, Masood Azhar hailed the fall of the tyrannical regime of Nawaz Sharif and demanded reforms, including an Islamic constitution that would proclaim the supremacy of the Quran and the Sunna. He also proposed a revision of the electoral system so that only good Muslims ready to make the greatest sacrifices for Islam could be candidates, as well as the Islamisation of the judicial system and of the economy, with the abolition of interest-bearing loans. He named the internal enemies of Pakistan: the politicians who had pillaged the country and left it in debt; the feudal landowners who had appropriated lands and oppressed the peasants; corrupt officials; merchants who sold sub-standard goods and operated on the black market; organisations which drew distinctions between Muslims on the basis of their ethnicity or language; those who wished to transform Pakistan into an American or Russian colony; the majority of foreign-controlled NGOs, which he regarded as ideological enemies of Pakistan whose personnel were mainly in the pay of the 'Jewish lobby'; writers and journalists who undermined the unity and security of the country, exploiting their right of freedom of expression to write against Islam—he accused them of responsibility for sectarianism, and alleged that they were supported from abroad; and finally those who disseminated obscenity and promoted an atmosphere of sinfulness.

Masood Azhar was very close to the Sipah-i-Sahaba-Pakistan and to Maulana Azam Tariq. In fact the SSP, the JM and the Lashkar-e Jhangvi appeared to be three wings of the same party: the SSP was a political umbrella while the JM and the Lashkar-e Jhangvi were the jihadi and domestic military wings respectively. A rumour which circulated in 2001 concerning a possible ban on the SSP was a further factor leading to the adherence of a number of its members to the Jaish-i Muhammad, although in fact only the Lashkar-i-Jhangvi was definitively banned, in August 2001. Soon after its creation the JM became involved in sectarian warfare in Pakistan in addition to its activities in Kashmir. A faction of the JM, led by Abdul Jabbar, carried out sectarian attacks in Islamabad's diplomatic enclave on a Christian church frequented by Americans in March 2002, and on a Shia mosque in Punjab in April 2002. His arrest for these specific attacks was announced in early July 2003. He is also said to have been behind the Taxila attack on a Christian hospital in August 2002. It so happened that the members of the JM had exactly the same profile as those of the SSP, since it recruited from the rural and urban lower middle class and from the madrasas. The JM recruited also in Britain among emigrant Kashmiris and Punjabis. The JM militant who on 25 December 2000 drove a car full of explosives into an Indian army base was a young man from Birmingham, Mohammed Bilal (alias Asif), who had converted to Islam after a having a vision of the Prophet Muhammad in a dream. This suicide attack was typical of the methods of Jaish-i Muhammad, which was one of the first jihadist groups in South Asia to import the technique of suicide missions from the Middle East. The JM also carried out a number of attacks against Indian forces in Srinagar in April 2000.

The Jaish-i-Mohammad was banned in January 2002. Masood Azhar had renamed his party Tehrik al Furqan in December 2001 after the US State Department had expressed concern about the 'terrorist' activities of the JM. After the ban of the JM he was placed under house arrest at Bahawalpur and the authorities granted him a monthly pension of 10,000 rupees. He was released by order of the court in December 2002 and has since kept a low profile. The JM has adopted the name of Tehrik Khuddam ul Islam (Movement of the Servants of Islam). The new organisation split in June 2003 after violent clashes over control of a mosque in Karachi between rival factions led respectively by Masood Azhar and Abdullah Shah Mazar, the Karachi amir of the movement. The latter, who was expelled, formed his own faction.

Salafism and jihadism

The other jihadist movement which carried out comparable operations in Kashmir was the Lashkar-i-Taiba, an offshoot of the Markaz Da'wa wal Irshad (the Centre for Preaching and Guidance). The latter organisation, which was ideologically affiliated to the Wahhabi Ahl-i-Hadith, was set up in 1987 by Abdullah Azzam (see below), Hafez Saeed and Dr Zafar Iqbal (Abu Hamza). The latter two were educated in Saudi Arabia at the Islamic University in Medina. Hafez Saeed taught at the faculty of engineering and technology at the University of Lahore. The base for Da'wa wal Irshad was installed at Muridke, close to Lahore, on a 190-acre plot donated by the government of General Zia-ul Haq. On the site, in addition to the Um al-Qura mosque, was an educational complex which included a university, a farm, a clothing factory, and a carpentry workshop. The intention was to create a model town in a purely Islamic environment wholly removed from the authority of the Pakistani state. Da'wat wal Irshad received a substantial amount of Saudi aid in its early years, particularly from a certain Sheikh Abu Abdul Aziz, who some sources say was Osama Bin Laden himself. The movement was essentially financed by private Arab donors (Saudi philanthropists discontented with the way the Royal Family governed the kingdom), as well as by the Pakistani diaspora of merchants and traders in the Middle East and Europe, including Britain, the Netherlands and, according to certain sources, France. It also received local gifts in money and kind, and enjoyed revenue from the processing of the hides of the animals sacrificed during Id al-Adha (Feast of the Sacrifice), which were sold at auction.

Da'wa wal Irshad had two explicit objectives. One was *da'wa*—preaching—and this was coupled with education and jihad, which were regarded by the movement as inseparable and of equal importance. This was what endowed it with its particular character relative to the other jihadist movements. Hafez Saeed said in August 1999: "Da'wa and jihad are of an equal and inseparable importance.... Da'wa and jihad are basic and we cannot prefer one to the other.... If beliefs and morals are left unreformed, da'wa alone can lead to anarchy.... It is therefore necessary to fuse the two. This is the only way to transform individual human beings, society and the world."[3]

In the tradition of the reformist Sunni movements of the region, Da'wa wal Irshad seeks to purify society and South Asian Islam from Hindu influences. It appeals to the authority of Ibn Taymiyya, of Muhammad ibn Abd al-Wahhab and of Syed Ahmed Barelvi (Ahmed Shaheed) and Ismail Shaheed, the leaders of the so-called "Wahhabi" movement, who waged a jihad against the Sikhs in the 1820s and founded the Islamic emirate of Peshawar; Ahmed Shaheed is an authority turned to by most of the jihadist movements. In 1994 the movement set up a network of schools which spread rapidly throughout the entire country—especially, in recent years, in Sind, where it has purchased real estate. Arabic and English are taught in addition to the Quranic sciences,—the aim being not merely to purify society by the teaching of the Quran and the Sunna, i.e. to promote a Wahhabi version of Islam as distinct from popular Pakistani Islam, but also to prepare individuals to be receptive to the *da'wa*, to relate the faith to modern knowledge, and to teach children in such a way as to repair the damage done by secular education. The content of school texts is centred on the jihad, so that for example in the Urdu textbook for the second year of primary education there are the last testaments of mujahidin about to go into battle.

The schools, situated in the poorer quarters of the towns and in the villages of rural Sind, attract an increasing number of children. Their success is due to the weakness of state education, which has occasioned a proliferation of private establishments. These are often openly commercial enterprises of very mediocre quality, but they are attractive to families because they offer education through the medium of the English language. It is noteworthy that the religious parties have invested extensively in this sector, especially in the sphere of English teaching and information technology. The Da'wa wal Irshad schools, which boast a total of 140 establishments and 20,000 pupils, are concerned to attract a different clientele from that of the madrasas: they offer a more modern education better adapted to the labour market, and are now beginning to attract the lower middle class—people who cannot afford to pay the high tuition fees charged by good private schools.

Da'wa wal Irshad insists that while the activities of many Muslim organisations relate to da'wa, jihad has been neglected. In its view the present situation demands that Muslims devote themselves to jihad. This is to be directed against the Hindus, whom it regards as the worst polytheists, and against the Jews, who are singled out by the Quran as enemies and are also enemies of Pakistan, since (as they allege) Israel assists the Indian army in Kashmir. Like its radical counterparts, the movement offers a selective reading of those verses of the Quran which relate to Jews and Christians. It thus brings together the main pan-Islamic concerns. The activities of the movement are as a whole directed towards arousing a passion for jihad within individuals, as the only remedy for the range of evils to which Pakistani society is prone. It is particularly seen as a counter to sectarianism, as manifested by conflict between Sunnis and Shias, and increasingly too between Deobandis and Barelvis, which is seen as yet one more conspiracy aimed at distracting Muslims from jihad against the infidels.

The armed wing of Da'wa wal-Irshad, the Lashkar-i-Taiba (LT—the Army of the Pure: Taiba is also an appelation of the holy city of Medina), has become the most active movement in Indian Kashmir, where it has supplanted both the nationalist Jammu and Kashmir Liberation Front and the Hizb ul-Muja-hidin, linked to Jamaat-i-Islami. It has rapidly become notorious for its spectacular 'missions impossible' such as the attacks on the airport at Srinagar and against Indian army barracks, such as that at Badami Bagh in November 1999. The attack in December 2000 against the Red Fort in Delhi was especially significant, since it symbolised the reconquest of the seat of the Moghul empire, occupied by the Hindus.[4]

The Lashkar-i-Taiba takes the position that in the absence of an Islamic state, the right to collect the *zakat* (the Islamic tax) has devolved upon it, and that it is entitled to wage jihad in any part of the world where Muslims are oppressed, that is to say not only in India but also in Palestine, Bosnia, Chechnya and the Philippines. The agenda of the Lashkar-i-Taiba is unambiguous: it intends to Islamise Kashmir and India, then embark on global conquest with the goal of restoring the Caliphate.

Hafez Saeed declares: 'Our jihad will continue until Islam becomes the dominant religion.... Kashmir is no more than the gateway to India, and we shall strive also for the liberation of the 200 million Indian Muslims.' Following the Soviet retreat from Afghanistan, the Lashkar-i-Taiba sent its mujahidin only to Kashmir, since the conflict in Afghanistan, where Muslims confront other Muslims, is in its eyes no longer an authentic jihad. It was banned in 2002, but till then in order to recruit volunteers it had set up a tightly-organised network throughout the country, with more than 2,000 local offices. Its militants were found throughout Pakistan, including the interior of Sind and Baluchistan. The monthly *Al-Dawat*, the most widely-read religious magazine in the Punjab, was printed in an edition of more than 80,000 copies and distributed through all possible outlets, notably in the English-language bookshops of the smart quarters of Islamabad and Karachi. The magazine reveals 'the evils of society, in order to lead young people away from them'. In addition to denouncing television, videocassettes and film music, it especially condemns Jewish conspiracies, the *qadiani* (the Ahmadi sect), and Barelvi practices which relate to the veneration of saints.

In contrast to other jihadist organisations which are active in Kashmir, 80 per cent of the combatants of the Lashkar-i-Taiba are Pakistani. The social profile of the mujahidin is identical to that of non-commissioned officers in the army, since recruitment is carried out—principally in the towns of the Punjab such as Gujranwala, Lahore and Multan,—among families of the lower middle class who, contrary to what is generally supposed, are not of Indian or Kashmiri origin. The majority of the mujahidin emerge from the Urdu-language system of public education, while only 10 per cent come from the madrasas. They are most frequently young town-dwellers who have left school without qualifications, and are either without work or are in low-paid employment which offers them poor prospects for the future. The Lashkar-i-Taiba has also made an effort to recruit in the universities and the high schools, since young men from the universities are more highly motivated and more aware of the significance of what they are undertaking. Young Pakistanis from Britain who join the Lashkar-i-Taiba are mainly university graduates and in skilled occupations. In the countryside the Lashkar-i-Taiba recruits from two social groups: families of Wahhabi inclination, who have often become converted to this school of thought after the head of the household has spent a period working in Saudi Arabia; and the poorer sections of society, since better-off and especially land-owning families do not send their sons to Kashmir. Finally, the Lashkar-i-Taiba takes in those who have been rejected by society; it makes considerable play of its rehabilitation of drug addicts and petty criminals.

The annual gatherings of Dawat wal Irshad brought together more than 100,000 people at Muridke over a period of three days, and foreign delegates attended in addition to the mujahidin and the families of martyrs. There was much oratory on the themes of jihad and the restoration of the Caliphate, and the speeches were accessible on the movement's website. The mujahidin and the martyrs' families themselves also delivered impassioned addresses on the subject of jihad. Military displays were also mounted during the gatherings, and every year these produced hundreds of volunteers.

What motivated recruits to join Lashkar-i-Taiba? Every Pakistani youth is exposed from childhood to intense propaganda on the issue of Kashmir—at school, in the media and within the family. It is not hard to imagine the cumulative effect on an adolescent of the daily portrayal on television of powerful images of Indian troops maltreating Kashmiris, and of appalling tales of extortion and humiliation, often of a sexual nature, committed by Indian soldiers, who are frequently Sikhs, against the Muslim women of Kashmir. All this serves to re-ignite memories of the horrors of the partition of India in 1947, which are still of great significance in the collective memory of the Punjab and are often alluded to.

Nonetheless propaganda, however effective it may be—added to the desire to protect the honour of 'their sisters and their mothers'—is not the only impetus driving young men to sign up with Lashkar-i-Taiba. Emigration, particularly to the Middle East, played the role of a safety valve between 1973 and 1986, after which it tailed off. It never in any case involved more than marginally either the southern Punjab or the poorest social classes, who were unable to muster the financial resources needed to fund emigration. People traffickers currently ask between 200,000 and 400,000 rupees for a departure to Europe, so that for the many Pakistanis who earn around 3,000–5,000 rupees a month travel abroad remains an inaccessible dream. However, the other safety valve for surplus workers is adherence to a religious party or jihadist movement which offers a degree of transformation of the individual's identity and some compensation for social frustrations, most of which stem from simple poverty. The political vacuum also contributes to the success of the jihad, since the Muslim League and the Pakistani Peoples Party have failed, and the traditional religious parties are believed to be too willing to compromise, and to be no less corrupt than other political organisations.

Young men without a future therefore say 'I want to be remembered as a martyr', just as they do in Palestine. Within Pakistani society, which is intensely hierarchical and focused on social status, and where social distinctions are increasingly marked, every individual strives to define his own status as superior in terms of either power, privilege or prestige. Under-achieving groups compensate for their inferiority in terms of power and privilege by adopting an ostentatious religiosity, and especially through the prestige which comes from participating in the jihad in Kashmir; this in turn reflects on all the family members of a combatant and even more on those of a martyr. In fact the family of a martyr acquires a privileged position, since it receives material benefits and often money. These considerations should not be under-rated, and they are especially relevant in the case of young men who were formerly unemployed, drug-addicts or petty criminals; their families might have been unable to cope with them but now, thanks to their sacrifice, they suddenly have a status which had previously seemed unattainable. Fathers have been heard to say, 'My son could have died of an overdose or in a traffic accident, or been killed by a thief in the street, but I have given him up voluntarily to be a martyr and to intercede with God on our behalf.' On the other hand, a careful study of the socio-economic profile of martyrs has shown that some of them at least did not join Lashkar-i Taiba until after they had married and were in steady employment, as if they could not envisage the jihad until they had already achieved some of their personal objectives.

The earliest mujahidin of Lashkar-i-Taiba were trained in Afghanistan in the provinces of Paktia, where there was a camp at Jaji from 1987, and Kunar (Nuristan) with the Muaskar Taiba under the aegis of Maulana Jamil ul-Rahman. Afghans from Nuristan are fighting today in Kashmir in the ranks of the Lashkar-i-Taiba, which maintains three training camps in Azad Kashmir, the part of Kashmir controlled by Pakistan. The principal one is Um al-Qura at Muzzaffarabad where 500 mujahidin are trained each month. The initial level of training, the basic course, lasts twenty-one days, candidates being selected by their local LT official who assesses their motivation. After this first session they go home and are kept under observation. They later take a further course lasting three weeks, devoted to religious indoctrination. Hafez Saeed was in the habit of saying that he would not put a weapon in the hands of any young recruit who had not first accepted a solid religious grounding, and who was not secure in his faith. If the candidates' behaviour at home appeared satisfactory—they were obliged to be model citizens and to have the general approval of those around them—they were allowed finally to take the three-month-long special course in the handling of light weapons, guerrilla tactics and survival techniques.

After completing this programme they returned home transformed. They kept their hair long, ceased to shave their beards, and wore their trousers short above their ankles. They also abandoned their own names and took the surname of a companion of the Prophet or a hero of the early days of Islam such as Abu Talha, Abi Huzaifa or Abu Hureira. A change of personality was in evidence. Militants themselves affirm that after the three-month course they were physically and mentally mature. This educational process therefore constituted a rite of passage. According to reliable sources, between 100,000 and 300,000 young men underwent military training. However, not all those go on to combat: many who receive training devote themselves to collecting funds or to propaganda, especially through the distribution of videocassettes of the atrocities committed in Kashmir. In any case, only those whose families give permission for them to go are sent to Kashmir, which implies that a process of persuading the relatives will be necessary when the latter have not themselves already accepted the Wahhabi ideology.

The Lashkar-i-Taiba adopted the strategy of suicide missions after the Kargil conflict between India and Pakistan in 1999. According to the supreme commander Maulana Zaki ul-Rehman Lakhvi, 891 Indian soldiers were killed in 2000 as a result of such attacks. Lashkar-i-Taiba itself claims to have killed 14,369 Indian soldiers between 1989 and 2000, and to have lost 1,100 mujahidin. These groups of *fidayin*, as they are designated within Lashkar-i-Taiba, differ from the suicide squads of the Tamil Tigers or Palestinian Hamas. Islam forbids suicide. Therefore, even if such martyrs are not regarded as having committed suicide, since the Quran declares that they are not dead but live at God's right hand, they nevertheless do not go on missions where death is certain, choosing rather operations where there is a chance, even if it is infinitesimal, of returning alive.

The objective of the *fidayin* is not to martyr themselves in their first operation. On the contrary, they aim to do as much damage as possible to the enemy to inspire fear in both present and future generations. This is why Lashkar-i-Taiba operations against the Hindus are so savage. Women and babies are killed, and victims are beheaded and eviscerated. The ultimate intention is always martyrdom, and families know that mujahidin leave their homes with the intention of dying. They return to combat repeatedly until they achieve martyrdom, the most sought-after death. Only a martyr speaks directly to God, and can intercede on behalf of his family and enable its members to enter directly into paradise.[5]

Martyrs are buried in Kashmir, and it is a traditional belief that their bodies remain uncorrupted, and that five or six months after death their flesh is still pink and fresh, and the scent of flowers emanates from their tombs. The district official of Lashkar-i-Taiba, accompanied by the regional official and a number of mujahidin, comes to announce the news to the family and to offer his congratulations. No display of mourning is allowed for martyrs, since—according to one of the hadiths regularly cited—the Prophet reproached women for lamenting the deaths of their husbands on the field of battle. Instead sweets are distributed, as at a festival. The Lashkar-i-Taiba has devised new rituals to accompany the prayer for the departed (*ghaibana namaz-i-janaza*): the ceremony is most often held on a sports field, and a large crowd assembles; this bestows great prestige on the family and on the village. Visiting senior officials of Lashkar-i-Taiba preside over the ceremonial, transforming it into a politico-religious meeting and, additionally, an opportunity for proselytisation and recruitment. Impassioned orations about jihad are delivered, and then the martyr's testament, routinely left with his next of kin, is read in public. This inevitably prompts further volunteers to come forward. The parents of the martyrs are proud to have been singled out to be blessed by God, and are given the chance to express their gratitude at the great annual gatherings of Lashkar-i-Taiba where they speak before tens of thousands of people.

The testaments themselves are usually quite short. All begin with more or less the same phrase: 'When you read this testament, I shall have arrived in paradise.' The themes covered are always the same. The combatants ask their parents' pardon for leaving them prematurely without having had the time to be of service to them. They also ask the pardon of all those whom they may at any time have harmed, and ask their family to reimburse any modest sums which they may have borrowed from their friends before leaving for Kashmir. They implore the women of their family to observe strict *purdah* (veiling and seclusion), the men to wear their beards, and all to observe scrupulously the five daily prayers. They also ask their families to give a strict religious education to the children, and in addition—this is a recurrent theme—to guard them against the harmful influence of television. They ask their brothers neither to listen to popular songs nor to watch films, and to destroy their television sets and CD players because of the Hindu culture of music, singing and dance which is conveyed through these media.

The family should prevent those who come to pay visits of condolence from weeping, since lamentation for the dead is a grave sin and causes pain to the deceased. The martyrs insist that their brothers must carry forward the banner ('Do not let my Kalashnikov fall') to avenge both their deaths and the humiliations to which the Muslim women of Kashmir have been subjected. All say that they will await their families at the gates of paradise on the day of the Last Judgement, stressing that life in the hereafter is all that counts, life on earth being no more than an ordeal that has to be borne.

The activities of the Lashkar-i-Taiba are not restricted to Kashmir. Its members have also carried out acts of terrorism in India, particularly in the cities of Bombay and Hyderabad. Their aim, which coincides with the interests of the ISI, is to radicalise particular Indian Muslim groups. The mujahidin are obliged to promise not to use their arms or their military skills within Pakistan and not to join any ethnic or sectarian group, for example the extremist Deobandi movements.[6] Until the American intervention in Afghanistan, the Lashkar-i-Taiba declared that it had no direct ambitions in Pakistan. Indeed it had no grievance against the Pakistani authorities, and had always enjoyed complete freedom of action within the country in the name of the jihad which it waged in Kashmir. However, the centre of Muridke served as an autonomous zone outside the jurisdiction of the state. Ramzi Yusuf[7] and Aimal Kansi[8] among others are said to have taken refuge there.

When the US invaded Afghanistan, the Lashkar-i-Taiba felt itself threatened. It had already been weakened in February 2000 by the Jaish-i-Mohammad's arrival on the scene, or rather its creation by the ISI. It feared, with reason, that it was one of the next targets of American vengeance, and placed little faith in the reassurances of the ISI that it would be permitted to resume its activities in Kashmir once the Afghan crisis was settled. It was for this reason that in October 2001, refusing to follow the instructions of its ISI patrons to keep a low profile, the Lashkar-i-Taiba launched a murderous attack in Kashmir, to match one carried out by the Jaish-i-Mohammad, and afterwards multiplied its attacks on the Indian army and on Hindu civilians. It was probably implicated in the assault on the Indian Parliament on 13 December 2001 which resulted in the deaths of fourteen Indians,— consistently denied by Hafiz Saeed—and in the operation on 14 May 2002 which targeted a garrison near Jammu and left some thirty dead.

Apart from its jihad in Kashmir, the Lashkar-i-Taiba may seem to be an advocate of 'jihad for jihad's sake', failing to take the immediate consequences into account. In December 2000 Hafez Saeed declared: 'Muslims are organising themselves everywhere in the world to participate in *jihad*.... People demand to know what the *mujahidin* have achieved by waging *jihad* in occupied Kashmir. It is true that we have not yet succeeded in liberating Kashmir, but in my opinion awareness on the part of Muslims of the necessity of *jihad* is much more important than any other outcome.' The Lashkar-i-Taiba was banned in January 2002, but in anticipation of this move the armed wing retired to Azad Kashmir and placed itself under an entirely Kashmiri command. It changed its name to Pasban-e Ahl-e hadith and continued its activities. Hafez Saeed became the head of the Jamaat ul-Dawat, based in Muridke, which restricts itself to preaching and education.

The case of the Lashkar-e Taiba demonstrates President Musharraf's ambivalence towards jihadi movements. The government has consistently maintained a lenient attitude towards groups focused on the jihad in Kashmir because the army will continue to need them as a proxy force for as long as the Kashmir issue remains unsolved. According to the authorities, the Lashkar-e Taiba is 'a real jihadi group'—in other words, a group preoccupied only with the jihad in Kashmir, which strictly controls its militants, does nothing harmful to the Pakistan government, and is no threat to the country's internal security—consequently the government sees no reason to interfere with its activities.

Hafiz Saeed was released in December 2002 on a court order after spending six months in detention, and immediately started travelling around the country to renew his call for jihad. He stresses that jihad is essential for the survival of Pakistan and says in interviews that suicide attacks are 'the best form of jihad'.

The annual gathering of the movement held in November 2002 in Pattoki attracted over 100,000 people. The magazine *Al Da'wa* has never ceased publication, and its content remains unchanged with a whole section devoted to the testaments of martyrs. Al Da'wa Model schools continue to instill the spirit of jihad in children's minds. In 2003 Jamaat ul-Dawat expanded its activities in the areas of health and welfare, notably in Karachi and the interior of Sind.

Other organisations include the Hizb ul-Mujahidin (HM—Party of the Mujahidin), directed by Syed Salahuddin, who came originally from Indian Kashmir and is now resident in Muzaffarabad. Eighty per cent of its recruitment is carried out in Kashmir. More liberal than the Lashkar-i-Taiba and the Jaish-i-Muhammad, it is very close to the Jamaat-i-Islami and demands the annexation of Kashmir to Pakistan. It was the first movement to unleash guerrilla warfare in the mid-1990s, but it declared a unilateral ceasefire in July 2000, which left it relatively marginalised, and led to a major rift inside the movement. Its former chief commander, Abdul Majid Dar, who held talks with the Indian government in Srinagar after this ceasefire, was assassinated in March 2003.

The Tehrik-i-Nifaz-i-Shari'at-i-Muhammadi (TNSM—Movement for the Application of the Sharia of Muhammad) was founded in 1994 in Malakand by Sufi Muhammad, a dissident member of the Jamaat-i-Islami. It was a tribal party active in the tribal zones and in the North-West Frontier Province, which demanded the application of the Sharia, and was a typical blend of tribal identity and fundamentalism. In the tradition of Pashtun tribal jihads in the nineteenth century, this movement sent at least 7,000 Pashtuns to fight on the side of the Taliban after the start of the American intervention. It was banned in January 2002. More than 5,000 of its members have died in battle or have disappeared in Afghanistan.

Meanwhile, in reaction to the rise of these sectarian movements of Sunni allegiance, the Shias of Pakistan have for their part also organised themselves into political and paramilitary groups. The Sipah-i-Muhammad Pakistan (SMP—Army of Mohammed-Pakistan) was a terrorist group which came out of the Tehrik-i-Jafria-e-Pakistan (TJP—Jafria [Shia] Movement-Pakistan). The TJP was banned in January 2002 and started functioning again under the name of Tehrik-e Islami (TI, Islamic Movement). Its leader Allama Sajid Naqvi is a member of the Muttahida Majlis-e Amal. The SMP was formed in 1994 by Ghulam Raza Naqvi and Murid Abbas Yazdani, who was assassinated in 1996, in reaction to the inability of the TJP to protect the Shias, and its members carried out violent attacks targeted at Sunnis. It recruited in rural areas, in the small villages of southern Punjab and in the Shia madrasas. This movement, financed by Iran till 1996 and concentrated in Lahore, was extensively infiltrated by the intelligence services, and fragmented by clashes between personalities and castes. It had an ambiguous relationship with the TJP, on the pattern of that between the Sipah-i-Sabaha-Pakistan with the Lashkar-i-Jangvi. Since 1998, the Sipah-i-Muhammad-Pakistan has virtually disintegrated, with its militants either in prison or in exile in Iran and southern Lebanon. What remains is a collection of uncontrolled and extremely violent elements without a unified structure of command, who carry out reprisals for anti-Shia attacks. The Sipah-i-Mohammad was banned in August 2001.

2

THE POLITICIZATION OF THE SHIA COMMUNITY IN PAKISTAN IN THE 1970s AND 1980s

Shias played a prominent role in the struggle for Pakistan, but as individuals rather than as Shias; most of the leaders were in fact Westernised and saw politics as a collective secular activity separate from religion. Today, having migrated in large numbers after the partition of the Indian subcontinent, Shias make up 15 to 20 per cent of the population of Pakistan, or a total of at least 25 million.[1]

Before 1977, the State was neutral and had no sectarian agenda. Shias were well represented in the army and the federal and local bureaucracy, and there were Shia ministers in each successive government. Communal disturbances erupted occasionally during the month of Muharram and tensions sometimes led to riots,[2] but most Shias did not feel discriminated against[3] and their position even improved under Zulfiqar Ali Bhutto (1971–7).

The Islamisation policy of General Zia-ul Haq's rule (1977–88), based on narrow Sunni interpretations of Islam,[4] alarmed the Shia community and contributed to the radicalisation of religious identities.[5] At the same time, the Iranian revolution emboldened the Shias; it also brought about a complete reshaping of the Shia leadership and empowered a new generation of clerics and students educated in Qom. Traditional ulama linked to Najaf, who were apolitical and concerned only with rituals, found themselves marginalised. Religious mobilisation led to political mobilisation as the 'new Shias' took control of the community and utilised old structures for political activism. Pakistan, with its sizeable Shia community, was seen as the mirror of Iran, and in the early 1980s, when Iran was trying to export its revolution, Pakistani government was unable—or unwilling—to restrict the internal impact of these new developments and of regional conflicts. Iranian interference in Pakistani politics was denounced by Sunni militants, while Shias were seen as disloyal to Pakistan and as a political and geo-strategic threat to Zia's regime. In an effort to contain the Shia resurgence, Saudi Arabia and Iraq patronised Sunni groups and Pakistan soon became a battlefield in a proxy war between Iran and Saudi Arabia.

The focus of this paper is the growing political mobilisation of the Pakistani Shia community between 1979 and 1988. It will first briefly describe the emergence of the student movement in the 1970s and the religious mobilisation following the Iranian revolution, then examine the formation of a political party under the leadership of Allama Husseini, and finally attempt to identify the reasons for the failure of the political movement and the subsequent upsurge in sectarian violence that has plagued Pakistan since the beginning of the 1990s.

Until the end of the 1960s, Shia students did not engage in student politics as Shias. Those who were politically conscious supported the Left and were affiliated to the National Students' Organisation (NSO), a socialist movement that was in decline by the early 1970s.

In 1966 a Shia Students' Association was created at King Edward's Medical College in Lahore, but its influence was only marginal, and it eventually petered out during the anti-Ayub movement in 1968,[6] when the colleges were closed and students returned to their home towns and villages. The colleges reopened in 1971, but students were kept busy with their exams and all political and union activities remained at a standstill.

The emergence of the Imamia Students' Organisation (ISO) in May 1972 was a turning point for the mobilisation of Shiite students on a religious basis. Students at the Engineering University contacted students at King Edward's (where Mohammad Ali Naqvi[7] was studying), with the aim of merging five smaller groups into a centralised organisation with a unified programme, along the lines of the Islami Jarmiat-e

Tulaba (IJT: Islamic Society of Students), the student wing of the Jamaat-e islami (JI). Few joined the new organisation at first, however, as Shias were more attracted to the People's Students Federation (PSF), the student wing of the Pakistan Peoples Party (PPP) that ruled the country from 1971 to 1977. Moreover, Shia organisations such as the All Pakistan Shia Conference and the Idara-e Tahaffuz-e Hoquq-e Shia (Organisation for Safeguarding Shia Rights in Pakistan) created in 1953, as well as the traditional clergy, were strongly opposed to the creation of the ISO. They feared that it would be a socialist or communist movement directed against the Jamaat-e islami, which they did not wish to antagonise. Starting from Lahore, which remained its stronghold till the 1980s, the ISO established itself at the Agricultural University of Faisalabad, then in Multan, Rawalpindi and Peshawar and finally, in 1978, in Karachi (Dow Medical College).[8]

The ISO won its first victory in 1972 during a campaign for a separate syllabus of *Islamiyat* (Islamic studies) for Shia students, when several of its members were part of a Shia delegation who met the minister of: religious affairs.[9] All Shia students' organisations were united in 1975 under the banner of the ISO, but the aims were still purely religious and social. ISO members organised rituals and *majalis* (mourning assemblies) on the campus and asked Shia students to wear a beard; they also helped poor students by providing them with free textbooks, cheap lodging and, if needed, financial assistance. Two categories of students joined the ISO in the 1970s: those who were disappointed with the Left, and those whose traditional families were impressed by the ISO's emphasis on rituals and feared that their children might be corrupted if they joined leftist organisations. From the beginning, caste and class factors played a great role: nearly all the ISO leaders were Syeds belonging to the urban professional middle class or to landed families from South Punjab.

Dr Mohammad Ali Naqvi's links with the ulama brought the ISO on to the international stage. In 1976 the organisation started denouncing the ill-treatment of Shia ulama by the Iraqi government.[10] And, although few students went to Iran before the revolution, the works of Ali Shariati were translated into Urdu and widely read in the universities. After the fall of the Shah, students became more assertive as they 'saw a light coming from Iran'. They recognised Ayatollah Khomeini as

their *marja-e taqlid* (religious authority) in 1979 and a first ISO delegation visited Iran in 1980,[11] Iranian cultural centres (*khana-e farhang*) in
Pakistan became very active, distributing works by prominent ulama
translated into Urdu as well as anti-Wahabi literature. Nearly four
thousand students received scholarships from the Iranian government
to spend a period of six months to a year in religious institutions—
mostly in Qom, where they came into contact with Shia students from
the Middle East. By the time of their return to Pakistan they had
adopted the doctrine of *wilayat-e faqih* (guardianship of the jurist).
Filled with enthusiasm, they toured the countryside in Punjab and the
Northern Areas and showed films on the oppression of the Shah's
regime and the success of the revolution. They criticised the traditional
ulama and their links to Iraq and accused them of being apolitical,
quietist and opposed to the leadership of Ayatollah Khomeini. Although
the traditional clergy welcomed the revolution because it had replaced
a secular anti-ulama monarchy with a government of the ulama, it was
opposed to Khomeini's revolutionary rhetoric and saw the students'
activism as a threat to its own authority.

The students also campaigned against the *zakirs* (religious specialists
who recite *majalis*), accusing them of being illiterate, spreading lies and
concerning themselves only with money-making. There are few real
mujtahids (ulama authorised to make binding interpretations of Islamic
law) in Pakistan,[12] but there are many *zakirs*, who may or, more often,
may not be well-grounded scholars of Islam, These skilled performers,
famed as much, if not more, for their personality and eloquence as for
their learning, have always been more important than the *mujtahids* to
the religious education of the community, especially as the great majority of the Shia population in Pakistan accepted *Shaikhiyya* doctrines and
gave a very high status to the *ahl-e bait* (the family of the Prophet). The
anti-*zakir* campaign of the ISO was thus seen by many as an attack on
the very foundation of Shiism as it was practised in South Asia. The
traditional clergy, who promoted *Shaikhiyya* beliefs, denounced the
campaign against *zakirs* as linked to the so-called 'Dhakko party' and
accused the students of being Khalisis[13] or Shia Wahhabis.[14]

Throughout 1979–80, Shia leaders mobilised the community against
the Sunni Hanafi laws that General Zia intended to implement. Mufti
Jaafar Hussain, a respected apolitical cleric from Gujranwala, resigned

in protest from the Council of Islamic Ideology. A Shia convention held in Bhakkar in April 1979 to protest against the implementation of Sunni Hanafi law elected Mufti Jaafar Hussain as *Qaid-e Millat-e Jaafria* (Leader of the Jaafari [i.e. Shia] People). The creation of the Tehrik-e Nifaz-e Fiqh-e Jaafria (TNFJ: Movement for the Implementation of Shia Law) as a religious pressure group was announced during this convention. Mufti Jaafar warned of the launching of a national movement if the government refused to accept the still purely religious Shia demands: recognition of Shia law by courts of law and the lifting of restrictions on *azadari* (the distinctively South Asian mourning rituals central to the expression of Shia religiosity in Pakistan).[15] Tension mounted after the promulgation of the *zakat* (compulsory almsgiving ordinance) in June 1980. Shias started to realise that, in an Islamic State, their political and religious interests were different from those of the majority. Zia's Islamisation was seen as the beginning of tyranny, and Shias felt that they had a duty to revolt against this manipulation of Sunni Islam directed against their interests.

The protest culminated in a three-day siege of Islamabad in July 1980, which those who took part in it saw as a kind of re-creation of Karbala. The ISO played a prominent role in bringing 100,000 Shias from all over Pakistan to the capital. Students wearing shrouds and shouting '*Ya Hussain*' and '*Zia Yazid*' demonstrated in front of the Iraqi embassy against the assassination on 19 April 1980 of Ayatollah Baqr ul Sadr and his sister Bint al Huda by the Saddam regime. Government buildings were under siege for two days. But Zia-ul Haq capitulated after significant Iranian pressure,[16] and an agreement signed on 6 July exempted Shias from the deduction of *zakat* from their bank accounts.

This was seen as a great victory by the Shias, who had alone dared to challenge the martial law regime. It brought them into politics, giving them a new visibility and empowerment; huge *imambaras*[17] and madrasas were built, in some cases with Iranian money. *Julus* (processions) and *majalis* became occasions for a competition over status and a reaffirmation of the superiority of Shia beliefs and devotion to the *ahl-e-bait*.

In response to these developments, which they regarded as provocative, Sunnis castigated Shias as *kafirs* (infidels)—on the grounds that *zakat* is a pillar of Islam—and denounced the Iranian revolution as a Zionist conspiracy to capture holy places. Leaflets citing nineteenth-century Deobandi fatwas that had declared Shias to be *kafirs* were pasted up on the walls. A large amount of Saudi-funded sectarian literature began to appear: for instance, *Shiites and Shiis* by Ehsan Elahi Zaheer[18] (head of the Ahl-e Hadith [19] party), a book published in 1980 in Lahore denouncing Shias as *kafirs* and Zionist agents,[20] and *Imam Khomeini aur Shiaya* (Imam Khomeini and Shiism) with a foreword by the head ot the *Nadwat ul ulama* school of Lucknow—closely linked to the *Rahita-e Alarn-e Islami* (World Islamic League)—were translated into English and Arabic and distributed by Saudi embassies around the world. The government sought to contain Shia activism and Iranian influence by strengthening Sunni institutions. Madrasas funded by foreign donors were established across Pakistan, and the Inter-Services Intelligence (LSI) organised Sunni militant groups to contend with the 'Shia problem'.[21]

The riots in Karachi in 1983 were orchestrated by the Sawad-e Azam-e Ahl-e Sunnat (The Great Sunni Majority), an Iraqi-funded movement led by Pathan extremists that was the precursor of the Sipah-e Sahaba Pakistan (SSP: Army of the Companions of the Prophet-Pakistan) created in Punjab in 1985. Anti-Shia riots in Kurram Agency and Gilgit in 1986 were seen as acts of revenge sponsored by the Zia regime to teach Shias a lesson.

Mufti Jaafar had given his community a degree of unity, but his death in 1983 led to a split between the traditional quietists and the modern reformists. Radicals saw this split as a conspiracy by Pakistani intelligence to weaken the community and divide it along the lines of the Sunni division between Deobandi and Barelvi,[22] Traditional ulama strongly opposed to the ISO, whom they described as a group of 'wahhabis bent on destroying the faith', campaigned for the election of Maulana Syed Hamid Ali Musavi, a cleric from Rawalpindi with Shaikhi leanings, to replace Mufti Jaafar.[23] At the same time, the ISO and the new generation of Qom-educated clerics united around the charismatic leadership of Allama Arif Hussein al Husseini and elected him as *Qaid-e Millat-e Jaafria* at a convention in Bhakkar in February Musavi's followers did not recognise Husseini's election and formed a TNFJ splinter faction concerned only with *azadari* that was willing to compromise with the Zia regime. Thus, Musavi and his followers enjoyed the support of General Zia and the army, whose aim it was to divide the community. Whereas the traditional clergy launched a campaign against Allama Husseini, describing him as this 'Pathan nominated as head of the community who is against *azadari*', he received the support of Hassan Taheri, Khomeini's official representative in Pakistan. Husseini tried in vain to bring about a reconciliation between the two groups, but Musavi rejected his offer to refer the problem to Ayatollah Khomeini or Ayatollah Khoi.

Allama Husseini, a Turi Pashtun[24] born in Parachinar (Kurram Agency) in 1946, was educated in Najaf and Qom.[25] In the early 1970s he stood apart from other Pakistani students in Iraq as a disciple of Ayatollah Khomeini.[26] He travelled to Pakistan to marry in 1973, and the next year, because of his political activities, the Iraqi authorities refused to issue him with a visa enabling him to return to Najaf. He then went to Qom, where he studied under Ayatollah Murtaza Mottahari, among others. Although he wished to stay in Qom, he was sent back to Pakistan in 1977 with a mission to mobilise the community on the pattern of what Imam Musa Sadr had done in Lebanon. Allama Husseini was the first cleric to recite a *majlis* in Pashto, in Peshawar in 1977. In 1978, he mobilised the students to organize a demonstration against the Shah of Iran in Peshawar, and he launched a social movement in the semi-autonomous Kurram Tribal Agency against the *maliks* (tribal representatives) and the Political Agent representing the federal government), which led to his arrest and detention. He created the Alamdar Foundation, a group of young people dedicated to social welfare and the fight against drugs, and also opened a school and a hospital in his hometown of Parachinar with funds collected from local Shias working in the Gulf. After the Islamabad agreement of July 1980, Allama Husseini became a member of the Supreme Council of the TNFJ and started working in close cooperation with the ISO. He used to say that ISO members were his wings and that he could not fly without them.

After his nomination as Khomeini's *wakil* (representative) in Pakistan, Allama Husseini gained legitimacy not only in Pakistan but in the eyes of the Shia community internationally. Traditionally the *maraji* of Iraq and Iran authorised their *wakils* in South Asia to collect *khoms* (religious tax of one fifth of income incumbent on all faithful Shias) and to spend it for the benefit of the community. Allama Husseini could now, as the representative of the *wali-e faqih*, intervene in political and religious affairs.

Allama Husseini transformed the TNFJ from a religious pressure group into a non-sectarian political party advocating '*ittihad bain al Muslimin*' (unity among Muslims), in order to fight tyranny and establish a just Islamic order. Openly at war with the Zia regime, he accused it of being the agency of American imperialism in the region and of 'busily spreading *fitna* (internal discord) and sectarian troubles in Pakistan at the behest of the Nejdis'[27] while Muslims were oppressed in Palestine, Afghanistan, Kashmir, India, Eritrea and the Philippines.

Allama Husseini's call for a boycott of the referendum in December 1984 made it clear to Zia that he would not limit himself to defending the rights of the Shia community. When the information minister announced In the same month that the government had implemented the Islamabad agreement, Allama Husseini protested and called a press conference in Lahore to announce the entry of the TNFJ into politics; 'we have formed a committee for the restoration of democracy which will contact the other parties and will elaborate an agenda to put an end to Imperialism.' He visited a number of cities to win Shias over to his new policy, which he explained clearly at one of the rallies:

> We have two types of problems, first as Shiites and then as Pakistanis. If we want to solve our religious problems without taking into account our political problems, it is absolutely certain that we will fail notwithstanding our efforts because these problems cannot be taken separately. If we remain apart from other Muslims at both national and international level, we will not only shirk our legal responsibility but go against the Koran and Islam. If we separate the political problems from the religious ones, the results will be terrible. The link between religion and politics is very deep and we must deal with them together.

The movement grew more radical after the Quetta incidents of July 1985. Shias had been demonstrating each year on 6 July to denounce the non-implementation of the Islamabad agreement of July 1980, but in 1985 the demonstrations turned violent in Quetta and resulted in at least 15 deaths and more than a thousand arrests. It was again a recreation of Karbala: water and electricity were cut off in the Shia neighbourhoods and a curfew enforced for sixteen days. This was denounced by Allama Husseini as an act of revenge by the Zia regime for the fact that the TNFJ had called for a boycott of the referendum in December 1984. The Quetta incidents transformed a moderate religious pressure group into a militant movement and paved the way for its transformation into a full-fledged political party.

On 6 July 1987 in Lahore, Allama Husseini announced the transformation of the TNFJ into a political party. He said that, by fighting only for their religious rights and remaining aloof from politics, Shias had been marginalised and considered unimportant. The charter of the Sabiluna party (*Hamara Rasta*, Our way) is very similar to the charter of the Lebanese party Amal. It advocates the Iranian model and claims that American imperialism is the cause of Pakistan's ills. Allama Husseini called on all Pakistanis to join him to fight injustice and exploitation and to rid the country of American imperialism and western influence. He gave a new definition of 'true religion', which embraced political, social and economic issues.

A kind of 'Qomization' of Pakistan took place under the charismatic leadership of Allama Husseini. Rituals (*majahs, julus, dua-e komail*) were rationalised on the Iranian pattern, and the didactic part of the *majlis* centred on *ihadat* (religious observances) and *aqidat* (dogma) was extended at the expense of *masaib* (or *gham*[28]). *Majalis* were also politicised, as Mohsin Naqvi[29] and Irfan Haider Abidi gave speeches depicting Zia as Yazid or an American agent and describing martial law as a war against God and His Prophet. Young clerics focused in their sermons on *mazlumiyat* (oppression), referring to the enemies of Shiism and to the experiences of Shias in Iran, Lebanon and the Gulf. Iranian diplomats openly participated in rituals, and the stalls erected in front of the *imambaras* sold Iranian books and cassettes. A pan-Islamic sentiment gained ground after the Iranian revolution: the Karbala paradigm was constantly reinterpreted and linked to Palestine, Kashmir and Bosnia. Religious symbolism was used to justify political action under the slogan *Kul yom Ashura, kul ardh Karbala* (Every day is Ashura, the whole earth is Karbala). Boys and girls educated in Qom adopted Iranian-style dress, and black cloaks, black turbans and hijab became commonplace. Iranian rhetoric (*taghut* [despotism, tyranny], *mustazafin* [dispossessed], *mazlumiyat*) was used and slogans such as *Amerika murdabad* (Death to America), *Islam ka dushman Amerika* (America is the enemy of Islam), *Pakistan ka dushman Amerika* (America is the enemy of Pakistan), *Russia murdabad* (Death to Russia) and *Israel murdabad* (Death to Israel) were heard after prayers in Shiite mosques. Just as in Iran, *Yom al Quds* (Jerusalem Day) was celebrated by the ISO on the last Friday of Ramadan and *Yom marg bar Amerika* (Death to America Day) on 16 May, when children dressed in fatigues would trample on Israeli and American flags.[30]

The transformation of the TNFJ into a political party was met with hostility by other Shia organisations, which claimed that the party's charter was an expression of communism and contrary to the Quran and the Sunna. The divide between old (or black) and new (or Wahhabi) Shias became deeper: the new generation accused the traditional clergy of being passive, of spending its time lamenting and waiting for the *mahdi*, whereas the Iranian revolution had shown that the world could be changed.

During the hajj in 1988, Dr Mohammad Ali Naqvi and several other Shia leaders were arrested by the Saudi authorities and deported to Pakistan. At the same time, pressure was exerted on Allama Husseini to tone down his rhetoric: the American authorities grew alarmed, and on 4 August a religious dignitary returning from the hajj conveyed a message to him that the Saudi government's patience was exhausted and that he should keep a low profile. Finally, on 6 August 1988, Allama Hussaini was assassinated in Peshawar, most probably at Riyadh's instigation and with the collusion of General Zia's aide de camp.

On 4 September 1988, Allama Sajid Naqvi was elected to replace him. From then on, the TNFJ lost its revolutionary zeal and became more moderate and pragmatic. It entered into an alliance with the Pakistan Peoples Party (PPP) for the elections of October 1988 and changed its name in 1993 to Tehrik-e Jaafria Pakistan (TJP: Jaafri Movement of Pakistan). The TJP failed to unite the Shia community and a number of splinter groups developed as a result; some of these were violent, like the Sipah-e Mohammad (SMP: Army of Mohammad), whose young militants believed that the TJP was too moderate and did not protect the community against Sunni extremists.

Several factors may explain the failed mutation from a sectarian group into a political party. Under the leadership of Allama Husseini, Shias in Pakistan forgot that they are only a small minority and that, living as they do in a complex religious environment that mostly disagrees with their beliefs and practices, their position cannot be compared with that of fellow Shias in Iran; the public nature of *azadari* also means that Shias impinge upon the religious sensitivities of the larger Sunni community. The new generation of ulama supported by the students emerged as a new power centre, and the activism they generated was perceived as a threat by Sunnis. Although Barelvis share their devotion to *ahl-e bait*, Shias could never gain their support against Deobandi extremists who wanted them declared *kafirs*; Barelvis simply stayed neutral. Their newfound assertiveness after the Iranian revolution and the impact of regional conflicts on the domestic scene led to the rise of sectarian violence, which has continued unabated since the early 1990s.

The heterogeneous nature of the community must also be considered in an analysis of the reasons for failure. Ethnic and linguistic divisions exist among Punjabis, Pathans, Baltistanis and Urdu-speaking Muhajirs of Karachi. Rituals and practices take different forms from one region to another and are a significant source of controversy: Muharram rituals in Karachi, largely imported from North India, are different from Muharram rituals in Lahore and even more from those performed in rural Punjab or the North West Frontier Province (NWFP). In a place like Jhang, which was a hotbed of sectarian violence in the early 1990s, there is not only a deep division between Sunnis and Shias but also a cleavage inside the Shia community between locals and Muhajirs for reasons partially linked to ritual and linguistic differences; the locals are rural and Siraiki-speaking, while the Muhajirs are urban and Urdu-speaking.

Pakistani society is highly fragmented, and so caste and class divisions are also part of the explanation. The traditional clergy belongs to prestigious religious families from Punjab or to families who migrated from North India after Partition. This caste-conscious and class-conscious establishment, linked to the big feudal families, felt threatened by the emergence of quite young new leaders who, though claiming to be Syeds, came from a totally different social and ethnic background. The people around Allama Husseini were Pashtuns from a modest rural background in the tribal areas, and their families were not part of the religious establishment; many student activists belonged to lower middle-class families from rural Punjab or were recently urbanised. This was not an acceptable situation to the traditional clergy. Moreover, the opposition between Musavi's and Husseini's followers also reflected a class conflict: the status gained by Qom-educated clerics and their appropriation of a religious discourse for social liberation[31] threatened the status quo. Allama Hussaini wanted to give the ulama the leading role: he intended that they would replace the feudal lords and the politicians as leaders of the community. The influence of the feudal lords diminished but, on the whole, they managed to keep the activists' influence away from the countryside and to preserve the status quo.

The caste factor also played a prominent role inside the TNFJ (later TJP). While the 'old' Shias referred to the Shia community as *Millat-e Jaafria*, the 'new' Shias insisted on using the word *Qaum* (nation) which, interestingly, is also the one used for caste or tribe in Pakistan. This terminological preference implied that they were first Shias and that they identified with the Shia community worldwide. Allama Husseini used to say: 'We are first Shia and then Pakistanis' but, as is nearly always the case in Pakistan, the local prevailed over the global and caste and class differences remained an obstacle in the way of unity.[32]

But probably the main reason for the failure is that clerics educated in Iran had no experience of the Pakistani political system; they entered politics without knowing its dynamics. Unable to act independently of Iran, they were eliminated from sensitive crimination in the army and the state but the backlash of the Afghan conflict, and positions at a time when the Pakistani government was seriously at odds with Iran.

In the 1990s, as dissatisfaction with Sajid Naqvi's style of leadership increased and gave rise to violent splinter groups, Iran stopped its counterproductive funding of the TJP and the ISO.[33] The 'new' Shias felt betrayed as they became aware that Iran had been using them for its own political interests. Pakistani Shias continue to pay a heavy price for their shattered dream. They find themselves without a sense of direction, while sectarian assassinations have claimed the lives of religious dignitaries, of ordinary citizens whose only fault is to have a Shia name, and of hundreds of Shia doctors, lawyers and businessmen. It has reached a point where some commentators say that the risk of being killed is now an occupational hazard for Shia professionals in Pakistan.

PART TWO

SECTARIANISM: THE SHIA/SUNNI CONFLICT IN PAKISTAN

3

SECTARIANISM AS A SUBSTITUTE IDENTITY

SUNNIS AND SHIAS IN CENTRAL AND SOUTH PUNJAB

Conflicts over identity are a major source of internal tensions in South Asia. Identities are defined in terms of boundaries, that is in reference to another group, to the 'Other'. The main contradiction of Pakistan—a modern secular state founded on religious sentiments-—has not been resolved.[1] Pakistan has never been a nation-state; highly fragmented, it has failed in integrating the people into a nation by making their Pakistani identity their most treasured possession. People had to find other identities whether ethnic group, caste, language, *biradari*[2] or sect. The political vacuum created in the Zia era was filled by the emergence of ethnic and sectarian organisations.[3] In the 1970s, ethnicity became a substitute identity, but it was branded as treason and violently suppressed. The environment in the 1980s was religious; religious identity was fostered by the state and official sanction was given to the religious organisations during the Afghan war in the name of Islam.

Sectarianism in Pakistan

Sectarianism which is, in Pakistan, a Deobandi-Shia[4] rather than a Sunni-Shia conflict comes from the belief that the sect which one professes is the only true one and that the followers of other sects should be converted to one's own sect or exterminated. The 'Other', the person who does not share your beliefs and religious observances is seen somehow as a danger to you because, being different, he cannot mean well for you.[5] Sectarianism, which was traditionally mostly confined to verbal attacks and clashes during the month of Muharram, has now degenerated into violence.[6]

More than 1000 serious incidents were recorded between 1987 and 1997, 478 persons were killed and some 2300 were injured.[7] The year 1997 was the worst so far—97 serious incidents were recorded claiming over 200 lives,[8] and 1998, which started with the Mominpura massacre, was another year of sectarian violence.[9] There has been a change in the pattern of violence: till 1995, the killings were confined to leaders and activists of both sects. Targeted attacks on religious gatherings and specific mosques followed, then it was hand-grenade attacks and time devices. In 1996, there were targeted killings of office bearers of organisations and government functionaries. The year 1997 saw a total change with indiscriminate gunfire on ordinary citizens not involved in sectarian activity, and tit-for-tat killings targeting doctors, lawyers and traders.[10]

Sectarian clashes were rare before Partition in the areas which now form Pakistan. Nobody thought in terms of Shia and Sunni at the time of the Pakistan movement.[11] Sectarian consciousness and some prejudice has always existed but has never prevented co-existence. Sectarianism does not exist at the community level even if some intolerance can now be felt: Shias and Sunnis live together in the same neighbourhoods, they speak the same language and share the same culture. This evokes the narcissism of minor differences described by Freud: the smaller the difference between two peoples, the greater it is bound to loom in their imagination. Why is there a need for a sectarian outlook on life, why has it become much more meaningful for certain people to identify themselves as a Sunni or a Shia and why do people adhere to the principles avowed by sectarian organisations?

The roots of sectarianism

Sectarianism is often seen as the consequence of Zia-ul Haq's Islamisation policy which meant state monopoly on religion and dominance of a particular sect, and which brought theological differences to the fore,[12] Religion without sectarian domination has little meaning for the common man in Pakistan. The imposition of *zakat* (compulsory tax deducted by the government) in 1980 mobilised the Shia community against Zia-ul Haq.[13] External factors are also enhanced: sectarianism is described as the outcome of the Iranian revolution and of the Afghan war and the ensuing influx of funds and arms, and it is often seen as a proxy war between foreign powers financing the mushroom growth of madrasas and using Pakistani territory to further their own interests.[14] It cannot be denied that the Iranian revolution gave a new sense of identity to the Shia community which became more assertive and entered the political arena in the 1980s. The development of sectarian Sunni organisations was partly a reaction to this new Shia militancy[15] and religion was seen, by Sunnis and Shias alike, as a means of power after the Iranian revolution. These explanations are obviously relevant but the external environment has perhaps been no more than the enabling factor which gave scale and sustenance to the sectarian phenomenon.[16] The 'foreign hand' and the intelligence agencies are inevitably blamed every time there is a crisis[17] and people are often ready to believe such stories, but this rationale too easily absolves the government and society of all responsibility.

The roots of sectarianism in Central and South Punjab go back to the political polarisation of the early seventies. The rapid social and economic change leading to the emergence of new classes (without any change in the system of power which remains under the control of the elite drawn from the landed and the urban upper class) was accompanied by an extremely rapid urbanisation without any industrialisation. Sectarian militancy in this context can be described as a reaction to a growing sense of insecurity and hopelessness resulting from the uneven distribution of resources, and as a revolt of the uprooted and marginalised periphery deprived of access to the political arena. It is the result of extreme poverty in South Punjab[18] coupled with illiteracy and the population explosion. In a context where the traditional structures are collapsing or dysfunctional, sect has become an identity marker, a temporary refuge and a platform to articulate grievances and get access to power.[19] Sectarianism can thus be described as a phenomenon of collective anger, an emotional outburst against structures of power which must be pressurised or done away with.

The social cost of mechanisation and the Green Revolution

South Punjab has been neglected since Partition. This economically deprived region had the lowest education rate according to the 1981 census. Large landholders in Central and South Punjab have managed to retain their power.[20] To escape land reforms, they converted their estates into orchards which were exempted from the limits on holdings. This was accompanied by a marked increase in mechanisation which created unemployment and semi-employment, while there was already surplus labour in the Punjab. Mechanisation was a substitute for labour and it displaced landless labour: a study based on sixty mechanised farms in the Punjab and Bahawalpur found that permanent labour declined from 2000 to 340 out of which 100 were employed on tractors. Another study revealed that the labour force per acre had been reduced about 50 per cent from the premechanisation period.'[21] The big landlords have sold vast tracts of land and a new class of middle capitalist landlords has appeared. They did not hesitate to eliminate those who could not compete with them and a large number of smaller landholders were displaced.[22] Land previously cultivated by tenants was resumed, many were transformed into wages' labourers on the feudals' or new middle capitalist landlords' farms, working as tractor drivers or seasonal workers as mechanisation had increased the need for casual workers. Many more were forced to migrate to the cities and this traumatic experience changed the social and political outlook of people who had been traditionally tied to the land. While in the *barani* (rain-fed) regions of north-west Punjab, there was a tradition of emigration to towns or employment in the army, such a relation with outside employment does not exist on a significant scale in the Canal Colonies of Sargodha, Multan and Bahawalpur. Allotment of land to military and civil officers at the expense of the locals has also produced a strong feeling of being neglected. Small farmers, owning between 12.5 and 25 acres, could not keep up with the increased competition. They sold their lands and moved to the towns and cities or became small shopkeepers. A comparison of the 1960 and 1972 census figures for the Punjab shows that the category of farmers owning between 7.5 to 25 acres has decreased both in area and numbers.[23] Although the Green Revolution has increased the prosperity of some, it has impoverished many in the rural areas.[24] Due to landlessness and unemployment the peasantry has been proletarianised:[25] 30 per cent of the population is now considered as living under the poverty level compared to 20 per cent ten years back.[26] Most of the people of South Punjab could not afford to pay recruitment agencies to get a job in the Middle East—anyway this safety valve does not exist anymore[27]—and Karachi has become more and more problematic because of the law and order situation. In traditional rural society, everybody was employed and had a place in village society, everyone had something to do and had some social utility. Traditional functions have been eliminated, auxiliary professions (blacksmith, carpenter, etc) are not needed anymore. Farmers have opted for cash crops—mostly cotton in South Punjab—they hardly grow vegetables anymore, and food has to be bought from specialised shops. There has been a realignment of the class structure: due to the traditional sense of superiority among the farming classes, they are reluctant to enter other professions. However, manual labourers have entered different professions and have made profit as entrepreneurs, merchants and intermediaries. Many *kammi*[28] families are now more prosperous than small farmers and their income is more stable. If there had been industrialisation, many people would have left the villages to work in factories thus reversing the trend of land fragmentation,[29]

The market towns are in the hands of Punjabi immigrants,[30] especially the *mohajirs* from Rohtak, Hisar and Karnal districts who control most of the trade.[31] For the locals displaced from their lands, no jobs are available which gives rise to much bitterness. The region has not been industrialised, as the Seraiki belt concentrates on agriculture. The South (Rahim Yar Khan) has witnessed the development of agro-based industries; the traders have invested but certain landlords have resisted the growth of industry which they see as a threat to their vested interests.[32] The Pakistan Peoples Party (PPP) was the main beneficiary of the discontent,[33] but its image of defender of the downtrodden suffered a lot after it allied itself with the feudals of the Multan area. The sense of hopelessness was channelled for some time into nationalist sentiment (Seraiki identity) which traditionally appeared every time the locals felt that they were left out of the power structure. People felt that they had been colonised economically and also psychologically, which resulted in a deep sense of alienation.

The mushroom growth of madrasas in South Punjab

Educational facilities were absent because the landlords did not allow the establishment of schools[34] and also because it carried the threat of alienation: educated sons were likely to leave the village, attracted by a job in town.[35] According to the survey of 'ghost schools' conducted in 1998 by the army, there are over 5000 such schools in Multan division and 800 in Sargodha division, the buildings being used by feudals as *dera*[36] or cowsheds. This explains why madrasas proliferated in South Punjab. According to an official report published in 1995, out of a total of 2512 registered madrasas in Punjab,[37] 1619 were located in South Punjab. Bahawalpur, a very poor area, had the highest number in the province (883), Dera Ghazi Khan came next (411) and Multan had 325. It should be recalled that West Pakistan had only 137 madrasas in 1947. The total number of students at any time is about 214,000 with Bahawalpur division on top. About 100,000 students graduate every year. The number of unregistered madrasas is thought to be much higher, according to some sources, Jhang district has over 500.[38] Not all madrasas are sectarian but the sectarian ones have multiplied.[39] In a feudal environment where violence is part of the sociopolitical culture and is even valued,[40] the sectarian madrasas identify with the parties which protect them, preach violence for enforcement of their kind of Islam and the elimination of other sects.[41] The students are taught a faulty interpretation of jihad (holy war): if they kill a member of the other sect, called a *kafir* (infidel), God will reward them because they have protected the true faith.

The sons of these uprooted peasants did not go willingly to the madrasas, they were forced by poverty. Parents send their children to the madrasas because they have no other alternative to ease their financial burden. Students come from the poorest and faraway places. They are lodged, get two meals a day and receive an average of 100 rupees a month. This means less mouths to feed for their parents. Madrasas are also the only means of social advancement for these children and the only hope for a career in the future. The parents gain the respect of the local mullah for sending their children to these schools, a *hadith*[42] says that the parents of a *hafiz-e Quran*[43] will be blessed with a luminous crown on the Day of Judgement. Madrasa students are taught in a language they do not understand—all the books studied in Sunni madrasas are in Arabic, a language which many of the mullahs hardly know. Physical abuse is the norm: it is considered a good method of ensuring discipline and attaining excellence and the parents agree to it most of the time. Children are chained 'to put the fear of God in their minds' according to a mullah. More than 80 per cent of the students in the madrasas of Lahore[44] studying the *hifz*[45] and *dars-e nizami*[46] courses do not come from the city. The mullahs say that those with families in the city would find it easier to escape from the madrasa so children from Lahore study in other cities. The young students are completely cut off from the outside world; they cannot watch television and newspapers and magazines are prohibited.[47] Their attitude towards secular education is one of contempt. However, they are often conscious of their low status in society, so they seek to compensate by serving the cause of religion,[48] According to Eqbal Ahmed: 'The madrasas have provided the religious parties with a potential constituency and a pool of cadres, workers and martyrs.'[49]

For madrasa graduates, the surest way of earning a livelihood is to become the imam of a masjid.[50] The mosques have become business enterprises with adjoining shops which can be rented out. The proliferation of mosques is due both to urbanisation and the high number of madrasa graduates: Okara had one Sunni mosque in the early fifties, in 1994 there were over 160 Sunni Barelvi[51] mosques and dozens of other Sunni mosques and Shia *imambafgahs*.[52] Investing in a mosque is a tremendous source of social prestige, more than half of them are built on public or disputed land. Mosques are no more open houses where everyone can come and pray, there is a system of sectarian apartheid and the names of the mosques often indicate their affiliation clearly. Sectarian interpretations of Islam have replaced traditional perceptions and the mosques have been taken over by extremists who are outsiders, the local community being marginalised.

Some madrasa graduates become teachers of Arabic and Islamic Studies. Zia-ul Haq had compelled the University Grants Commission in 1980 to recognize the *Wifuqs*[53] and treat their degrees as equivalent to M.A Arabic/Islamiyat. Only Peshawar University accorded recognition to these degrees and the practice virtually stopped after Zia's death. But most of the graduates remain unemployed and feel bitter.

Held in contempt by the westernised elite, they burn with rage against it. Without any connections and no links to their own village, they feel a deep sense of alienation in a society where they have lost their way.

Sectarianism as the outcome of poverty and unemployment

Not all sectarian extremists have a madrasa background, many are drop-outs of the Urdu medium system of education, half educated, and with no qualifications and no connections to get a government job.[54] Full of anger and frustration with the corrupt system, they are ready to join a sectarian organisation which will give them a sense of belonging and power.[55] They will have access to arms in a society where the display of arms and their utilisation to intimidate one's rival is a widely accepted practice.

They are misfits in society because they have no skills and no relevance to the job market. They cannot go back to their families who are too poor to support them, so they find themselves rootless, with no place in traditional society. Frustrated and bitter, they do not believe in politics and elections, they cannot identify with the corrupt elite which has failed to deliver, and place no trust in the traditional religious parties, too ready to compromise. They are looking for a messiah, a charismatic leader who blames everything on another group and exhorts them to exterminate it.[56]

In South Punjab, where the Sunni-Shia divide was previously blurred by the pir[57] factor and where 80 per cent of the population was Barelvi, the puritanical brand of Islam was not favoured before the proliferation of madrasas and the proselytism of the Tablighi Jamaat which promotes a certain kind of sectarianism. The young madrasa graduates and those who had been 'converted' by the Tablighis became staunch Deobandis and harboured strong anti-Shia feelings. It is then not surprising that the Sipah-e Sahaba (SSP, the Army of the Companions of the Prophet), a sectarian party which appeared as an offshoot of the Jamiat-i-Ulema-i-Islam (JUI) and defined itself as the defender of the downtrodden—and later the terrorist movement Lashkar-e Jhangvi—were born in Jhang where Shia landowners have traditionally held power.[58] Religion has become a tool and a social demarcation rather than a faith, the members of the other sect are viewed as rivals and as a threat to the material status of one's community.[59] Sectarianism has been used as an umbrella for the struggle of the emerging classes against more entrenched interests and the beginning of a challenge to feudalism.[60] The new middle class—Sunni immigrants from East Punjab with a strong sectarian tradition[61] controlling 80 per cent of the trade and business of the cities—,[62] who were in competition with the traditional elite,[63] were compelled in the ideological environment of the 1980s to use anti-Shia rhetoric and they found allies in the ideologically motivated madrasa graduates. Most people joined the SSP for political interests because it was the only party which provided a political platform against the powerful feudal families and which could give them access to the political arena. Sectarian politics thus became a surrogate for political empowerment and material gains.[64]

Religious violence as a means of empowerment

Jhang was the first city to fall prey to sectarian violence in the mid-eighties,[65] it then spread to the poor parts of the region, notably Leiah and Muzaffargarh[66] then to Bahawalpur and Bahawalnagar where the percentage of Shias is minimal and where there was no separate *imambargah* till 1970,[67] It all started when Maulana Haq Nawaz Jhangvi, the provincial *amir* of the Jamiat-i-Ulema-i-Islam (JUI)—who founded the SSP in 1985—hailing from a poor rural background and being an ordinary *maulvi* of a local mosque,[68] gained prominence when he persuaded poor Sunnis to send their young sons to his madrasa to be educated free of cost.

The presence of a large number of Muhajirs* in the small towns became a catalyst for violence. This new under-class of small, traders finances the SSP while physically staying out of the conflict.[69] While Shia militants belonging to the Imamia Students' Organisation (ISO) or to Sipah-e Mohammad (SMP) are locals, mostly middle class, and financed by the landlords,[70] Sunni militants belong to the lower and lower middle classes. Many of them, Sunnis and Shias, are unemployed

---

* Although most East Punjabi immigrants do not call themselves Muhajirs, the 'locals' refer to them as such. There is a very strong divide in South Punjab between the Seraiki-speaking locals and the Muhajirs—both Urdu and Punjabi-speaking. This divide together with the caste factor plays a central part in the sectarian conflict and should not be underestimated.

or do not have a steady job. But Sunnis are convinced that they are discriminated against and that the government supports the Shias.[71] Maulana Ziaul Qasmi, Chairman of the Supreme Council of SSP, said recently: 'The government gives too much importance to the Shias. They are everywhere, on television, on radio, in newspapers and in senior positions. This causes heartburn. The jobless Sunni youths find all doors closed; they have no option but to join extremist groups.'[72]

The traditional religious parties have no control over the sectarian organisations and anarchy prevails. The rivalry has degenerated into a chain reaction of vengeance and tit-for-tat killings in a society where revenge is viewed by most as a natural sentiment linked to one's identity and ones honour.[73] Determined gunmen, who are trained in the same camps as the Harkat ul Ansar[74] militants who fought in Kashmir or in Afghanistan and have firearms at their disposal, have taken the lead. They are often recruited as bodyguards for the leaders or 'muscle men' for political rallies.[76] A gun gives them a sense of power, violence is a thrill and when they have tasted blood, they are transformed overnight. They resort to robberies to finance their activities[76] and rely on the network of madrasas to hide. Highly motivated and committed to a cause, most of them do not kill for money although they need it when they are on the run. They feel that the religious parties have failed to defend their faith and they are disillusioned. Bitter and indignant at the hypocrisy and injustice found in society, they have become desperate. They have seen that the religious parties are corrupt, that they compromise and think only of making money. They are willing to kill and to die. They believe that they are waging a jihad to cleanse the ummah (Muslim community) of impurities from within, certain that they will go straight to Paradise, that martyrdom is at their doorstep, and that they do not have to travel far to fight an alien enemy.[77] Jihad has come to be identified with the cult of violence. They are persuaded that they have a religious mission and that violence is legitimate to accomplish that mission. They are sure that they are defending their faith in a war which has been imposed on them and that it is permitted by the Sharia. They want to take the message of Islam all over the world. When asked why his group targeted specifically doctors, lawyers and traders, a militant said; 'It is useless to kill the *malangs*.[78] We kill people who pollute their minds.'[79] They want to spread terror and for that purpose killing community leaders is very effective. They have no material or social stakes, no hope. They are ideologically opposed to the state. Unable to fit into society, they try to create a society where they will be useful. They have in some cases succeeded in creating territories independent of state control, 'no-go areas' such as Niaz Beg in Lahore.[80] They want to avenge alleged wrongs and settle a succession controversy which took place 1400 years ago.

The culture of sectarian violence

Maulana Ajmal Qadri from the Jamiat-i-Ulema-i-Islam (JUI) said recently: 'Sectarian violence has become a culture and it is here to stay'.[81] Students and staff of educational institutions supported by religious leaders have started exploiting sectarian differences to extort concessions from teachers and the administration. Blackmailing by students' organisations who exploit sectarian differences to get their own ends is becoming commonplace, as illustrated by a recent case in Multan.[82] The government is backing off; it fears the street power of the religious organisations and does not want to disavow those who fight in Kashmir. More than 120 sectarian cases are pending in the courts and very few have been adjudicated, while judges and policemen are under threat.[83] Society seems to have learned to cope with the sectarian violence, it does not resist either physically or intellectually, there is no rational interpretation of Islam as a counterweight. Political parties believing in secularism are on the defensive and have sometimes entered into alliances with the sectarian organisations.[84]

Conclusion

There are still some reasons to be optimistic: society does not approve, sectarian organisations have only a marginal appeal and no roots in the population. They have not succeeded in radicalising the population on sectarian lines. The Sunni-Shia conflict has never assumed the proportion of Hindu-Muslim riots in India, and sectarian hatred has not penetrated to the grassroots level of Pakistani society.[85] People do not blame the other sect when sectarian motivated killings are perpetrated, they turn their anger towards the state: no Sunni home or shop was attacked after the Mominpura massacre in Lahore but the crowds burned the district commissioner's office and the district court. The limits of sectarian movements might have been reached as they have no permanent source of financial support and they cannot last without foreign funding as the decline of SMP shows. The idea of Islam as a religion which will provide social justice and punish criminals is what appeals to the population. The solution lies in creating a new culture through an education which emphasises nationhood, teaches tolerance and restores Islam to what it truly is and what it was when it first came to the subcontinent; a message of love and peace as propagated by the Sufis.

4

THE SUNNI-SHIA CONFLICT IN JHANG (PAKISTAN)

Introduction

Although sectarian[1] issues were not prominent in the course of the freedom movement in Pakistan, these identities surfaced soon after independence. Violent clashes were isolated and mostly happened during Muharram when the Shias perform mourning rituals (*azadari*) in public and take out huge processions. Since the mid-1980s, parties and violent groups, often sponsored by Islamic states, have emerged with a narrow sectarian agenda and, thanks to the easy availability of weapons and to the training facilities in Afghanistan and in Kashmir, the level and intensity of violence has tremendously increased, claiming hundreds of lives. Every region of Pakistan has been affected—Sunnis and Shias have killed each other in the name of religion in the Punjab, in the NWFP, in Karachi and in the Northern Areas of Gilgit and Baltistan—but the conflict has been particularly violent in the Punjab, especially in the south of the province.

Much has been written on the internal and external causes of the emergence of the sectarian conflict in Pakistan at the macro level. Therefore, we will neither insist on Zia-ul Haq's policies of Islamisation and its consequences nor on the regional dimension of the sectarian conflict fuelled by the Iranian revolution and the Iran-Iraq war which assumed the character of a proxy war between Iran and Saudi Arabia on Pakistani soil. Such analyses, although relevant, fail to explain why sectarian violence affected some areas of Punjab more than others.

This chapter will focus on the Sunni-Shia conflict at the micro level with a study of Jhang, a city of central Punjab where the Anjuman Sipah-e Sahafaa (later renamed Sipah-e Sahaba Pakistan, SSP), an extremist Sunni movement, was founded in September 1985.[2] The case study reveals that a multiplicity of factors, most of them not related to religion, have to be taken into account while analysing sectarianism at the grassroots level.

The aim of this chapter is to analyse the factors that led to the rise of sectarianism in Jhang. Our assumption is that the sectarian conflict in Jhang is mainly the result of the struggle for political power between the traditional feudal families who are primarily Shia and rural-based and the emergent middle class which is largely Deobandi or Ahl-i-Hadith and urban-based.

This chapter will examine the religious dimension, which is not the main reason for the conflict but only a pretext which proved to be a powerful means of mobilisation in the 1980s. We try to analyse the complexity of the social conflict in Jhang, which is not limited to a class struggle between feudals and the urban middle class but should also be analysed as a conflict between the locals and the Muhajirs and as a conflict inside the Sunni community between two dominant castes or *biradaris*. We will describe the rise of the SSP which emerged as a credible alternative to the feudals and was instrumentalised both by local Sunni landlords and businessmen and by the Muhajir emergent middle class who used it to mobilise the urban youth in the defence of their own interests. Finally, the criminal dimension (the Islamisation of criminality) should not be overlooked as it played a major role in the mobilisation of the militants and in the persistence of the violence.

Geographical context

Jhang is located about 200 kilometres south of Lahore. It had historically a great politico-strategic importance for two reasons: the Sial dynasty was once powerful and Jhang was situated on the main communication line between Lahore and Multan. Parts of the vast district were taken away by the British and later by the Government of Pakistan when they created new districts. Today Jhang district consists of three tehsils: Jhang, Chiniot and Shorkot. According to the 1998 census, the total population of the district is 2,835,000 out of which 655,000 (1/5) live in the urban areas. Jhang itself has a population of 292,000 inhabitants.

The municipal area of Jhang is divided into 3 parts: Jhang City (the walled city known as Jhang Sial), predominantly Hindu before 1947 and where the Muhajirs are in a majority, Jhang Saddar (Jhang Maghiana) with a sizeable Muhajir population (both Sunnis and Shias) and the satellite town with a mixed population. Jhang City and some mohallas of Jhang Saddar have also been affected by sectarian violence.

The Social structure

Jhang is the centre of Punjabi folk culture, the famous epic Hir-Ranjha took place in Jhang where the shrine of Hir attracts many devotees. Many prominent academics and politicians[3] hail from the district, and it was also the home of the only Pakistani Nobel prize winner, Dr Abdus Salam, a nuclear scientist who happened to also be an Ahmadi.

Jhang is one of the most backward and feudal districts of Pakistan. The feudals—more precisely the Shah Jewna family[4]—and the Pirs have dominated political life in the district since the days of the Raj; the local population is convinced that they have deliberately kept the district backward, refusing the opening of schools and the building of roads. In 1947, a sizeable number of refugees from India, many of them hailing from Panipat, were settled in Jhang;[5] they occupied the properties left by the Hindus and started business activities. The large influx of refugees provoked a negative reaction among the locals, some of whom had occupied the properties of Hindus and Sikhs which were later taken back from them to be distributed to Muhajirs. Contrary to what is generally assumed, even those who settled in the rural areas could never assimilate although they came from East Punjab and shared the same language and culture with the local population. Although they do not identify themselves as Muhajirs, the local population considers them as such. The wounds of Partition have not healed, there is resentment even among those who were born much later, and everybody has a story to tell about who became rich overnight or about the kammis (lower caste people) who changed their caste during Partition to become Syed. Relations between the communities were always tense, even if violent clashes were few.

The religious communities

Although the majority of the population is Sunni, Jhang district has a sizeable Shia population, probably around 25 per cent (10 per cent in the city itself) although it is very difficult to make an accurate assessment. Shia communities had moved to Punjab and Sind after the conquest of Muhammad bin Qasim. Ismaili missionaries were also active in the area. Under the Abbasids, the governor of Jhang, Umar bin Hafas, was a clandestine supporter of the Fatimid movement and the Batiniya influence spread in Southern Punjab. Then, the Karamats, who had established contacts with the Fatimids in Egypt, set up an independent dynasty in Multan and ruled the surrounding areas till they were defeated by Mahmud Ghaznavi.[6] The Karamat movement left a deep impact on the local population. The small Shia Muhajir community settled in Jhang Saddar belongs mostly to the educated middle class, is often Urdu speaking, shares the Sunni hatred for the feudals and has few contacts with the local Shias who are mostly Siraiki speaking and rural based.[7]

While Muhajir Sunnis are often Deobandis, most of the local Sunnis are Barelvis, the shrine of Sultan Bahu is located in Jhang district and a Qadiri Pir belonging to the Gilani family who was previously settled in Azam Warsak (Waziristan) moved to Jhang in the early 1980s. According to Pir Syed Agha Kazem Shah Gilani, known locally as Pir Pathan, he chose Jhang because of the central geographical location of the city which made it much easier for his *murids* (followers) to visit him than when he was based in Waziristan.

Jhang has a history of sectarian conflict which goes back to pre-Partition days. After 1947, the relocation of the headquarter of the Ahmadi community from Qadian (today in the Indian state of Punjab) and the transformation of Rabwah (near Chiniot) into an 'Ahmadi Vatican', attracted militant Sunnis originally from Panipat, Rohtak and Hisar to Jhang and Chiniot. There they opened madrasas and have been active in the anti-Ahmadi movement since the 1950s. Maulana Manzoor Ahmed Chinioti, the head of Tehrik-e Khatm-e Nubuwwat, always took the lead in the anti-Ahmadi campaigns. The Muhajirs were also in the forefront of anti-Shia and anti-feudal activity but they were not yet economically powerful and they did not have enough support among the locals to challenge the monopoly of the Shia feudal establishment over political life. The Muhajirs whose religious identity had been sharpened by the revivalist movements of the 1920s in East Punjab[8] and by the sufferings experienced during Partition have always supported religious parties, namely Jamiat-e Ulema-e Pakistan (JUP) and Jamiat-e Ulema-e Islam (JUI).

Elections have been contested on a sectarian basis in Jhang since the 1950–1 provincial elections. Maulana Ghulam Hussain started an anti-Shia crusade in the 1950s; he opposed Colonel Syed Abid Hussain both as a feudal and as a Shia and was utilised by the small Sunni landlords who drew political benefits from this campaign (out of a total of 9 seats, Sunni landlords were able to secure 4 seats in 1951). The elections of 1954 were not fought on a sectarian basis: Syed Abid Hussain won the only seat from Jhang in the National Assembly and became the federal minister. But in 1970, there was an unprecented mobilisation of Sunni ulema against the Shia feudals of Jhang due to violent Sunni-Shia clashes in front of Khewa Gate (renamed Bab-e Umar by the Sunnis) during the procession of 7th Muharram (March 1969) which had caused the death of five Sunnis. Syed Abid Hussain was defeated by Ghulam Haider Bhawana, a Sunni landlord, and the three National Assembly seats were won by Sunni candidates elected on a JUP ticket.[9] The political activism of the ulema was however short-lived, their attention was focused on the Ahmadis and on Islamisation and they soon went back to their madrasas. The Sunni-Shia factor receded to the background for some time, the middle class was still very small and too weak to challenge the political monopoly of the Shia feudal establishment. Sunnis supported Sunni landlords, but they had a feeling of betrayal as the Sunni landlords were as indifferent to their interests as the Shia landlords[10] and they were not ready to share power with the emergent Muhajir middle class.

By that time, members of the Sunni business class, both Muhajirs and locals, had entered the municipal committee. Sheikh Iqbal, a local who claimed he belonged to the famous trading *biradari* of the Chinioti Sheikhs and who monopolised municipal politics for many years, became Vice-president of the municipal committee in the late 1960s and later the Chairman, a post which he held for almost 25 years. He was elected to the Provincial assembly on a JUI ticket in 1970 and joined the PPP in 1972. Since then, Sunnis have dominated the municipal committee while the district committee remained, except for a very short period, in the hands of the Shia feudal players—sometimes associated with the sajjada *nashins* of Sultan Bahu, as has been the case since the local elections held in 2001 under the devolution plan designed by General Musharraf.

In 1974, the Qadianis were declared non-Muslims by a constitutional amendment and in 1977 Zulfiqar Ali Bhutto banned alcohol and declared Friday as public holiday. General Zia-ul Haq, who took power in July 1977, soon started implementing a program of Islamisation. This emboldened the *ulema* and in the context of Jhang, the Shias were likely to be their next focus. The consequences of Zia-ul Haq's politics of Islamisation and the politicisation of the Shias after the Iranian revolution and the imposition of zakat[11] led to a new phase of sectarianism in Jhang.

The formation of the Tehrik-e Nifaz-e Fiqh-e Jaafria (TNFJ) in 1979, later renamed Tehrik-e Jaafria Pakistan (TJP), with a purely religious agenda in the beginning, was a turning point for the sectarian conflict in Pakistan. This party, whose name sounded offensive to Sunnis, became much more militant from 1984 under the leadership of Allama Arif Hussain al Hussaini, a charismatic leader who empowered the Shia community and transformed this religious movement to a political party in July 1987. The young ulema who had been educated in prestigious religious schools in Iran promoted a more rationalised and puritan version of Shiism. They were branded as 'Wahabi Shias' by the traditional clergy who accused them of destroying the religion, but surprisingly enough, they soon became very popular among the community and their *majlis*, often politicised, attracted crowds.[12] The young ulema opened madrasas with Iranian support and became an inspiration for the Shia community, especially for the students who joined the militant Imamia Students Organisation (ISO). Although the feudal class had no influence on these ulema who were financed by Iran, the Sunnis blamed them for the new assertiveness of the Shia community.

It is in this context that the Anjuman Sipah-e Sahaba was founded on 6 September 1985 in Jhang by Maulana Haq Nawaz Jhangvi (1952–90). There are lots of rumours about the role of the agencies in the creation of the SSP—a parallel can be drawn with the foundation of the MQM in Karachi, both parties being the product of the political vacuum created by Zia-ul Haq's regime—and about the financing of the party by Iraq and Saudi Arabia and by zakat money.[13] It is obvious that the SSP was a retaliation to Shia militancy and that Zia was only too happy to get an opportunity to teach the Shias a lesson. It can also be assumed that Haq Nawaz, who was at that time vice-amir of the JUI for the Punjab,[14] had political objectives as the SSP was created a few months before the lifting of martial law on 1 January 1986.

The SSP's goals are to defend the honour of the Sahaba (companions of the Prophet), to strive against rafiziyat (Shiism) by all legal and constitutional means, to proscribe Muharram processions, Shia azan (call to prayer) and all forms of azadari and matam (chest beating) in public, to get Shias declared as non-Muslims and Pakistan declared a Sunni state, and to make efforts to unite Sunni sects.[15]

Born in a poor rural family of the Khoja (pathfinders) caste of 'Chela, a village of Jhang district, Haq Nawaz received a madrasa education[16] and, in 1973, he became the khatib and imam of a Deobandi mosque in the mohalla of Piplianwala in Jhang Saddar. Before he started mobilizing Sunnis against Shias, he had participated in the anti-Ahmadi movement and had also denounced Barelvi rituals.[17] Haq Nawaz, who was a fiery orator, launched a crusade against Iran which he accused of supporting the Shias in Pakistan and of wanting to export its revolution, his attacks were as much directed against Khomeini as against Shia beliefs and rituals. Locally, he particularly targeted the Shah Jewna family and the district administration. Besides appealing to anti-Shia sentiments, Haq Nawaz started addressing social problems, becoming involved in thana-kutcheri issues, which made him extremely popular even among local Shias. He emerged quickly as a credible alternative to the feudals and won the support of persons who were not otherwise sympathetic to his personality or ideology[18] as he was much more accessible and more efficient than the feudals to solve people's problems.

The class struggle rhetoric of the SSP was largely borrowed from the JUI which remained closely associated with the SSP at least till

1989. The SSP denounces the Shia jagirdars who received lands from the British and the 'black laws'[19] and claims that nothing has changed since the days of the Raj as the poor have simply become the slaves of the 'Brown sahibs', that is those feudals who supported the Raj and were the slaves of the British. With such a rhetoric, the SSP attracted the downtrodden who had voted for the PPP in 1970 and had seen their hopes frustrated.

The causes of the conflict

The conflict has a religious, or rather a cultural, aspect. Although he had denounced Barelvis till the early 1980s, Haq Nawaz was later careful to avoid antagonising them and he managed to win their electoral support for the SSP to some extent. Haq Nawaz criticized the peasants for their ignorance of 'true' Islam which he linked to the influence of Shiism, he accused them of being devoid of religious identity and wanted to make them aware of the differences between Sunnis and Shias, which are quite blurred in the rural Barelvi society. The SSP wants to convert Sunnis to a rationalised Islam, to replace customary practices by the Islam of urban ulemas and madrasas, their struggle is directed as much against local rituals seen as Shiism as against the influence of *pirs*, both Sunni and Shia. They want to purify Islam from all external influences and their rhetoric often borrows from the reformist literature of the nineteenth century to which they constantly refer to give legitimacy to their anti-Shia campaigns. The SSP preaches a total social boycott of the Shias, relying on famous fatwas of the founders of Deobandi Islam. It denounces Shias as Zionist agents and as the 'other' responsible for all the problems of the country. The SSP's rhetoric equates local forms of religious beliefs and cultural practices to the influence of Shiism. However, these rituals have hardly anything in common with Shia rituals in Iran or Lebanon, they are a local expression of the tragedy of Karbala which is deeply rooted in the Punjabi culture and often evokes Sikh or Hindu rituals. It is true that up to now Sunnis and Shias, and even Ahmadis, participate in Shia rituals in Jhang, just like the Hindus participated before Partition,[20] because they do not equate *majlis* or processions with Shiism but with their local culture. By assassinating prominent zakirs, the SSP militants are destroying part of the Punjabi culture transmitted orally from father to son. Those zakirs are targeted because they are popular with Barelvis who share the same devotion to the Ahl-i-Bait (the family of the Prophet); they are seen as more dangerous than the Iran-educated zakirs who preach a rationalised form of Shiism which appeals only to a fraction of the Shia community.

This religious aspect is however not the main reason for the conflict; these themes were not new, the Deobandi madrasas and ulema had been promoting the same anti-Shia sentiments for many years and they had promulgated anti-Shia fatwas but these ideas never penetrated the society in South Punjab and did not lead to large scale violence.

Religion was only a pretext as anti-Shia rhetoric proved to be a powerful means of mobilisation in the mid-1980s and also a way to get support both from the state and from foreign sources. The Sunni emergent middle class, both local and Muhajir, who had been trying to enter the political arena made full use of this situation and quickly understood the benefits it could draw from supporting Haq Nawaz. Sunni landlords and the emergent under-class of transporters, contractors,[21] intermediaries and shopkeepers who had benefited from the liberal economic policy of the Zia regime and who supported the SPP to further their own political and economic interests. Most of the Muhajir businessmen dealing in animal skins and distributors of ghee, sugar and flour who had prospered under the Zia regime financed the SSP. Haq Nawaz gained the support, both financial and political, of the rich businessmen of Jhang who wanted an access to the political arena and also wanted to break Sheikh Iqbal's monopoly on municipal affairs. Muhajir businessmen and shopkeepers supported the SSP, either directly or through the powerful Anjuman-e Tajiran (Association of Traders). It is not surprising that shops belonging to Sunni Muhajirs were set on fire at the instigation of Shia feudals players as retaliation. Those who wanted to stand for the provincial elections against the feudals and could not get a Pakistan Muslim League (PML) ticket also supported the SSP. Sheikh Iqbal[22] and Sheikh Yousaf were competing to support Haq Nawaz. Sheikh Iqbal, who wanted to keep Haq Nawaz away from local politics, financed discreetly his electoral campaign for the national elections of 1988, which ironically gained him the support of the local Shias who shared the same interests.

Sheikh Yousaf, once a small contractor of Jhang settled in Lahore, had become very rich in the 1980s. He now owns Hasnain Construction Company to which the contract of the Islamabad-Lahore motorway, among other lucrative contracts, was awarded. This former MPA, well connected in army circles, was the major financier of Haq Nawaz and of the SSP in general, providing Pajeros and the like and financing the election campaigns. Richer than Sheikh Iqbal, he had the support of all those, Sunnis and Shias, who were opposed to Sheikh Iqbal. Haq Nawaz thus became a pawn in this rivalry between local Sunni businessmen and his assassination in February 1990 was most probably perpetrated at the instigation of Sunni leaders as they were competing for the same constituency. Some sources argue that Haq Nawaz wanted to stand for the provincial assembly elections against Sheikh Iqbal and that he resented the fact that Sheikh Iqbal had convinced him to instead contest the National Assembly elections in 1988.

After the assassination of Haq Nawaz, Sheikh Iqbal, who was MPA at that time, made a mistake which contributed to the cycle of violence. The police had wanted to launch an operation against the SSP which was postponed at the request of Sheikh Iqbal. When he refused later to finance the purchase of weapons for the SSP activists, they attacked his home.[23] From that time, Sheikh Iqbal and his family became the enemy of the SSP and they have since been the target of many acts of violence perpetrated by the SSP militants.[24]

The social conflict has thus several levels: feudals versus the emergent middle class, Shias versus Sunnis, local Shias versus Muhajir Shias, local Sunnis versus Muhajir Sunnis, Syed (local and Muhajir Shias) versus *julahas* and *kammis* (Sunni Muhajirs), Sheikh *biradari* (local Sunnis) versus Arain *biradari* (Muhajir Sunnis) and also competition for power inside the local Sheikh *biradari*. The local-Muhajir conflict can also be analysed in terms of a conflict between two dominant castes (Sheikh versus Arain).[25]

If the biggest financiers were local, the cadres of the SSP come mostly from the Muhajir community and belong to the Arain biradari as did many of the settlers who migrated from East Punjab to the Canal Colonies at the end of the nineteenth century. Many of them had fought in Afghanistan and most of the terrorists who caused a lot of bloodshed between 1990 and 1993 in Jhang were Muhajirs.[26] The SSP militants belong to the emergent 'under-classes', semi-urban, often unemployed, who are at the margin of the middle class, and whom the SSP has empowered by giving them an aggressive Sunni identity.

During Haq Nawaz's lifetime, there was not such a high level of violence in Jhang as after his death. This can be attributed to the fact that he was a local. His successors as leaders of the SSP were Muhajirs, outsiders imported in Jhang,[27] and it can be said that the SSP thrived on the dead body of Haq Nawaz. The criminalisation of the sectarian conflict in Jhang, which could be observed since the creation of the SSP, became much more obvious after the death of Haq Nawaz thanks to the weaponisation of society and to the power of the local mafias.[28] Muhajir goondas who had joined the SSP—Anwar alias Gaddu, Haider Butt, Saleem Fauji[29] to name but a few—played a prominent role in the bloodshed which followed the assassination of Haq Nawaz. They became heroes when they vowed to avenge his death. They got political protection from the SSP and a lot of local drug dealers gave them protection money which means that the SSP utilised them to maintain a certain level of tension in the street. In exchange for financing the SSP, Sheikh Yousaf is also alleged to having used SSP activists and goondas to threaten and sometimes kill people.

The sectarian situation was also manipulated by the drag mafia—Jhang is at the crossroads of drug and arms distribution networks. The drug mafia had an interest in maintaining a certain level of tension and resorted to provocations whenever the situation was too calm for its activities. Heroin smuggling became a main commercial activity in Jhang after the onset of sectarian violence[30] and electoral campaigns were financed by the profits of the drug business. Both sides were involved: a Shia feudal figure who is an ex-MNA is regularly denounced as one of the drug mafia bosses and the SSP apparently controlled the retail sales with the connivance of the police. When Jhang experienced the worst violence in 1992, drug dealers and drug users were the only persons who could move freely between the different parts of the city.

The SSP tried to get rid of the goondas after Azam Tariq was elected MNA for the first time in a by-election in 1992, and adopted a soft line, insisting on welfare (development projects, Sui gas, etc.) and on the necessity of maintaining peace in Jhang. The extremists, who felt betrayed, created the Lashkar-e Jhangvi headed by Riaz Basra in 1994 and the violence spread to other districts, becoming more terrorist in nature.

Azam Tariq was elected as an independent MNA in October 2002—the authorities tried, so far in vain, to get his election invalidated—after spending a whole year either in jail or under house-arrest after the SSP was banned in January 2002. Although the Shia feudal establishment have lost some of their influence,[31] Faisal Saleh Hayat, a powerful Shia landlord and *sajjada nashin* of Shah Jiwana, has been rewarded with the Ministry of Interior for having left the PPP to join the PML(Q). Sughra Imam, the daughter of Abida Hussain, has been elected MPA and Asad Hayat, a Shia feudal and brother of Faisal Saleh Hayat, is naib nazim of the district. The results of these elections held in August 2001 demonstrated that, at least at the local level, it is power and the traditional Punjabi rivalry between factions which count rather than ideology. The SSP supported Sahibzada Sultan Hamid of Sultan Bahu and Asad Hayat, a PPP-backed panel, against Sughra Imam who was defeated. This shows once again that when the game is about power and money, Shia feudals and Barelvi Pirs are acceptable to the SSP.

Local Sunnis have retained their power at the local level as Sheikh Akram, the brother of Sheikh Iqbal, was elected tehsil nazim despite the efforts of the SSP to take over this seat. Given the enmity between Sheikh Akram and the SSP, there is every reason to fear a new outbreak of violence in Jhang.

Conclusions

This short study of the many aspects of the sectarian conflict in Jhang demonstrates that sectarianism is linked with the power struggle and that, due to the lack of confidence in the state and the absence of channels of political participation, primordial identities come to the forefront and are instrumentalised by the protagonists in conflicts involving class, *biradari*, factions, or ethnic identity. It shows that in the context of Jhang the conflict cannot be explained in religious and ideological terms alone and that it is primarily the result of the socioeconomic tensions among different classes of society. Sectarianism can thus be defined in this particular context as a temporary substitute identity and as a vehicle of social change.

5

THE SSP

HERALD OF MILITANT SUNNI ISLAM IN PAKISTAN

In the context of Pakistan, 'sectarianism' denotes the conflict between the Sunni and Shia communities, which make up about 80 and 20 per cent of the population respectively. South Asia has a long tradition of sectarian violence between Sunni and Shia Muslims, especially in the form of isolated incidents during the Muharram processions.[1] Until recently, doctrinal differences were largely confined to theological arguments and concerned a relatively small segment of the population. In general, Sunni and Shia[2] co-existed peacefully, and marriages between the two communities were frequent.

The latent tensions between Sunni and Shia were exacerbated by the Islamisation policy introduced during the rule of General Zia-ul Haq (1977–88), an approach based on a narrow interpretation of Hanafi Sunni Islam[3] and favouring the Deobandi school of thought.[4] However, numerous external factors also contributed to the radicalisation of religious identities: the Iranian revolution (which reinforced the Shia identity and triggered a religious and later political mobilisation of the community);[5] regional rivalry between Saudi Arabia and Iran; the war between Iran and Iraq (which was perceived in Pakistan as a war between Sunni and Shia); and the launch of jihad in Afghanistan. This context was conducive to the emergence of sectarian movements that maintained ambiguous links with traditional religious parties and were often accused of conducting a proxy war on behalf of foreign powers, from whom they received money and arms. In the 1990s, these groups launched a violent campaign to protect the interests of their respective communities. Some 4,000 people, most of them Shia Muslims, were killed; thousands were injured during targeted assassinations and indiscriminate attacks on mosques and processions.

Is the often quoted theory of outside interference enough to explain the scale of sectarian violence? Or should we accept the interpretation advanced by the International Crisis Group (ICG)—'Sectarian conflict in Pakistan is the direct consequence of state policies of Islamization and marginalization of secular democratic forces'[6]—and attribute the conflict to purely internal factors?

While acknowledging the importance of external factors, one of the arguments advanced in this chapter is that the scale and intensity of the violence owe much to the exploitation of sectarian movements by two elements: social groups competing for local power, and successive governments pursuing short-term domestic and regional political goals.

What is the historical and ideological background of these groups? What goals do they hope to achieve? What constitutes their support base? What forms of violence do they employ? What is their relationship to the Pakistani state? We shall attempt to answer these questions through an examination of the Sipah-e-Sahaba Pakistan (SSP, Army of the Prophet's Companions), a Sunni extremist movement created in Jhang, a town in central Punjab, in 1985.

The origins of the SSP

The SSP appeared in Punjab in 1985 in the context of an Islamisation policy which, by identifying the version of Islam promoted by the state as the 'true Islam', institutionalised religious discrimination and paved the way for the politicisation of religion.

The SSP has often been described as a reaction to aggressive, Iranian-backed Shia militancy. In reality, outside interference had a catalytic effect on one of the most fertile areas in Pakistan at a time when politico-religious entrepreneurs had grasped the power of anti-Shia rhetoric as a means of mobilising communities.

The social structure particular to Jhang was highly conducive to the emergence of the SSP. In this specific context, the conflict between Sunni and Shia may be interpreted as the outcome of a struggle for political power between rural Shia feudal landlords and an emergent urban middle class adhering to the Deobandi school of Sunni Islam.[7]

The SSP sprang from the Jamiat-e-Ulema-e-Islam (JUI), a Deobandi Sunni party founded in 1945 by pro-Pakistan ulema who had broken away from the Jamiat-Ulema-e-Hind (JUH), which opposed religious nationalism. Formally established as a political party in Lahore in 1968, the JUI fielded candidates in the first national elections in 1970, taking 25 per centof the vote in North West Frontier Province (NWFP), where it formed a short-lived coalition government (1972–73) with a Pashtun nationalist party, the National Awami Party (NAP). The JUI, also firmly embedded in the Pashtun regions of North Baluchistan, had access to a vast network of madrasas, seminaries which played a major role in the Afghan jihad and the subsequent emergence of the Taliban. Like other Deobandi groups, the JUI participated in the anti-Ahmadi movement,[8] which in 1974 culminated in the adoption of a constitutional amendment that reclassified the Ahmadiyya community as a non-Muslim minority. The anti-Ahmadi movement was particularly active in Jhang, for at Partition the community had established its headquarters at Rabwah, near the city of Chiniot, in the same district. The anti-Ahmadi controversy fuelled the development of sectarian discourse and was thus a key factor in the rise of the anti-Shia movement.

Precursors of the SSP also include the Majlis-e-Ahrar, a less well-known movement founded by a group of reformist Punjabi ulema in 1929. The Ahrar, which recruited its members from Punjab's urban lower-middle class, campaigned against British rule, the feudals[9] and the Ahmadiyya. In the early 1930s, it launched a movement for the defence of Islam in Kashmir. The Ahrar became notorious for its participation in anti-Shia activities in the late 1930s, notably in Lucknow, where its Punjabi members took part in violent clashes between Sunnis and Shias in 1937 and 1938. The movement went into decline after Partition and its members (followed by their sons) were 'reconverted' to violence, first against Ahmadis and later against the Shia. This trajectory explains the sectarian education received by many SSP members, who continued a family tradition that the teaching in Deobandi madrasas simply reinforced.

Finally, in Karachi, there was a predecessor of the SSP in the Sawad-e Azam Ahl e-Sunnat (the Sunni Majority), a virulently anti-Shia organisation created by Pashtun clerics in the early 1980s. This group, believed to have been set up by the martial law authorities, also counted Haq Nawaz Jhangvi, founder of the SSP, as a member, and was the first to call publicly for Shia Muslims to be classed as *kafir* (infidels).

The SSP has always maintained ambiguous relations with the JUI, skilfully playing off the rivalry between the Maulana Fazlur Rehman and Maulana Sami ul Haq factions. Interaction is very strong at madrasa level. The links with the JUI have never been broken; the party's leaders claim to agree with the SSP's ideas, but differ as to its methods.

Haq Nawaz Jhangvi was born in Jhang district in 1952. A fine orator, he attended a madrasa in Multan and, like other SSP leaders, launched his career during the anti-Ahmadi agitation in 1974. He also denounced the beliefs and practices of the Barelvi school[10] and the influence of Shia Islam on the rural Sunni population through the agency of Shia landowners, most of whom, in Jhang district, claimed a spiritual power derived from their status as the descendents of saints. Haq Nawaz was vice-president of the Punjabi branch of the JUI when the SSP was created.

The SSP's founders, almost all of whom were shopkeepers, local residents and Mohajirs,[11] held meetings in a mosque in the Piplianwali quarter of Jhang. Aware of the possibilities afforded by anti-Shia propaganda, they recruited and manipulated a number of extremist mullahs, notably Jhangvi.

The Zia regime, anxious to counter Shia activism triggered by its attempts to impose Hanafi Sunni Islam and punish the community for its defiance of martial law and successful resistance to the state collection of *zakat* (alms tax), encouraged the SSP's formation. Zia also saw it as a way to break the Pakistan Peoples Party (PPP), with which many Shias identified. The anti-PPP strategy also gave rise to the Mohajir Qaumi Movement (MQM), created in Karachi in 1984. It should be noted that both movements emerged shortly before the lifting of martial law (1 January 1986), and that Jhangvi—or at least his mentors—clearly nursed political ambitions despite the SSP's insistence that it was a non-political, purely religious movement. Jhangvi himself always referred to separation between politics and religion as a plot devised by the enemies of Islam.

Furthermore, Saudi Arabia, concerned by Iran's eagerness to export its revolution and the level of Shia activism in Pakistan, was inclined to provide financial support for movements like the SSP. The United States, whose relations with Iran had deteriorated considerably following the embassy hostage crisis, made no objection. Iraq, competing with Iran in the massive dissemination of sectarian literature in Pakistan, also contributed to the SSP's coffers.

During the 1980s, SSP activity was generally confined to the denunciation of 'Shia heretics' and the large-scale production of sectarian literature, most of which was authored by Zia ul Rehman Farooqi, a Mojahir scholar employed at the Ministry of *awqaf* (endowments, a key Islamic institution).

The SSP seeks to combat the Shia by any means, have them declared a non-Muslim minority and, ultimately, transform Pakistan into a Sunni state. It advocates the defence, through constitutional and legal measures, of the honour of the *Sahaba* (*namus-e-Sahaba*, Companions of the Prophet), and the death sentence for anyone who insults them. This is aimed at the Shia, who are accused of cursing the first caliphs (*tabarra*) during their mourning ceremonies. The organisation calls for the restoration of the caliphate system of government (*Khilafat-e Rashida*, which is also the title of its monthly journal) and for the anniversaries of the deaths of the first caliphs—particularly on Muharram, the death of Caliph Omar—to be declared public holidays. In order to eliminate sectarian violence, it demands a ban on Shia public mourning ceremonies (essentially the processions involving flagellation and other physical manifestations of mourning), which are judged offensive to Sunnis. Other demands include an end to Iranian interference in Pakistan's domestic affairs, and the prohibition of Shia sectarian literature distributed with the support of Iranian cultural centres and the Iranian embassy in Pakistan.

The SSP and the electoral process

In 1988, Haq Nawaz stood as a JUI candidate against Abida Hussain, the dominant Shia figure in Jhang. He obtained 38,995 votes, but Abida Hussain was elected with 47,374 votes. Note, however, that during non-partisan elections in 1985, Sheikh Yusuf—a local industrialist and member of the Sheikh caste[12] who would later become the SSP's principal source of local financial support and exploit it to break the monopoly in municipal politics of his rival Sheikh Iqbal[13]–had won a seat on Punjab's Provincial Assembly. Yusuf was backed by the same people who would go on to form the SSP a few months later.

Haq Nawaz's successor as head of the SSP, Maulana Isar ul Qasmi (born in 1964), came from an Ambala Mohajir family which had settled in the Samundri district. Educated at three madrasas in Lahore, he abandoned an unsuccessful business career to become *khatib* (preacher) in an Okara mosque, where his reputation owed more to his clashes with the police than to erudition concerning religious matters.

A JUI cadre, Qasmi joined the SSP in 1986 and was elected as a JUI representative to the National and Provincial Assemblies in 1990, defeating Sheikh Iqbal. Abida Hussain did not stand in this election but supported Sheikh Iqbal against the SSP. Iqbal, however, was unable to attract the Shia vote. Qasmi was assassinated in January 1991. In a move that revealed the competition between the SSP and local Sunnis for the same electoral base, the SSP, despite the lack of evidence, chose to accuse Sheikh Iqbal's family of the murder rather than attribute it to Shia elements. For security reasons, the authorities did not organise a by-election until April 1992. In the meantime, outbreaks of sectarian violence in Jhang claimed many lives.

The 1992 election, successfully contested by the SSP candidate Maulana Azam Tariq, signalled the movement's emergence as a political force. For the first time in Pakistan's history, a sectarian organisation had won an election. The campaign unfolded in a climate of terror; the SSP announced that it would not accept defeat, and participation was around 40 per cent.[14]

In the context of Jhang, Azam Tariq was an outsider. Born in 1962 to a Mohajir family which had settled in a village near Chichawatni, he attended the celebrated Binori Town Deobandi madrasa in Karachi, obtaining a double MA in Arabic and Islamic studies. He was an outstanding orator—it was said that he could ignite water—and his teachers advised him to use language as a weapon. He taught in a Karachi madrasa before joining the SSP in 1987. Shortly afterwards he travelled to Afghanistan, where he displayed little aptitude for combat but inspired the fighters with his preaching. Returning to Pakistan, he became imam of the Siddiq-e-Akbar mosque in north Karachi (still an SSP bastion), where he was spotted by Haq Nawaz and Zia ul Rehman Farooqi, the SSP ideologue, and invited to take over the Jamia Mahmudia madrasa, the organisation's base in Jhang.[15] He was re-elected to the National Assembly in 1993, obtaining 55,004 votes as opposed to the 36,278 votes garnered by the independent candidate Sheikh Iqbal.

From the time of his arrival in Jhang and the SSP's formal entry into politics, Azam Tariq devoted considerable energy to creating a respectable image for the movement and distancing it from the thugs it attracted in large numbers. During the 1993 election campaign he stressed the need to maintain law and order in Jhang, denounced unemployment as a cause of disorder and claimed to have furthered the town's economic development, notably by securing its connection to the gas network. These campaign themes won him a number of Shia votes. Two SSP members, natives of Jhang, also won election to the Punjab Provincial Assembly in 1993: Sheikh Hakim Ali, who in 1995 would become Fisheries Minister in the pro-PPP provincial government of Sardar Arif Nakai, and Riaz Hashmat Janjua, who would be appointed adviser to Manzoor Wattoo, the head of the provincial government. Manzoor Wattoo, whose father was Ahmadi, was susceptible to pressure from the SSP, which partly explains the impunity enjoyed by militants at that time.

However, the SSP's political influence in Jhang began to decline in 1997. Azam Tariq, defeated in the National Assembly elections by Amanullah Sial, a Shia feudal landlord, succeeded in winning a seat on the Punjab Provincial Assembly. He took over the leadership of the SSP that same year, after sustaining serious injuries when the group was attacked in Lahore (Zia ul Rehman Farooqi died in this attack). A Shia, Mehram Ali, was subsequently convicted of these crimes and executed.

The SSP's social base in Jhang

Jhang is the only district in which sectarian strife and class conflict (between landowners and other social categories) coincide to the extent that they structure the political dimension. Anyone seeking to enter the political arena but lacking the necessary capital—land, a modern education or family networks—uses religion as a lever.

A number of Mohajir entrepreneurs, middlemen and businessmen with interests in pesticides, fertilisers, leather, textiles, flour, sugar, vegetable oil and transport saw their wealth increase considerably in the 1980s under the economic liberalisation policy implemented by General Zia. This group formed a new middle class; it existed on the margins of the traditional urban middle class (many of whom had enriched themselves at Partition by seizing the wealth of Hindus and Sikhs in Jhang) and lacked representation in the traditional political parties. Unable to influence the local population, which was locked into a clientelist relationship with the landowners, Mohajir business communities began funding religious movements. Their initiative coincided with the development of clientelist arrangements between the state and clerics and madrasas, a network facilitated by the *zakat* and *ushr* (a religious tax on crops) committees, inspired by Zia's policy of Islamisation. The rising business elite realised the potential benefits of this ideological resource and supported the exploitation of Islam for political ends.

The Mohajir middle class was quick to grasp the advantages of joining—or at least supporting—the SSP: the movement had the potential to further its interests. Mohajirs who could not obtain the endorsement of the Pakistan Muslim League (PML) ran on the SSP ticket and attracted bloc votes. Local mullahs, for their part, secured votes for the SSP in return for services, and especially for jobs. Thus people who felt no particular hostility towards the Shia community were elected on the SSP ticket. When the organisation was outlawed in 2002, some of its cadres, clerics included, joined the pro-Musharraf PML-Q, a clear indication that their allegiance to the SSP had been determined more by access to power than by religious ideology.

The organisation also attracted the support of local Sunnis, Deobandis and even Barelvis, who owned modest estates and sought to contest the hegemony of the big Shia landowners.

Apart from Haq Nawaz, whose family was indigenous to the area, all the SSP's leaders were Mohajirs. Although educated in prestigious madrasas, they were 'peripheral' and indeed *lumpen* rather than traditional ulema. All had taken part in the Afghan jihad, and many belonged to the Arain caste which, while occupying a fairly low ranking in the Punjabi hierarchy, had become economically dominant in the province after Partition. The caste continued its social ascent under the regime of Zia-ul Haq, who was himself Arain.

Most grassroots activists were recruited from the madrasas which proliferated in southern Punjab and constituted an almost inexhaustible pool of recruits. One striking aspect of the demonstrators fielded by the SSP was their youth; this was particularly noticeable the day after 11 September and during the riots that followed the funeral of Azam Tariq in 2003. Despite abundant evidence to the contrary, the SSP constantly denied its links to the madrasas, although Mohammad Amir Rana counted 34 affiliated seminaries.[16] Apart from central and south Punjab, the SSP was particularly well embedded in Karachi, where it recruited Punjabi and Pashtun students from the madrasas. The SSP maintained a much lower profile in north Punjab, especially in the 'army belt' districts,[17] where sectarian loyalties were not as relevant in political terms.

The organisation also attracted the urban young who had attended Urdu-medium state schools, a group characterised by its poor education, lack of qualifications, inability to find work and vulnerability to indoctrination. These third-generation Mohajirs resented graduates of the English-medium private schools, had no prospects and were eager for an identity and a cause to fight for. They were ready to follow anyone who blamed an 'other' for their predicament—Shia Muslims in this instance—and offered them a way out of it. Moreover, by claiming to speak in the name of Islam, they could compensate for their social marginality.

The SSP also recruited criminals, a practice that began before 1992. Such people—especially drug traffickers—were quick to grasp that the SSP provided the perfect cover for their activities. The arrangement was mutually beneficial: criminals gained political protection and were able to operate with impunity, while the SSP used them to maintain a certain level of mobilisation in the streets and intimidate its rivals.

Drug traffickers used the SSP to conduct their business. This was the case in Jhang and also in Karachi in 1995, where the SSP formed an alliance with the MQM-Haqiqi[18] in order to share the benefits of the drug and arms trades with mafia syndicates.

In sociological terms, the similarity to the MQM in Karachi is striking. But whereas the MQM offered the youth of Karachi a substitute ethnic identity, the identity on offer in Punjab was that of a Sunni militant. Ethnic identity was not a viable option for the Mohajirs of Punjab. In fact it was irrelevant, as most Punjabis accepted their identity as Pakistanis. Moreover, Punjabi Mohajirs refused to be defined as such and referred to themselves as Pakistanis. On the other hand, the local population, many of whom spoke Siraiki, had not fully accepted the presence of settlers (*abadkar*) from northern Punjab, the people who had migrated south in the late 19th century when the Canal colonies were opened, and still regarded Mohajirs as outsiders.

Like some other social categories, Mohajir traders sought to break the stranglehold on the structures of power maintained by feudal landlords and local Sunni businessmen. They supported the SSP but kept their distance from it. The Jhang Chamber of Commerce also used SSP activists as an alternative police force. When crime rates increased, businessmen paid more to buy security.

Having consolidated its presence in Jhang, the SSP extended its activities to other towns in central and south Punjab. Faisalabad, the largest industrial city in the province, the centre of Sunni extremism and home to a large number of Mohajirs, soon became an SSP bastion.

In Pakistan, the state is perceived as illegitimate and institutionally weak, and is thus widely distrusted. The SSP attracted people who were looking for protection from corruption and nepotism. The organisation responded to this demand by setting up a form of patron-client relationship that functioned in the same way as traditional networks.

Haq Nawaz adopted a different approach to the madrasa- and mosque-centred activities of traditional ulema. He became involved in social work, attempted to resolve the population's material difficulties, arbitrated in conflicts between neighbours and found jobs for the unemployed. Within a very short period, he had established himself as a credible alternative to the feudals for purposes of protection and the distribution of wealth. He was also more accessible and more efficient, and was thus able to reach beyond the Sunni community and extend his electoral base. Azam Tariq adopted a similar approach, as we were able to observe when spending a day at his home in Jhang. By 6 a.m., a crowd had gathered outside his door to request a variety of favours. He stage-managed the event, sitting cross-legged on his bed, flanked by telephones and a fax machine. He listened patiently, offering advice, writing job references and helping to fill in hospital admission forms and applications for financial assistance. A single telephone call secured the release of a young man the police were holding in custody. His visitors, impressed by his charisma and effectiveness, insisted that the lot of the poor had improved considerably since his arrival in Jhang. The SSP was much more accessible than the feudal landlords, who had to be approached through an intermediary who would arrange an appointment and then keep the supplicant waiting; the setting in which the supplicant was received was designed to intimidate, and everything was done to ensure that he felt obliged to the feudal landlord. The SSP had also set up a mutual aid fund to look after prisoners and their families. It was located in the Piplianwali mosque, next door to Azam Tariq's modest house.

In order to spread its message and mobilise its recruits, the SSP relied on local mosques and Deobandi madrasas. The function of these establishments was twofold: they provided the manpower which kept the conflict alive, and also reproduced the ideology behind it through a brand of teaching that focused on denouncing the 'other', and the production of sectarian literature.

The SSP was the first movement to fully exploit sectarian literature as an instrument of mobilisation. Besides the monthly *Khilafat-e Rashida* published in Faisalabad, it distributed pamphlets and booklets containing extracts from Shia texts attributed to anonymous Iranian authors. For the most part, these texts concerned the allegedly dissolute life of the wives of the Prophet and the *Sahaba*, and were intended to arouse hatred towards Shia Muslims. The young men who read this literature were horrified, and felt duty-bound to defend the honour of the *Sahaba* and of Aisha, the Prophet's favourite wife. Zia ur Rehman Farooqi produced a compilation of some two hundred Shia works entitled *Tarikhi Dastawez* (Historic Documents). In 1991, this was presented to Nawaz Sharif, then head of the Punjab provincial government, with a view to securing a ban on such material. The introduction to the collection contained anti-Shia quotations from Sunni texts as well as fatwas approved by 400 ulema from the various branches of Sunni Islam.

Audio and video cassettes were also used extensively to recruit new members, as we were able to note when we asked militants about the circumstances that had led them to join the movement.

In January 2001, as electoral support declined, Azam Tariq changed tactics and announced a five-point programme for the application of Sharia law in 20 Punjabi towns. The programme was primarily aimed at re-mobilising activists and keeping them occupied. The militants would ensure that shops closed for half an hour for prayers and boycott those that did not comply. Shops would also close on Friday and open on Sunday. Other targets included satellite and cable TV stations; establishments involved in this 'immoral' culture would be boycotted. Finally, militants were to urge the population to reject courts that applied the British-based judicial system and turn to ulema and mosques which meted out justice in accordance with Islamic law. As Azam Tariq was imprisoned once again in February 2001, the programme was not launched.

Funding

The SSP's principal financial backer in Jhang itself is Sheikh Yusuf, a local small businessman who amassed considerable wealth in the 1960s. Based in Lahore and very well connected in military circles, Yusuf owns the Hasnain Construction Company, which won the contract to build the Peshawar-Islamabad motorway.

Some of Faisalabad's leading Mohajir industrialists have also funded the movement. The main task of the 17 branches the SSP claims to maintain overseas—in countries such as the United Arab Emirates, the United States and Britain—is to raise money from the businessmen of the Punjabi diaspora. Grassroots members contributed very little money. Like other religious movements, the SSP collected the hides of animals sacrificed at Eid (the festival of sacrifice) and sold them to the tanneries at auctions. Criminal activities—armed robbery, kidnapping and ransom, *qabza* operations (groups seizing land by force and very often staking their claim to it by erecting a mosque), and even drug trafficking—provided another source of income.

Finally, the SSP is said to have received Arab funding (from sources known as the 'powerful external godfathers'), although this cannot be verified.

Anyway, the SSP had considerable financial resources at its disposal. Large sums were spent on bailing out militants or bribing the police to release those under arrest. In 2001, Azam Tariq offered the family of Sadiq Ganji[19] a large sum in blood money in order to prevent his murderer's execution. The rifts and infighting that followed the assassination of leaders were usually triggered by arguments over the control of the group's financial assets. This was notably the case in 2001, when one of the sons of Zia ul Qasmi (director of the Qasmia madrasa in Faisalabad), a member of the SSP Supreme Council, joined the JUI's Qadri faction and denounced Azam Tariq, accusing him of stealing the proceeds from the sale of hides as well as donations from other countries. The recurrent and often violent conflicts between Azam Tariq and the sons of Haq Nawaz—one of whom was murdered in 2002 in Karachi in unexplained circumstances—were also about financial matters. The power struggles that followed Azam Tariq's murder revolved around the distribution of the movement's funds.

Violence and the Lashkar-e-Jhangvi

Membership of the SSP provided young Sunni Muslims with a refuge in the form of a different identity. Their parents had envisaged Pakistan as a Muslim paradise on earth, a land free of injustice and oppression. Having suffered rejection and humiliation when looking for work, they realised that the SSP, which blamed Shias for their predicament, offered them a way to defend their interests. These young people were eager to acquire social status and saw membership of the SSP as a means of inspiring respect, even if only through the fear the organisation aroused. In a society which regarded violence as a legitimate way to settle differences, considerable power accrued to those prepared to use it. Moreover, the militants regarded violence against the Shias as a perfectly legitimate activity, since the aim was to purify the religion. They believed in the rightness of their actions, and the encouragement they often received from their families reinforced their conviction that nothing could stop those who acted in God's name.

Sectarian violence is often seen as an acceptable way of expressing discontent. The police do nothing to stop militants rampaging through the streets after the funerals of murdered leaders. In October 2003, we witnessed the riot that followed the funeral of Azam Tariq in Islamabad: militants, many of them very young, attacked and looted shops, set fire to a cinema, smashed the windows of hundreds of cars and stole trunks containing the gifts of worshippers from a nearby Shia sanctuary. The police made no attempt to intervene. The Ministry of the Interior subsequently stated that as the young people had been enraged by their leader's murder, it was natural for them to express their anger. The disorder and the targets selected strongly suggested a revolt by the have-nots against a Westernised urban middle class.

The violence began in 1986, with anti-Shia riots in Lahore. In 1987 Ehsan Elahi Zaheer and Habib ul Rehman Yazdani, leaders of Ahl-e-Hadith, the Pakistani advocates of Salafism, were assassinated. Ehsan Elahi Zaheer was the author of *Khomeini and the Shia*; translated into many languages, the book is still popular in Saudi Arabia, where it is distributed to pilgrims in Mecca and Medina. In 1987, clashes between Deobandis and Barelvis in Jhang resulted in the deaths of two Barelvis. Twelve SSP cadres, including Haq Nawaz, were arrested and later released on bail. Haq Nawaz retained bitter memories of the humiliating treatment he received while in police custody.

A turning point was reached in Peshawar in August 1988, with the assassination of Allama Arif Hussaini, a Parachinar Pashtun and leader of the Shia party Tehrik-e-Nifaz-e-Fiqh-e-Jaafriya (TNFJ), which became Tehrik-e-Jaafriya Pakistan (TJP) in 1993. Allama Hussaini acted as Khomeini's *wakil* (representative) in Pakistan. His activities aroused great concern in Saudi Arabia and Iraq. Among those implicated in his murder was a close colleague of General Zia and a native of Jhang, which indicated that Inter-Services Intelligence (ISI) had played a part in the affair. Haq Nawaz Jhangvi himself was assassinated in February 1990, probably at the instigation of Sheikh Iqbal. However, the SSP attributed the crime to Shia elements, a tactic that enabled it to mobilise the Sunni community in Jhang. Sheikh Iqbal and his family were targeted by SSP militants, and Sheikh Iqbal himself was killed by members of the organisation in March 1995.

In December 1990, the murder of Haq Nawaz was followed by that of Sadiq Ganji, the Iranian consul general in Lahore. The diplomat was killed by a man who was a member of the SSP at the time and who was allegedly accompanied by a junior air force officer seconded to the ISI.[20] Another SSP member, a resident of Jhang who had changed his name to Haq Nawaz, was convicted of the murder and executed in February 2001.

During the 1990s, the SSP spawned numerous dissident splinter groups, many of which were led by local mullahs and served the interests of the feudal lords. The most violent of these groups, Lashkar-e-Jhangvi (LeJ, Army of Jhangvi), emerged in 1994, soon after the SSP's entry into politics. The LeJ's founders criticised SSP leaders for having abandoned Haq Nawaz's mission, and were committed to its continuation through violence.

The LeJ developed into the armed wing of the SSP and carried out attacks that would have been too costly for the SSP in political terms—the murder of Iranians and Shia dignitaries, and reprisals for the killing of Sunni dignitaries, SSP leaders and militants. Azam Tariq told us that the LeJ was created by SSP militants who had suffered at the hands of the police during the violence in Jhang in 1992 and had subsequently been forced to go underground. These claims were repeated by other SSP leaders, who maintained they had expelled extremists like Malik Ishaq, a LeJ ideologue and member of the SSP supreme council, for their espousal of armed violence following the government's persecution of militants. They also pointed out that those expelled for indiscipline had been trained by the SSP and shared its values; it was therefore hardly surprising if they reacted whenever sectarian violence claimed the life of an SSP militant.

In public, Azam Tariq's statements were far more categorical: he totally denied the existence of any link between the SSP and the LeJ, and condemned members whose opposition to the peaceful campaign for the application of Islamic law had created the rogue organisation.

The LeJ's founder, Riaz Basra (born in 1967), came from a poor family in the Sargodha region and attended a madrasa in Lahore before joining the SSP in 1986. Rising to become the movement's head of information, he stood for election in 1988 in the same Lahore constituency as Nawaz Sharif, obtaining 9,000 votes. Arrested in 1992 for the murder of Sadiq Ganji, he escaped in 1994 when being transferred from prison to court. 'Influential friends' (the ISI) are alleged to have facilitated his escape. Basra fled to Afghanistan, where he established his own training camp, although he often quarrelled with the Taliban. LeJ militants, who probably never exceeded 100 in total, used Afghanistan as a sanctuary until November 2001, entering Pakistan to stage anti-Shia operations and returning immediately. The LeJ specialised in the murder of Iranian diplomats, leading Shia officials, lawyers, doctors, wealthy businessmen and high-ranking police officers, including Ashraf Marth, the brother-in-law of Chaudhry Shujaat, the Interior Minister at the time. Marth had conducted a detailed investigation of the attack on the Iranian cultural centre in Multan, and had revealed the LeJ's links with foreign elements. The group also attempted to assassinate Nawaz Sharif in January 1999. Riaz Basra regularly crossed the border into Pakistan and even attended a Tabligh rally in Raiwind. In telephone calls and faxes to newspapers, he claimed responsibility for the attacks carried out by LeJ militants.

In Afghanistan, the LeJ took part in the massacres of Hazara Shias and Iranian diplomats at Mazar-e-Sharif in 1998. The movement was outlawed in August 2001. Riaz Basra, whose links with the intelligence service were notorious, fled Afghanistan and was arrested in the tribal zone in December 2001. He was handed over to the intelligence services, which eliminated him in May 2002. The Pakistani government subsequently portrayed the LeJ as the Pakistani branch of al-Qaeda and blamed it for every attack on foreigners and religious minorities, although many of these claims were scarcely credible. By 2000, the group was torn by arguments, notably over the management of funds and the appropriateness of continuing sectarian attacks under a military government. This last point demonstrates, if need be, how the relationship between the group and certain sections of the army was at least ambiguous. The attacks on Shias in Quetta in 2004 may have been the work of the LeJ, although the leaders of its two main factions—Akram Lahori and Qari Asadullah alias Qari Abdul Hai—had been arrested in 2003. The LeJ benefited from rifts in the SSP following the assassination of Azam Tariq: grassroots militants, disillusioned by the arguments, were inclined to join a group that remained loyal to the ideals of Haq Nawaz and Azam Tariq.

The Jaish-e-Muhammad (JeM, Army of Muhammad), founded (with ISI support) in February 2000 by Maulana Masood Azhar, a graduate of the Binori Town madrasa and a close confederate of both Haq Nawaz and Azam Tariq, emerged as the jihadist façade of the SSP. In October 2000, Masood Azhar addressed a conference on jihad and declared: 'We march hand in hand; the SSP pursues jihad alongside the JeM'.

The social base remained unchanged, and many activists shifted from one movement to the other. Moreover, the JeM maintained close links with the SSP. From the outset, the JeM not only competed with the Lashkar-e-Taiba in Kashmir, but took part in sectarian attacks, particularly against Christians.

Tools of the state

Each successive Pakistani government has used the SSP to achieve short-term goals. The Zia regime backed it in order to combat ethno-nationalism, strengthen Muslim identity in Pakistan and bring down the PPP, which had been attracting Shia votes since the 1970s.

Following the country's return to democratic rule in 1988—and particularly during the second Benazir Bhutto government (1993–6)—the PPP, a party which lacked Islamic legitimacy and sought to defeat the PML, formed two alliances: one with the JUI at the federal level[21] and another with the SSP in Punjab. In return, the SSP was allowed to pursue its violent activities with impunity.[22]

The government took no firm action against sectarian movements—especially the SSP—until 1998, when the PML held a majority in Punjab and in the federal parliament. The antiterrorist unit within the Special Branch of the Pakistani police had been transformed into a separate service and given the task of combating sectarian terrorism in April 1995, but it did not begin to function until the appointment of Tariq Pervaiz as its head in 1997. By 1998, it was clear that anti-terrorist laws had failed, and that threats against police officers and politicians were on the rise. Given the impossibility of obtaining guilty verdicts in the courts, the police in Punjab were ordered to eliminate 'terrorists' instead of trying to arrest them. As a consequence, 37 alleged 'terrorists' were eliminated in Punjab. But not all police officers approved of the policy. Some believed it actually exacerbated the situation, for militants were prone to even greater violence when they knew they would be killed even if they surrendered. In addition, their deaths denied the police the opportunity to elicit information concerning their networks. The policy had yet another perverse effect: extremists formerly shunned by the religious parties were welcomed back into the fold when the manhunt began.

The fact remains that many policemen, including some high-ranking officers, were sympathetic to the SSP[23] and therefore susceptible to bribery and intimidation. Junior officers often complained that they were unable to arrest SSP militants, or were forced by their superiors to release those in custody.

In the mid-1990s, the police discovered that collaborating with SSP militants was generally more lucrative and less dangerous than the alternative. The antagonists arrived at a tacit understanding: if the police did not delve too deeply into SSP affairs, they would not be targeted. They also received large sums of money from businessmen in return for releasing SSP militants in their custody.

The policies adopted by Nawaz Sharif's government had very little impact, however, for the country's leaders could not stem the support the SSP received from abroad, notably from the Taliban. Moreover, during the 1990s the army ceaselessly exploited the instability bred by the violence, pressurising democratic governments by claiming that they were incapable of maintaining law and order. Both Benazir Bhutto and Nawaz Sharif were forced to appeal to the army when violence reached a critical level.

The 1999 military coup did little to alter the situation. General Musharraf outlawed the LeJ in August 2001, a measure that would probably have come to nothing had it not been for the events of 11 September. The SSP then came under strong pressure from the government. President Musharraf accused it of training its militants in Afghanistan and destroying Shia property in Peshawar during anti-American demonstrations, charges that Azam Tariq was hard put to deny.

On 12 January 2002, President Musharraf banned the SSP. The organisation maintained a low profile for several months, then resumed its activities under the name Millat-e-Islamia Pakistan (MIP). Azam Tariq, placed under house arrest and later transferred to prison, was elected as an independent in October 2002 and immediately declared support for President Musharraf. He refused to join the Muttahida Majlis-e-Amal (MMA), the alliance of religious parties, on the grounds that it tolerated the presence of Sajid Naqvi, leader of the Shia party Tehrik-e-Jaafria (TJP), which had resurfaced as Tehrik-e-Islami after being banned in January 2002. Once elected, Azam Tariq played by the establishment's rules, obtaining the release of SSP militants and a lenient approach to the movement's activities in return for his support. The authorities seemed interested in using it to create a religious alliance to rival the MMA. The SSP then adopted a new charter which laid great emphasis on unity between Muslims and harmony between the Sunni and Shia of Pakistan.

Azam Tariq was assassinated in Islamabad on 6 October 2003, in circumstances that will probably remain shrouded in mystery. There are indications that the killing, ostensibly a result of strife within the movement, was approved at the highest level of government.[24] The MIP was banned in November 2003, but as in the past, prohibition appeared to have no effect.

Since 2004, the tribal areas and the Kohat district of the NWFP have been a sanctuary for members of the SSP, and sectarian attacks have become commonplace in Kurram and Orakzai tribal agencies as well as in Peshawar and Dera Ismail Khan, notably after the assault on the Red Mosque in Islamabad in July 2007, which had a strong sectarian dimension as the Red Mosque had long been an SSP stronghold.

Meanwhile, restrictions were relaxed and in April 2006, the SSP organised a rally in Islamabad; the participants, under police protection, chanted anti-Shia slogans with impunity. Once again, it seemed that rather than crack down on the SSP, the authorities preferred to hold it in reserve.

In 2008, the SSP was active again in Karachi. It organised a public demonstration in March against the Danish cartoons, and two other meetings in June and August, at which weapons were displayed. It was believed that the government was using it to exert pressure on the MQM.

Conclusion

The dynamics of sectarian strife demonstrate that religion is nothing more than a pretext. Above all, the conflict is the reflection of the socio-economic tensions that pervade a society in transition, and an expression of the complex trajectories of modernisation. Emergent categories have used the SSP as a vehicle for social change; they have exploited the claims of the disaffected to further their own interests, a strategy not dissimilar to those employed by Hindu nationalist movements. Moreover, state exploitation of the SSP and other jihadist movements has led to an increase in the level of violence against Shia Muslims, which intensified after the invasion of Iraq in 2003.

Pakistanis appear to have understood the ambivalent role played by the state. Shias do not blame Sunnis for the violence—their anger is directed at the state. Mobs do not target Sunni houses and establishments after attacks on Shia Muslims—they target public buildings and the symbols of the state.

Sectarian organisations have therefore failed to radicalise the population. Nor has the conflict between Sunni and Shia Muslims ever reached the scale of the violence between Hindus and Muslims in India. But the Talibanisation of the tribal zones, encompassing as it does the entire North West Frontier Province and even parts of Punjab, indicates the extent to which sectarian groups constitute a threat to both state and society. The authorities' insistence that the violence is the work of hostile foreign elements is a convenient way to divert attention from their inability to put an end to it. Measures such as banning movements will not solve the problem, for they offer the disaffected young, the very people who feel excluded from society, no alternative. Pakistan is faced with a challenge to its survival. In order to combat religious extremism effectively, the government must revive the economy, restore political parties to their rightful position and strengthen its own institutions. These are the only means by which the tendency can be reversed.

PART TRHEE

TALIBANISATION AND JIHAD IN THE PASHTUN BELT AND THE PUNJAB

6

SALAFISM IN PAKISTAN

THE AHL-E HADITH MOVEMENT

Salafis are known as Ahl-e Hadith in South Asia and have relatively few followers in Pakistan, where they have been active since the nineteenth century. They have maintained close ties with the Saudi religious establishment since the 1960s, ties which were reinforced when thousands of Arabs came to Pakistan after the Soviet invasion of Afghanistan. Although there has been some convergence of Salafi theology and Deobandi sectarian political ideology in recent years, along with an overlapping of personnel in organisations belonging to different schools of thought, the focus of this paper is on the Ahl-e Hadith movement and its jihadi expression in Kashmir.

The historical context

The Jama'at Ahl-e Hadith, an elitist politico-religious movement aimed at *islah* (reform), has its origins in the early 1870s. Like other Sunni reform movements, it claims to continue the tradition of Shah Waliullah Dehlavi (1703–62) whom it regards as the first modern Ahl-e Hadith member and draws on ideas of Syed Ahmed Barelvi (Ahmed Shaheed) (1786–1831), follower of Shah Abdul Aziz (1746–1824), the son of Shah Waliullah, and the Yemenite *qadi* Mohammad ibn Ali al Shawkani

(1775–1839).[1] In the late nineteenth century, the princely state of Bhopal became a centre for the Ahl-e Hadith around Siddique Hasan Khan (1832–90) and Maulana Syed Nazir Hussain (1805–1902). The former belonged to a prominent Shia[2] family from Awadh State; his father had converted to Sunnism under the influence of Shah Abdul Aziz who taught the religious sciences, particularly *hadith*, in Delhi with his three brothers. Maulana Nazir Hussain, the first ideologue of the Ahl-e Hadith, had studied under Shah Muhammad Ishaq (1782–1846), the grandson of Shah Waliullah and his khalifa. Thus they constructed a spiritual-cum-genealogical 'Ahl-e Hadith family tree'.[3]

The leadership of the movement belonged to socially eminent families,[4] descendants of the Mughals and Awadh aristocracy, many of them *sayyid*. But most of these families had fallen on poor times after the British colonisation of India; they had a sense of social dislocation and were disturbed by what they felt to be the decadence of the Muslim community. In order to unite the Muslims and to revive and strengthen their faith, they insisted on a return to the original sources of the faith, the Qur'an and the *hadith*,[5] 'they drew on them as their major marker of identity'[6] to restore Islam from what they perceived as *bida'* (innovations), deviations and superstitions.

Doctrines and principles

The Ahl-e Hadith recognise only the Qur'an and the *hadith* as legal sources—with *qiyas* (analogy) and *ijma'* (consensus). They claim not to follow any specific school of jurisprudence and proudly call themselves *ghayr muqallid* (non-conformists). For them, following a *madhhab* (school of jurisprudence) is tantamount to the personality worship of its founder.[7] In addition, they advocate *ijtihad* (independent reasoning), making it 'the focal point of their identity',[8] but confining it to the sufficiently qualified.

Puritanical in matters of faith and practices, they criticise Sufism as being a wrongful innovation and are hostile to the syncretic practices of most South Asian Muslims, particularly the Barelwis, who are regarded as *bida'*-akin to *shirk* (associationism). They want to purge the religion of 'un-Islamic' Hindu borrowings and of all customs that could be criticised by non-Muslims. They accuse Sufis of including non-

Muslim traditions in their practice and of compromising the Sharia. As for the Barelvis, who place emphasis on Sufi saints as intermediaries, have cults centred on shrines and holy relics, and venerate the Prophet as being made of light (*nur*) and having supernatural powers, Ahl-e Hadith consider them ignorant shrine-worshippers, or even heretics.

According to the Ahl-e Hadith, the major problem in South Asia is not irregularity in prayers, but *shirk*[9] which is why such efforts are being made towards installing the concept of *tawhid*. The Ahl-e Hadith condemn the invoking of the Prophet or of a saint in prayer, as this is considered to be *shirk*. Other customs they condemn are: supplication at graves, including the grave of the Prophet; the celebration of the death anniversary (*urs*) of a saint (*qawwali*), including the *giyarwin sharif* of Abdul Qadir Gilani;[10] the wearing of *taawiz* (amulets) and the belief in their healing power; the practice of magic; the fast on particular days dedicated to saints; the distribution of food for marriages, funerals and religious festivals; the recitation of *durud* (praise of the Prophet) in mosques; the celebration of *Milad un-Nabi* (birth of the Prophet) and of Hindu festivals, and Shia customs.

They also introduced a new, highly visible, style of *namaz* (prayer) that makes them distinct from the Hanafis. The Ahl-e Hadith say *amin* out loud (*amin bil jahr*), lift their hands as they bow (*rafa' al yadayn*), fold their hands above the navel and repeat the *Fatiha* out loud along with the imam, claiming that Shah Waliullah prayed that way.[11] As a result, they have faced regular opposition and expulsion from Hanafi mosques.

They oppose all those whose beliefs differ from theirs, including the Deobandis, convinced that they alone embody the authentic faith. Both the Ahl-e Hadith and the Deobandis are the product of the colonial context. And although they share a reliance on Shah Waliullah with the Deobandis, the Ahl-e Hadith do not recognise the Hanafi school of law, on which the Deobandi doctrine is based.[12] The Deobandis place the *hadith* at the centre of their education but unlike the Ahl-e Hadith, they accept Sufism. The Ahl-e Hadith accuse Deobandis of fabricating *hadiths* and do not accept the interpretative tradition of Hanafis. The Ahl-e Hadith target Deobandis as *mushrikin*, worshipping graves (*quburiyin*) for their practice of offering *fateha*[13] on shrines and their veneration of the Prophets.

To justify themselves, they have, from the outset, engaged in big public debates against the reformist Hindus of the Arya Samaj and the

Christian missionaries and have been very active in preaching and publishing pamphlets in Urdu, Arabic and Persian.

The Arab connection

Due to certain similarities with the Wahhabis, questions were asked of their connections as, like them, the Ahl-e Hadith greatly valued Ibn Taymiyya and translated his writings into Urdu. Furthermore they met Wahhabis during the pilgrimage, read their books and associated with the Arab ulema who had migrated to India and settled in Bhopal. However the influence of the Arab Wahhabis was denied, and it was pointed out that as the Wahhabis were Hanbali they were not real Salafis, instead they emphasised their links to Shah Waliullah. This was mainly to avoid being suspected by the British of political activism and of following the jihadi tradition of Syed Ahmed Barelvi, the so-called 'Wahhabi movement'. But, 'at the same time, they retained connections to the local networks of the Indian "Wahhabis", suppressed by the British in 1863 and sentenced in the so-called Wahhabi trials between 1868 and 1871'.[14] Nazir Husain was even suspected of links with the mujahidin and imprisoned. The Ahl-e Hadith eventually persuaded the British colonial administration to drop the word Wahhabi from official correspondence. Until about 1910, they actively engaged in religious reform and professed loyalty to British rule. Gradually, they grew into a sectarian movement and by holding all-India conferences became more visible.[15]

'From the 1920s onwards, accelerating after the 1970s, [the Ahl-e Hadith] developed international connections with the *Salafiya* and the *Wahhabiyya* in Arabia, building on old networks of personal contacts with the *Hijaz*."[16] One of the prominent Ahl-e Hadith scholars was Sheikh Abdul Ghaffar Hassan (1913–2007). Born in Umarpur, near Delhi, he migrated to Pakistan after partition in 1947. Interestingly, he was associated with the Jamaat-e Islami from 1941 to 1957 and left due to differences with Maududi about the way to establish an Islamic state, through elections or by educating the masses. Abdul Ghaffar Hassan was in favour of education. He then established a school in Faisalabad. In 1964 a delegation from Saudi Arabia came to Pakistan and he was selected, together with Hafiz Mohammad Gondalavi, the father-in-law of Ehsan Ellahi Zaheer, to teach at the Islamic University in Medina. He replaced Sheikh Nasir al-Din al-Albani and taught *hadith* for sixteen years in Medina; he was very close to Ibn Baz and among his most famous students were Safar al-Hawali and Sheikh Muqbil al-Wadi'i. Back in Pakistan he was engaged in *da'wa* activities till his death.

Since the 1980s, this elitist group with an urban following has made inroads into Pakistani society as migrant workers and alumni of Medina University have introduced Salafi ideas from Saudi Arabia. The appeal of literalist Islam is due to the Afghan jihad, sponsorship by the state and the expansion of madrasas financed by Saudis.

After the Gulf War in 1991, Saudi Arabia shifted its patronage from the Jamaat-e Islami[17] to Ahl-e Hadith and created Salafi establishments in Pakistan. The Ahl-e Hadith received millions of dollars and developed a publishing empire with worldwide distribution.

The Markazi Jamiat Ahl-e Hadith (MJAH)

There are 17 Ahl-e Hadith organisations in Pakistan, six of them taking part in politics and three engaging in jihad, the others focus on *da'wa* and the establishment of a network of madrasas.[18] The Ahl-e Hadith suffer from significant fragmentation and there is intense internal strife over differences in ritual and strategy; much time is spent refuting other groups. Some reject the political system as *batil* (false) and do not take part in politics while others participate in elections. There are also differences over jihad, some advocating *jihad bi-l-nafs* (effort to better oneself) and others *jihad bi-l-sayf* (violent jihad), some considering jihad as a *fardh-e ain* (individual duty) and others as a *fardh kifaya* (collective duty).

The Markazi Jamiat Ahl-e Hadith (MJAH) is the main Salafi organisation in Pakistan. It traces its origins to the All India Ahl-e Hadith Conference which took place in Arah (Bihar) in 1906. This organisation came to the forefront in 1986 in Lahore under the leadership of Allama Ehsan Elahi Zaheer,[19] who transformed the Jamiat into a political party closely associated with the Pakistan Muslim League. The MJAH is part of the Muttahida Majlis-e Amal (MMA), the alliance of religious parties, where it is represented by its chairman, Professor Sajid Mir.

The MJAH has several subsidiary organisations, one of which is the Ahl-e Hadith Youth Force, a group with a great ability to mobilise the youth, they take part in sectarian disputes against Shias and Barelvis and take over Barelvi mosques. The other important subsidiary is Tehrik-e Mujahidin, a jihadi outfit that emerged in 1989 in Indian-held Kashmir and sent its recruits to Afghanistan for training.[20] Linked to the MJAH since 2000 (the MJAH absorbed Tehrik-e Mujahidin in response to objections that it was not militant and was only interested in politics), it has a training camp near Muzaffarabad (Azad Kashmir). Apart from fighting the *kuffar*, Tehrik-e Mujahidin, which is funded by the Haramayn Foundation, strives to defend the pure *'aqida* (faith) in Indian-held Kashmir where it has converted many Barelvi mosques into Ahl-e Hadith mosques. The contact with Saudi Arabia was established when the Ahl-e Hadith started the Tahaffuz-e Haramain-e Sharifain Movement in 1985 after Iranian pilgrims demonstrated in Mecca during the Hajj.

The madrasa network

The greatest asset of the MJAH is the Wifaq ul Madaris Salafiya, which controls Salafi madrasas all over Pakistan.[21]

According to the Ministry of Interior, there were some 20,000 madrasas in Pakistan in 2000. In 1947 there were only 245 madrasas in West Pakistan. Although it is generally taken for granted that the mushroom growth of seminaries was linked to the Afghan jihad, their number increased considerably between 1988 and 2000 and the proliferation of madrasas during General Musharraf's rule, notably in Islamabad.[22] The largest number of madrasas are Deobandi (65 per cent) with only 6 per cent Ahl-e Hadith, but the increase in the number of Ahl-e Hadith seminaries has been phenomenal, going up from 134 in 1988 to 310 in 2000 (131 per cent). According to some sources, they now number 500 of whom about 300 are affiliated to the Wifaq ul Madaris Salafiya and the Islamic University of Medina. In 2006, according to the Pakistani government, 34,000 students[23] were studying in Ahl-e Hadith madrasas compared to 18,800 in 1996.

Interestingly this massive increase coincides with a similar growth of Shia madrasas since 2000 as if there was renewed competition between Saudi Arabia and Iran on Pakistani soil. The Ahl-e Hadith madrasas teach the *dars-e nizami*—the curriculum developed in the eighteenth century by Mulla Nizamuddin and which is taught in Pakistani madrasas, including Shia madrasas—but with an emphasis on Qur'an and hadith.[24] Contrary to madrasas affiliated to other schools of thought, the Ahl-e Hadith madrasas merge Islamic education with a modern curriculum and have been teaching Pakistan studies, English,[25] mathematics and science for a long time. Many madrasas have a high school that follows the national curriculum and prepares students for matriculation (secondary school certificate) and B.A. exams.

The main Ahl-e Hadith madrasa[26] is Jamaa Salafiya in Faisalabad, whose director is Sajid Mir, and which is also the headquarter of Wifaq ul Madaris Salafiya. It is a centre of *tablighi* (missionary work, preaching) and jihadi activities and of the Ahl-e Hadith Youth Force that is involved in sectarian activities. The Jamaa Salafiya in Islamabad is affiliated to the Medina and Umm al-Qura universities. The madrasa of Mamun Kanjan, in Faisalabad district, founded in 1921, has the biggest religious library in Pakistan. Jamaa Dirasat ul Salafiya in Swat, founded in 1994, has become a centre of Tehrik-e Mujahidin and the administration of the Mansehra training camp has been shifted to the madrasa after the crackdown on jihadi groups in 2002. The Ahl-e Hadith madrasa of Quetta (Baluchistan), founded in 1978, is closely linked to the Islamic University of Medina, all the teachers graduated in Saudi Arabia and courses are taught in Arabic. It controls 25 madrasas in the province. In Peshawar, Jamaa Asaria, built in 2006, is considered among the best Salafi madrasas in Pakistan. The fees are very low for the 1,200 students, thanks to the generosity of donors in Saudi Arabia, Kuwait and Qatar.

The Markaz Da'wa wal Irshad (MDI)[27]

The MDI (Centre for Preaching and Guidance) was set up in 1986 by three Pakistani university professors belonging to the department of Islamic studies of Lahore Engineering University—Hafiz Mohammad Saeed,[28] Dr Zafar Iqbal (*nom de guerre* Abu Hamza), and Hafiz Abdul Rehman Makki (Hafiz Mohammad Saeed's nephew), all linked to Saudi ulema and the Medina Islamic University—and to Sheikh Abdullah 'Azzam.

The Markaz's headquarters are located in Muridke, 30 kilometres from Lahore. It is a big complex of 200 acres, allegedly donated by the government of Zia-ul Haq, with schools, a farm and factories, and is meant to be a pure city (*Medina al Taiba*) in a purely Islamic environment. In the beginning, the Markaz received considerable Arab funds, including some from Osama bin Laden, who also sent telephone messages from Sudan and later Afghanistan for several of their general meetings. It is also funded by the large Pakistani diaspora in Europe—mostly in Britain, France and the Netherlands—and in the Middle East, it also collects donations in Pakistan.[29]

The Da'wa wal Irshad movement can be described as 'Salafi-jihadi', in that it has two proclaimed aims: *da'wa* and jihad, which have a symbiotic relationship and cannot be separated, and to which it gives equal importance. Hafiz Saeed sees jihad and education as complementing each other. The characteristic of the Markaz is to integrate *da'wa* with jihad and to advocate that modern education is not in conflict with religious education. But without military training, education is meaningless because 'when the Muslims gave up jihad, science and technology also went into the hands of others'.[30] For Hafiz Saeed, the main problem facing Muslims as a whole is their subjugation to the West; jihad is thus a means of challenging oppression and establishing the rule of Islam. Contrary to the other Ahl-e Hadith movements of Pakistan, who consider jihad as *fardh kifaya*, Da'wa wal Irshad considers jihad as a *fardh-e ain* in the prevailing situation.[31]

Da'wa wal Irshad affirms that many organisations are engaged in *da'wa*, but that they have forgotten jihad. This criticism is aimed directly at the Markaz Jamiat Ahl-e Hadith whom Hafiz Saeed reproaches for its inertia with regard to jihad. For the movement, the current situation where Muslims are perceived as oppressed throughout the world demands from Muslims that they engage in jihad against Hindus who are the worst of polytheists and against Jews who are their allies, with the aim of first Islamising India and then conquering the whole world. Jihad is also presented as essential in preserving the Islamic identity of Pakistan and as the only solution to the evils that plague Pakistani society, notably sectarianism (the Sunni-Shia conflict), which is seen as another conspiracy to divert Muslims from waging jihad against the infidels. Besides, jihad is also justified in terms of *'izzat* (honour) to take revenge for the 'rape of sisters and mothers'.[32]

Apart from jihad, Da'wa wal Irshad wants to purify Pakistani society in particular and Muslim societies in general and purge South Asian

Islam of Hindu influences. According to Hafiz Saeed, 'the majority of Pakistanis have been unable to pull themselves away from Hindu customs and traditions'. He quotes as examples the popularity of the Basant kite-flying festival and the *Jashn-e Baharan* (spring festival) in the Punjab, adding: 'It is shameful that our rulers are wasting the money of Muslims to celebrate this Hindu festival, and they should fear Allah's wrath for doing so.'[33]

Their success in 'converting' Muslims from different schools of thought to the Ahl-e Hadith has indeed, been phenomenal. They have set up a huge network of over 2,000 recruitment centres across Pakistan and have, since 1994, been developing a network of Al Da'wa model schools under the leadership of Dr Zafar Iqbal, where children receive Islamic and modern education, with an emphasis on Arabic, English and computer science. The aim is to utilise modern technology to spread the message of jihad and prepare children from a young age to become mujahidin. Textbooks insist on jihad and train young children to focus on the spirit of sacrifice (*qurbani*): Urdu readers for second year children contain the wills (*wasiatnamah*) of martyrs and exhort children (both boys and girls) to prepare to give their life for the great nuclear power that Pakistan has become. In 2002, Da'wa wal Irshad claimed to have 200 primary schools and 20,000 students, including 5,000 girls.[34]

The following advertisement for Al Da'wa schools appeared in *Ghazwa*, a magazine published by the MDI: 'Do you want your children to grow up to become a doctor, engineer, economist, officer, businessman or leader? But do you also want that they should not become "slaves" of the English people? Then you should put your children in the Al Da'wa System of Schools (ADSS). At ADSS, they will become guardians of Islam and Qur'an. They will become leaders of the Muslim world besides becoming a professional in medicine, engineering, law, business, etc. At Da'wa's school, we also prepare your children for *jihad*. We offer classes of martial arts. Please call [phone numbers in Lahore]."[35]

The Lashkar-e Taiba (LeT)[36]

The Laskhar-e Taiba, which is the military wing of the Markaz Da'wa wal Irshad, is the jihadi expression of the Ahl-e Hadith movement and the largest private jihadi army in South Asia.

The LeT was established in early 1990 to train young Pakistanis willing to fight against the Soviet occupation in Afghanistan. In 1987, the MDI had set up a training centre known as Muaskar-e Taiba in Jaji (Paktia province, Afghanistan, bordering Pakistan), and a second one known as Muaskar-e Aqsa in the Kunar province in Afghanistan.[37] It claims that some 1,600 of its trainees participated in the Afghan jihad but that only five were martyred. It shifted its focus to Kashmir after the Soviet withdrawal from Afghanistan as it did not want to involve itself in factional fighting within Afghanistan. After the Soviet withdrawal, the LeT decided to 'take a leaf from the book of the Afghans [...] and lit the torch of the jihad movement.'

Although the LeT claims that the mujahidin are recruited from all social classes, most of them belong to the lower middle class and come from the towns and cities of central and south Punjab and from semi-urban neighbouring villages whose populations grew exponentially in the 1980s through rural-urban migration. In their late teens or early twenties, mostly between 18 and 25 years of age, the recruits tend on the whole to be more educated than the average Pakistani and certainly more so than members of Deobandi jihadi groups, such the Sipah-e Sahaba or Jaish-e Mohammad. The majority of them have completed secondary school with high grades and quite a few have studied for BA or BSc at college, and have come into contact with the LeT through *da'wa* programmes which have in turn led them to attend the big annual congregations organised every year in Muridke by the MDI. The proportion of madrasa-educated boys is minimal (about 10 per cent), but includes boys who studied in a madrasa after studying in an Urdu medium school. It is difficult for the LeT to recruit in Ahl-e Hadith madrasas due to its differences, notably on the concept of jihad, with the MJAH, which controls the great majority of Ahl-e Hadith madrasas.[38] The MJAH considers jihad *fardh kifaya* while the LeT considers it to be *fardh-e ain*. The MJAH considers that the Tehrik-e Mujahidin fulfills the conditions to wage jihad. It also condemns the behaviour of some of the LeT recruits who loot banks, make money out of jihad and embezzle huge sums of money collected under the name of jihad.[39]

Apart from the madrasa in Muridke, the LeT controls a dozen others, the two main ones being located in Karachi—Jamia Abu Bakr which follows the same curriculum as the Islamic University of Medina[40] and Jamaa Dirasat ul Islamia where half of the 500 students come from South East Asia. The LeT prefers to recruit educated boys as they are more motivated and well aware of what they are doing. With its call to erase centuries of superstitions, the Ahl-e Hadith school of thought appeals to the educated youth who have become dissatisfied with traditional Islam but who also reject Western ideas. Belonging to this highly structured movement gives a substitute identity and a feeling of moral superiority to young men who feel despised by the Westernised elite of their country and marginalised in a society which they consider impure and corrupt and where they do not see any opportunity for upward social mobility. Two teenagers caught after running away from their boarding school to join the LeT made the following statement: 'The jihadi man who brought us to Muridke told us we would become great by fighting jihad. We knew we could never become great if we stayed in Buner. I wanted to become great. [...] We were told to fight against Israel, America and non-Muslims. We are so unhappy with our lives here. We have nothing. We wanted to go to the Muridke madrasa so we would have a better life in the hereafter.'[41]

Recruits are not sent to Kashmir immediately, but after a long period of training.[42] Most of them are Hanafis, they often do not know which *maslak* (rule of conduct) they belong to and it is only during religious training that they find out that they are Deobandi or Barelvi. First they attend an ordinary course (*daura–e amma*) that lasts 21 days and focuses on religious education and more precisely on the principles of the Ahl-e Hadith school of thought; two weeks are devoted to religious education and one week to practical *da'wa* and *tabligh*. They are then sent back home to resume their former activities, and to engage in *da'wa* work in their neighbourhood, with the particular task of recruiting their friends. They remain under the scrutiny of the local LeT leaders who only agree to send them for the three-month special course (*daura-e khassa*) after assessing their level of motivation. The aim of this course is to demonstrate the superiority of the Ahl-e Hadith to the other schools of thought and to prepare the recruits for *tabligh*.

The LeT after the ban of 12 January 2002

As a result of pressure from India and the USA, President Musharraf banned the LeT, in his landmark speech of 12 January 2002. However, in anticipation of this declaration, Hafiz Saeed reshaped the MDI on 25 December 2001 into a missionary (*tablighi*) organisation named Jamaat ul Da'wa Pakistan (JUD), an organisation that was completely separate from the LeT, and in doing so announced that he would devote himself to education and social welfare activities with the aim of reforming Pakistani society. Yahya Mujahid, spokesman for the Jamaat ul Da'wa, was reported as saying: 'We handed Lashkar-e-Taiba over to the Kashmiris in December 2001. Now we have no contact with any jihadi organisation. We, the Jamaat ul Da'wa, are only preachers.'[43]

The Jamaat ul Da'wa is building a support base across the entire country. Meanwhile the Idara Khidmat-e Khalq (Service of the People), a front for LeT, has become highly visible, setting up Taiba hospitals in Muridke and Muzaffarabad (Azad Kashmir), 51 dispensaries plus mobile medical camps for patients in poor areas and in the Afghan and Kashmiri refugee camps: 'We are a welfare organisation and are working on various projects in health, education, provision of clean drinking water, advancing financial help to orphans and families of those martyred in jihad in Kashmir and Afghanistan.'[44] They provided relief after the tsunami of December 2004 and were the first group to offer aid after the earthquake in October 2005 with a stated policy 'to win the hearts and minds of people'.[45] The earthquake was described by Hafiz Saeed as the wrath of God: 'The earthquake is the result of the rulers' sinful policies. They wanted the women to abandon hijab [...] at Bush's behest, they wanted to purge our school books from verses on jihad, befriend India and recognise Israel. They banned all the jihadi groups and abandoned jihad [...] thus they invited the wrath of God.'[46]

As their training camps were near the epicentre of the earthquake, they were the first to reach the affected people and to offer aid. They were praised by the Pakistani government, and even by some Western NGOs, for their efficiency and these legitimate relief activities boosted their position locally.

Al Da'wa Medical Mission, which had previously focused on the urban poor, has now extended its activities to the least privileged areas of Sindh (Tharparkar) and Baluchistan (Makran belt) with the double aim of countering the activities of the NGOs and of fulfilling a religious duty. According to Hafiz Saeed, NGOs have hidden agendas that aim to weaken faith in God and the spirit of jihad. 'These NGOs are working on an anti-Islamic agenda and after the invasion of Afghanistan and Iraq by the US and European countries, their agendas have been exposed.'[47] Nonetheless, Jamaat ul Da'wa uses the same techniques as NGOs and Christian missionaries, with doctors extending *da'wa* to patients while they treat them.[48]

After keeping a low profile for a short time, the LeT became active again, this time under the name Pasban Ahl-e Hadith (Guardians of Ahl-e Hadith), though is still known as LeT. Its offices had been closed or turned into Jamaat ul Da'wa offices—who meanwhile continued to recruit mujahidin for the LeT—but remained operational in Azad Kashmir under the pretext that the ban was not enforceable there. The Jamaat ul Da'wa is targeting not only the youth but is giving equal importance to 'converting' women, as without them it cannot realise the dream of establishing the kind of society it wants to create in Pakistan and elsewhere. Despite divisions in the leadership due to personality clashes, accusations of nepotism[49] and unfair distribution of funds, Hafiz Saeed has expanded the membership of the JUD.

After the beginning of the rapprochement between India and Pakistan, the LeT mujahidin were compelled by the Inter-Services Intelligence, (ISI, the intelligence services of Pakistan) to keep a low profile, but it was at this time that their international links became clear and a process of deterritorialisation was started. The arrest in March 2002 of the Arab militant Abu Zubaidah in a LeT safehouse in Faisalabad, a Pakistani Islamist hub, put the spotlight on the connections between the LeT and Arab militants linked to al-Qaeda. Similarly, in September 2003, Indonesian and Malaysian students linked to the Jemaah Islamiyyah were arrested in Karachi from the Jamaat ul Dirasat ul Islamiya, a madrasa that is affiliated to the Jamaat ul Da'wa. It was also reported that students arrested in the Philippines in October 2003 had received training in LeT camps. Western converts and people of Pakistani origin settled in the United States and Australia, who had been trained in LeT camps in Azad Kashmir, were also detained in 2003.

In the beginning, they supported the clerics of the Red Mosque (Lal Masjid) in Islamabad because they wanted to enforce Sharia,[50] but when the situation turned nasty, they distanced themselves claiming that 'the people of Lal Masjid and Jamia Hafsa belong to a different school of thought' (Deobandi Hanafi)[51] and that no group had the legal, constitutional or religious right to forcibly implement Sharia in the country.

The ambiguity of the LeT is plain for all to see: it looks beyond Kashmir, at least in its rhetoric, and promotes transnational activities in the name of jihad against infidels anywhere in the world where Muslims are perceived to be oppressed, and aims at creating a new deterritorialised identity based on Islam (i.e. the ummah). Hafiz Saeed reiterated in August 2007 its call for jihad: 'It is obligatory that every Muslim rise for the defence of oppressed Muslims regardless of which part of the world they are in, whether they are in Kashmir, Palestine, Iraq, Afghanistan, India, or in any other part of the world.'[52] The LeT pays great attention to the links between global and local scenarios and its publications focus on developments in other countries and in the USA that are seen as a threat to the Muslims.

But as is the case with every jihadi movement in Pakistan or elsewhere in the region (Afghanistan, Central and South East Asia), local considerations always prevail over global ones. The jihadi movements have to some extent Islamised a nationalist struggle but, notwithstanding the presence of foreign delegates in the congregations and the rhetoric about the oppressed Muslims in every part of the world, the main objective of the LeT recruits waging the Kashmiri jihad is to complete the unachieved partition of 1947 and integrate Kashmir into Pakistan. Recruitment is still driven by the dynamics of the India-Pakistan conflict and strategic interests in Afghanistan rather than by global events. The mujahidin are more concerned with liberating Kashmir from Indian occupation and through martyrdom gaining a place for themselves and their family in Paradise, than waging jihad in distant lands.

The Ahl-e Hadith have limited appeal beyond certain urban commercial and professional middle classes. Although they have gained strength since the 1990s and are more organised than the other groups, they remain a tiny minority, a puritanical group in matters of faith and practice, and an elitist group that worships in separate mosques, many of them refusing to pray behind imams belonging to other Sunni sects. The Ahl-e Hadith madrasas are located in the cities of Northern Punjab that have a large Muhajir population such as Gujranwala, Faisalabad, Sheikhupura, Kasur. Their unique approach, merging Islamic education with modern curricula, is attractive for the lower middle classes who cannot afford private English-medium schools. These hybrid madrasas boast excellent exam results, which in turn encourages parents to send their children to these schools.

The Ahl-e Hadith devote considerable energy to combating Sufism and other so-called 'Hindu practices', particularly on the internet. This is the reason why the Ahl-e Hadith is particularly appealing to young people from the diaspora who want to break away from the South Asian Islam of their parents which they often consider as superstition. The emphasis on individual scholarship and the rejection of 'blind *taqlid*' is attractive to young people, which explains the success of Zakir Naik (an Indian medical doctor by training who has become a religious preacher inspired by Sheikh Ahmed Deedat) in Pakistan and in the diaspora.

KASHARS AGAINST MASHARS

JIHAD AND SOCIAL CHANGE IN THE FATA[1]

Socio-political change in traditional Pashtun tribal society has sped up during the last three decades. Such changes in the society's dynamics go back to the 1970s when tribals started migrating to Karachi and to the Gulf, enabling minor lineages to become rich and to challenge the power hierarchy.[2] The open economy of the 1980s, the boom of smuggling during the Zia-ul Haq regime and the tremendous inflow of remittances[3]—which benefited predominantly the disadvantaged and traditionally subordinate segments of the rural society—led to wealth accumulation by emerging classes who invested mostly in construction of huge new houses and shops and also in the purchase of land and weapons. The old inequalities based on Pashtun values of hospitality and manhood were replaced by new inequalities based on money; these transformed the character of tribal society. During the Afghan jihad of the 1980s, the flow of US dollars and weapons, as well as smuggling, drug peddling, gun running, car theft and abduction for ransom, became extra sources of money. The consequence was social disruption and polarisation rather than adaptation.[4] Wealth and power started coming from other sources than land and this changed the dynamics of the old system that had existed under the British Raj.

The breakdown of tribal authority began in the 1980s when the agencies marginalised the *malik*s (tribal elders) and used mullahs to unite feuding tribes against the Soviet occupation of Afghanistan. Islam was also seen as a counterweight to the internal threat of Pashtun nationalism. The gradual weakening of traditional rural institutions and the political scenario in Afghanistan led to the empowerment of religious groups who became autonomous as the writ of the Pakistani government was ineffective in the tribal areas.[5] There was virtually no international border between Pakistan and Afghanistan and the settlement of Afghan refugees in the tribal areas affected the demographic balance and the power structure. Moreover, training camps and Deobandi madrassas supported by Arab donors promoted religious militancy in a traditionally secular society.

Most studies dealing with the tribal areas explain the developments of the last three decades by focusing on the external factors without taking local dynamics into account. The importance of external factors should not be underplayed, but they can only work in an atmosphere conducive to their influence.

In this chapter I discuss the change in the sociology and patterns of leadership in the Federally Administered Tribal Areas (FATA) since the arrival of al-Qaeda in the area after 9/11.[6] It must be emphasised that my focus will be on South Waziristan which has become the hub of al-Qaeda and the Taliban—local and Afghan elements—and also of Uzbeks, among other foreign jihadis; this means that the developments in other tribal areas will not be considered here. My key argument is that the Talibanisation of Waziristan might be analysed as the outcome of a social movement among the Wazir tribesmen which started in the 1970s and was accelerated in the post-9/11 context by the emergence of 'tribal entrepreneurs' who took advantage of a change in political opportunities and of their access to resources to challenge the traditional tribal leadership. I argue that it is a movement of the *kashars* (the young, the poor and those belonging to minor lineages or powerless tribes)[7] against the *mashars* (the tribal elders)[8] and the Political Agent. It is also a movement of the *kashars* against those who have an interest in the status quo—the so-called 'mafia of maliks, transporters and traffickers', in other words the emergent under-class of the new rich.

The first part of the paper will provide an outline of the changes which have occurred in the last three decades in the social structure of the FATA. The second part will look at the social and demographic changes in Waziristan. I will then attempt to analyse the shift in the traditional structure of power—from the political administration to the military and from the *maliks* (elders who are the mediators between their tribes and the Political Agent) to the militants who call themselves the Pakistani Taliban and the emergence of an alternative leadership. Finally I will address the attempts of the old elite to counter the movement. The aim of this chapter is modest, but I hope that it can be a starting point to develop the understanding of the internal dynamics of Pashtun tribal society.

Changing patterns of social and political life

Pashtun tribal society, widely considered by earlier ethnographers as classless and egalitarian, has gradually changed and class is now an important dimension of social life and relations. Five categories of class-like social groups can be identified.[9] First, there are the traditional leaders (*mashars*)—land owning elders and *maliks*—who gradually allied themselves with the administration to pursue their personal interests and have been the sole beneficiaries of the system. They have lost influence over time and are discredited; tribal elders are still respected, but their roles and views are increasingly being questioned. Second, there are the new rich—traders, wholesalers, contractors, timber merchants, transporters, drug/arms traffickers. Many of them have acquired the status of *malik* to contest the elections and register themselves as contractors and suppliers; they are the main beneficiaries of the war economy.[10] Third, the educated and professionals (doctors, engineers, college teachers, journalists, students, NGOs' employees, active and retired members of the military and the bureaucracy) who oppose the status quo and are the self-defined agents of social change. Fourth, the common people (farmers, sharecroppers, landless peasants, artisans, workers in the transport sector, unemployed youth), in other words the *kashars* who have no civil and political rights and are dissatisfied with the existing political and administrative set-up; the state has not provided people belonging to this group with basic rights—education, health and most important, justice. Fifth, migrants settled in Karachi and the Gulf who, just like the third and fourth categories, are dissatisfied and oppose the status quo and desire to be agents of social change.

PAKISTAN

The administrative structure

At the Bannu tribal *jirga* (council of elders) in January 1948, Pakistan accepted the autonomous character of the Federally Administered Tribal Areas, FATA, and continued to follow the policy of the colonial rulers towards the tribal areas. There has been little change in the administrative set up of Waziristan since the creation of the agencies of North and South Waziristan during British rule.[11] This area which is geographically, economically and socially at the extreme periphery of Pakistani society has been historically independent of any central authority, owing to its inaccessibility, and has often looked towards Kabul. The Wana Wazir gave much trouble to the British. In 1920 J.M. Ewart wrote: 'Their behaviour throughout had been worse than that of any tribe on the Frontier, showing a combination of treachery, lawlessness and fanaticism'.[12]

After Partition, partly because of strained relations with Afghanistan, the Pakistani government allowed the FATA administration to become entrenched in its colonial past; it continued to deal with the *malik*s through the Political Agent, and the system of allowances and subsidies has survived.[13] Zulfiqar Ali Bhutto initiated policies aimed at the development of the FATA, but there was no change in the administrative system. He introduced quotas in educational institutions[14] and federal jobs and facilitated the issuance of passports, which had far reaching socio-economic and political implications.[15]

In 1996, the caretaker government of Malik Miraj Khalid introduced universal adult franchise in the tribal areas.[16] A large number of candidates contested elections in 1997 and in October 2002; these elections, however, were held on a non-party basis in the tribal areas. The introduction of local government institutions under the Devolution plan and the FATA reform plan announced in January 2002 by President Musharraf was shelved on account of the War on Terror, as the government thought that a centralised command structure was more suitable for the military operations. The tribals were not given any representation in the North West Frontier Province (NWFP) assembly during the October 2002 election, judicial powers were not separated from executive powers, and the necessary amendments were not made in the Frontier Crimes Regulations (FCR) of 1901.[17]

A reform package was announced in August 2009 lifting restrictions on political parties' activities and excluding women and children from collective responsibility, among other things.[18] These reforms which should be a first step towards bringing FATA into the mainstream have still to be implemented. Two decrees amending the FCR[19] and extending the Political Parties Order (2002) to the FATA were signed in August 2011 by President Zardari. Although some claim that it is too little too late, these steps towards bringing FATA into the mainstream are nevertheless encouraging.

The changing demographic structure of Waziristan

According to the 1998 census, North Waziristan had approximately 360,000 inhabitants, the increase from 1981 to 1998 being 51 per cent, while South Waziristan had 430,000 inhabitants, the increase from 1981 to 1998 being 39 per cent.[20] The unofficial estimated populations of North and South Waziristan are now around 600,000 and 800,000 inhabitants respectively. Tens of thousands of inhabitants of South Waziristan have been displaced by military operations.[21] This has led to forced urbanisation[22] and to the dislocation of whole communities, notably the Burki (Urmar) of Kaniguram.[23]

Half of the population of North Waziristan belongs to the Wazir tribe[24] and one third are Dawar, a minor tribe, a proportion that has been stable for the last three decades. The situation in South Waziristan is very different. Traditionally 75 per cent of the population were Mehsud and 25 per cent Wazir, the most important clan being the Zalikhel, a sub-tribe of the Ahmedzai Wazir which has links with Afghan tribes across the Durand Line.[25] According to the population census of 1972, the Mehsud were about 250,000 and the Wazir 50,000; since 1981 the number of Mehsud has constantly declined while the Wazir population has kept increasing[26] and is now on a par with the Mehsud. The Wazir, who control 70 per cent of business, are more affluent.[27] They also control some of the most fertile valleys and lucrative trade routes along the border. The Mehsud have achieved an impressive literacy rate and produced scores of civil servants and military officers, they have joined mainstream Pakistani society and moved to the settled areas of Tank and Dera Ismail Khan.[28] Many of them have also settled in Karachi where they have opened transport businesses. Well-placed in the power hierarchy of the state, they are inclined towards integration in the state rather than separation from it.

The rivalry between Mehsud and Wazir for control of the resources of South Waziristan goes back to the period preceding Partition. At the turn of the twentieth century, colonial administrators noted that 'the relations of the Darwesh Khel with the Mahsuds have never been cordial, and now they might be best described as being distinctly strained.'[29] Although they were the largest tribe in South Waziristan, the Mehsud are described in colonial literature as the junior lineage among the main Wazir tribes, therefore having the worst land—largely barren mountains—and living in the most crowded conditions, which partly explains why they looked southwards.

The Mehsud have long been in dispute with the Wazir over the ownership of the Gomal Pass:

> The Gomal Pass [...] has always been considered as belonging to the Mahsuds. Actually it is outside the limits of their country. The claim of the Mahsuds to the Gomal Pass is based on the fact of their using it from time immemorial as raiding ground which supplied them with a source of livelihood. The pass has been used for generations by the Powindah caravans that trade between India, Afghanistan and Central Asia.[30]

Although they inhabit two-thirds of South Waziristan the Mehsud are isolated geographically, having no direct access either to Afghanistan or to the settled areas.

In the 1950s, at a time when the Wazir were in the minority, a peace deal was struck and the political administration introduced the *nikat*[31] (loss and profit sharing) system on the basis of population. The Mehsud were given three quarters of the share of resources and development funds and the Wazir one quarter.[32] The government continues to follow this system in spite of the Wazir tribe's demand to do away with it. In December 2004, an Ahmedzai *jirga* denounced the elections to the Agency Council (two thirds of the seats were allocated to the Mehsud and one third to the Wazir according to the *nikat*) as being anti-democratic, while the Mehsud defended the status quo.[33] The administration is indifferent to the problem and has been seen by the Wazir as supporting the Mehsud. These claims are not new. A movement was launched among the Wazir in the early 1970s by Maulana Noor Mohammad who 'mobilised Islam to activate specific tribal ideology into a political movement against the Mehsud, accusing the administration of supporting them.'[34] The army moved into South Waziristan in May 1976 and dismantled the parallel administration he had set up; some 1,500 shops in the bazaar of Wana were destroyed, Noor Mohammad and his key followers fled to Angoor Adda but were arrested and jailed. He spent several years in jail and later joined the Jamiat-e Ulama-e Islam (JUI). He received Arab money and weapons in the 1980s which enabled him to build a madrasa.[35] Maulana Noor Mohammad was not only a cleric but also a respected tribal leader. He was elected to Parliament in 1997 and after 9/11 he kept a low profile and was seen by the local Taliban as pro-government. Opposed to suicide attacks and to attacks targeting the Pakistani army, he was killed on 23 August 2010 when a suicide bomber—a Mehsud affiliated to the Tehrik-i-Taliban Pakistan (TTP)—blew himself up inside a mosque in Wana.[36] He was delivering a sermon at the time.

The emergence of an alternative leadership after 9/11

The introduction in 1996 of adult franchise—although without political parties—was meant to bring tribal areas into the mainstream and to answer a long-standing demand from the emerging middle class. The participation of the tribals in the general elections of 1997 further eroded the power and authority of tribal elders.[37] Before, members of parliament were chosen by the *jirga*, and the *malik*s had political influence and could get rich.[38] The political system was centred on them and its effectiveness was linked to the competency of the Political Agent; the system was strong as long as the institution of the *malik*s was strong, but *malik*s are no more the representatives of the tribes. An alternative leadership, more charismatic and with access to considerable resources, has emerged from the war and filled the vacuum. The October 2002 elections, which coincided with the re-emergence of the Taliban, saw the destruction of the base of the *malik*s' power as mullahs linked to the JUI-F (Fazlur Rehman) were elected as members of parliament and transformed their religious authority into political power.[39] But the Muttahida Majlis-e Amal (MMA) disappointed, or indeed betrayed, the rural poor.

After the American intervention, foreign militants, Afghan Taliban and others who fled Afghanistan entered the tribal areas, and a sizeable number of foreigners settled in Waziristan where they developed deep links with Ahmedzai Wazir. From 2003 Waziristan, described by Ahmed Rashid as 'al-Qaeda central', became the focal point of the militant activities. Afghan Taliban and foreign fighters, mostly Uzbeks, were hosted in Wana by the Yargulkhel, a sub-clan of the Ahmedzai Wazir. Prominent among the Wazir who hosted them was Nek Mohammad who had been recruited by the Afghan Taliban in the mid-1990s, had ascended rapidly through the hierarchy and was promoted to lead a Waziri contingent in Bagram.[40] He built links with the Afghan Taliban and the foreign fighters to whom he provided safe passage and support after 9/11; he was generously rewarded by those who made it to the FATA.

After the arrival of al-Qaeda, unemployed locals—'tribal entrepreneurs'—discovered the lucrative business of harbouring foreign militants, which became a source of extra money. They rented compounds for shelter and training camps and provided food at inflated prices, which was a way of gaining influence. Criminals have joined them because of the tremendous influx of Arab money. The disintegration of the institutional structure provided them an open space; they borrowed Taliban rhetoric and contributed to the territorial expansion of the Taliban movement.

Almost every tribe supported al-Qaeda, actively or passively, as guests.[41] In the eyes of the Pashtuns standing by the weak reinforces one's honour. But this code of honour, known as Pashtunwali, is intended to protect the weakest members within the tribe. For outsiders the rules have limits: if a foreigner is a cause of war, he has to leave. *Melmastia* (hospitality), which is one of the stronger Pashtun traditions, has lost its meaning. It is no more a free hospitality but a way of acquiring wealth and influence.

The army and the Frontier Corps moved into Waziristan in June 2002 after long negotiations with the tribes, who agreed, reluctantly, to allow the military's presence on the assurance that it would bring in funds and development works.[42] After the traditional approach of using carrot and stick and tribal *lashkar*s to persuade the tribals to hand over the foreign militants failed, from 2003 onwards, under intense

American pressure, the army conducted military operations in the Wazir areas of South Waziristan.[43] The military raids have weakened the already eroded power of the tribal elders who, locked in negotiations with the political administration, saw it as a betrayal and a violation of the traditions and lost whatever influence they still had on the tribes.

The military operations also created conditions for the emergence of new actors who have deep influence on the society: charismatic young men who fought in Afghanistan and are not tribal leaders by lineage, and whose power and legitimacy are based on their recently acquired wealth—either Arab money or the exorbitant compensations paid by the army—as well as their ability to fight, filled the power vacuum.[44] They capitalised on the hostility towards the presence in the area of Pakistani forces, seen as American proxies, and used both reinvented Pashtun values and resistance narratives as mobilisation tools.[45] This dynamic is similar to the situation in Afghanistan in the 1980s, where the mullahs gained autonomy in the Pashtun rural areas after the elimination, or the marginalisation, of the khans and the absence of the government's writ. This led in the 1990s to the emergence of the Taliban as a social movement.

The debacle of Kalusha in March 2004 changed the dynamics, forcing the army to sign peace deals with the militants who have been empowered. Two deals were signed between the army and the militants, in Shakai in April 2004 with Nek Mohammad and in Sararogha in February 2005 with Baitullah Mehsud.[46] The tribal elders were sidelined and the Political Agent was made redundant by the army. Maulana Meraj Qureshi and Maulana Abdul Malik Wazir, both members of the National Assembly, acted as mediators between the militants and the army. The militants had refused to strike a deal through tribal *jirga*s that had attempted to make them surrender to the military authorities in exchange for amnesty.

Changing dynamics

Between 2004 and 2007 the centre of gravity of the Pakistani Taliban moved progressively to North Waziristan as the Pakistani intelligence establishment tried to exploit traditional tribal rifts to split the pro-foreigner front and gain proxies within the Taliban movement.[47] Tribal allegiances, which had given the Taliban an invaluable network to develop their organisation, were also the cause of their fragmentation along tribal faultlines.

In December 2007 the Tehrik-i-Taliban Pakistan (TTP), an umbrella of some 40 groups aimed at bypassing the tribal factor in the insurgency, was created around Baitullah Mehsud. The TTP was established on the basis of an anti-tribal or pan-tribal agenda after the assault on the Lal Masjid (Red Mosque) in Islamabad in July 2007, which led to the proclamation of a 'defensive jihad' against the Pakistani army.

Soon after this, a new group named the Maqami Taliban, aimed at 'defending the Wazir tribe's interests in North and South Waziristan,' was formed by Uthmanzai Wazir of North Waziristan and Ahmedzai Wazir of South Waziristan. The leader, Maulvi Nazir,[48] made clear that the movement was opposed to Baitullah's 'defensive jihad' against the Pakistani army and would continue to support the Afghan jihad from the FATA. This group was reported to have been devised by Pakistani intelligence as a proxy which could be controlled to stem the growth of the TTP.

Ahmedzai Wazir had a strong interest in playing the anti-Mehsud card and instrumentalising an external actor to challenge the domination of the Mehsud. The Wazir, who have stayed neutral since the launch of the Rah-e Nejat offensive in Mehsud populated areas in October 2009, have been rewarded for their pro-government position.[49] The US has sanctioned $55 million for quick impact projects in South Waziristan, including the construction of a road and the provision of water. In February 2010 General Kayani inaugurated the Wana-Tank road which allows the Wazir to avoid travelling through Mehsud territory. The Mehsud accepted the construction of the road with the condition that they be given three quarters of the Gomal land for construction of houses. The Wazir objected, arguing that the Mehsud wanted to keep them enslaved, as passing through a rival territory means that you have to accept that tribe's dominance.[50]

In February 2010, an Ahmedzai Wazir *jirga* demanded a separate administrative status for areas under their control. This demand was not new, and in fact it was reported in December 2007 that the government planned to divide South Waziristan into two zones to give the Ahmedzai Wazir a separate entity and end their dependence on the

Mehsud. Some officials argued that the construction of the Gomal Zam road to allow unhindered access to Wazir and the creation of a separate Wazir tribal agency would end the Mehsud's nuisance value. The Mehsud are opposed to such a measure, which will allow access to Afghanistan via Wazir territory for trade.[51]

According to a senior government official: 'The Wazir are satisfied with the government. Development projects are being implemented and three small dams are being constructed.'[52] In brief, the *nikat* has become irrelevant and by manipulating an external political actor the Wazir have, at least temporarily, achieved what they had been fighting for.

The redefinition of the jirga *and the new role of the mullahs*

While claiming to be the defenders of Pashtun values, the Taliban have attacked three key bastions of Pashtun male culture: the *hujra*, the mosque and the *jirga*.

Traditionally, every member of the tribe can participate in the *jirga*, the *malik* dominates the proceedings but everyone has a chance to speak. It takes place in the open, participants sit in a circle which symbolises and materialises their equality. There is no place for the mullah, he sits on the side and prays for the success of the *jirga*.

The concept of *jirga* has changed since the 1980s; it has lost its credibility after becoming a tool in the hands of the political administration and is riddled with corruption. The *jirga* is now artificial, it is no more egalitarian and has been converted into a state-manipulated gathering. Membership is restricted to men from powerful tribes, it does not provide justice to the poor and in most cases it favours the richer or more influential party.

Traditionally, the mosque was not used for tribal political activity. The mullah, who had a low status in Pashtun society, was subordinated to the tribal elders who had the monopoly of political activity conducted in the *hujra*, which acted as a counterweight to the mosque. The mullah acted as a mediator between parties in conflict but he did not handle the gun. When the threat came from a non-Muslim enemy, the mullah came to the front line and preached jihad, but once the conflict was finished, he went back to the mosque. New opportunities have enabled him to reject his traditional role and to move from the mosque to the *hujra*, or rather they have merged the mosque and the *hujra*. Mullahs participate in the 'new jirga' and guarantees which were given by the tribe are now given by the mullahs. *Jirgas*, which were traditionally held in the open, have been held inside madrasas and addressed by mullahs.

In the traditional system mullahs could not sustain a network of political patronage as they lacked financial means, but now they have access to money and have created a space for themselves in society. There are now two sets of competing elites: the *maliks* whose power has declined and the mullahs whose power has soared.

Jihad as a means of social empowerment

The shift in the structure of power—from the political administration to the army and from the *maliks* to the militants—and the new status of the mullahs as arbitrators between the tribes and the state gave assurance to the local Taliban who became an alternative leadership. The deals with the army gave the militants an upper hand. The Shakai deal was not a surrender: in tribal tradition, surrender means that you approach the rival group and meet it on its territory.[53] In Shakai, the army came to meet Nek Mohammad in a JUI-F madrasa: 'I did not go to them, they came to my place. That should make it clear who surrendered to whom.'[54] The militants described the deal as a 'reconciliation', which means, according to tribal logic, accepting the other group as equally powerful and legitimate. By signing the deals with the militants, the army has given them legitimacy and allowed them to consolidate themselves. Nek Muhammad emerged as a hero who had put up a tough fight against the army and forced it to strike a deal on his terms. He obtained the release of 163 local tribesmen and Afghan refugees who had been arrested by the army during the Wana operation of March 2004, compensation for all tribesmen whose houses had been destroyed or damaged, and the promise of more money for development work in South Waziristan.[55]

In a society where power is related to tribal identity, age and kinship, the militants' charisma, jihadi credentials and access to resources compensated for both their youth and their lack of tribal and religious legitimacy. Tribal society has been reshaped around the militants who succeeded where the government and the traditional institutions had failed and have been able to carve out enclaves of alternative power. They capitalised on the local anger at the general lawlessness and gangs of bandits and, in doing so, they became an alternative moral authority. The tribal structure has been replaced by a superimposed religious structure based on a local interpretation of the sharia which gives importance to *riwaj* (local custom).[56] The Pakistani Taliban have established alternative centres for the administration of justice and the settling of disputes. The role of the tribal elders was buried when the implementation of sharia was announced by Mullah Nazir in March 2006 in South Waziristan.

Attempts to restore the old order

The tribal social contract is broken, and the collapse of the *malik*s is one of the most important changes in the FATA. Over 200 *malik*s have been assassinated in South Waziristan since 2004 on suspicion of spying for the USA or for the government, and many others have left Waziristan to find shelter in the cities. Some members of the Pashtun elite who are in denial of social change argue that the tribal social fabric is intact[57] and that once the Taliban alternative model is eliminated, the old tribal order will be restored.[58] This is not realistic. The colonial model worked because the tribes were isolated and could tolerate poverty as long as their autonomy was respected. They are no longer isolated and austerity is no more a value. The system is discredited and has been unable to respond to social change. It enhances poverty and denies people access to opportunities of upward social mobility.

To prevent the collapse of the old system, the military is "collaborating with the maliks to form *lashkar*s to counter the movement waged by the rural poor under the guise of Islamism and led by the so-called Taliban."[59] *Lashkar*s are a way for dominant tribes or clans to get access to modern weapons and money.[60] The sociology of these *lashkar*s is telling: they are raised by the dominant tribes who just want to crush the ordinary poor people.[61] And this leads to further polarisation: *lashkar*s could get out of control, cause further violence and unending tribal feuds. They might also turn against the state once the elders have re-established their power over the people. By arming the tribes, the state is part of the process of its own marginalisation, and rather than mainstreaming the FATA the state is trying to keep it and its people apart, thereby only exacerbating the problem. The state cannot protect the people against social change.

Conclusion

This chapter has attempted to demonstrate that the dynamics of the insurgency in South Waziristan are not very different from those that characterise other social movements both within and beyond the Pakistan-Afghanistan borderlands. Islamist militancy in the FATA, as well as in South Punjab, retains a strong element of class conflict. There is a need to engage the tribals who have been alienated and have turned towards the Taliban, and particularly to create jobs to reduce social inequality and to implement political reforms aimed at ensuring participation of marginalised groups in the decision-making process. This is the only way to help them overcome their frustrations and to respond to their aspirations in terms of security, justice, political empowerment and socio-economic development.

Before the military operations, about half of the tribal population lived, temporarily or permanently, outside the FATA. Hundreds of thousands of people have been displaced since 2003. About 200,000 people were displaced from Waziristan in January 2008 during Operation Zalzala (earthquake) against Baitullah Mehsud's Taliban. According to Khalid Aziz, the displacement was 'one of the biggest in tribal history' and the human cost of the conflict in Waziristan 'has gone unrecorded'. From June 2009, the Pakistan army launched a massive operation to eliminate Baitullah Mehsud's Taliban. Kaniguram, Sararogha and Laddah were devastated in the fighting. The army declared victory in South Waziristan in December 2009. Owing to the blockade of South Waziristan in 2009 and the huge displacement it and other events created, a new Pashtun diaspora is in the making.[62] A process of re-invention of a Pashtun identity can be observed with particular clarity in Karachi. The old system cannot be restored and the FATA might not exist any more a few years from now. But as J.E. Ewart wrote in 1929: 'No man can say what the morrow will bring forth. But this after all is nothing new on the Frontier.'[63]

8

PASHTUN AND PUNJABI TALIBAN

THE JIHADI-SECTARIAN NEXUS

The Punjab and Karachi have been the primary hubs of sectarian violence in Pakistan since the 1980s, but in the post-9/11 environment
the Sunni-Shia conflict has assumed a new dimension. Sunni extremist
groups whose activities were focussed on Pakistani Shia targets have
formed shifting alliances with transnational networks in response to the
pro-US policy of President Musharraf's government and American
military operations in Afghanistan and in Iraq. Rising sectarianism since
2003 in the North West Frontier Province (NWFP)[1] and the Federally
Administered Tribal Areas (FATA) which is a direct offshoot of growing
Talibanisation—Sunni Deobandi groups with ideological affinity with
the Afghan Taliban having gradually taken control of the region—has
added a new dimension to the conflict. South Punjabi militants are a
growing presence in the FATA and provide manpower for attacks on
behalf of other networks in addition to continuing, or rather expanding, their own jihad against Shia Muslims. Different strains of militancy
have overlapped to the point where it might not seem relevant to treat
sectarian violence as separate from al-Qaeda attacks or militancy in
Punjab as different from that in FATA.

This chapter attempts to analyse the dynamics of the Pashtun-
Punjabi nexus and the areas of competition and cooperation between

Sunni sectarian groups and the Pakistani Taliban. It begins by outlining the links between Sunni sectarian groups and the Afghan Taliban, the impact of the collapse of the Taliban regime in Afghanistan and the implications of the relocation of Punjabi jihadi/sectarian groups in the NWFP and the FATA. It then focuses on the consequences of the storming of Islamabad's Lal Masjid (Red Mosque) in July 2007 and, finally, analyses the re-emergence of sectarian groups in Karachi and in the Punjab and its implications for Pakistan.

Sunni sectarian groups and Afghanistan

The Sipah-e-Sahaba Pakistan (Army of the Companions of the Prophet, SSP), founded in Jhang in 1985 as an offshoot of the Jamiat Ulama-e Islam (JUI),[2] and the Lashkar-e-Jhangvi (Army of Jhangvi, LeJ), a group which emerged in 1994 soon after the SSP's entry into politics and developed as its armed wing, found a sanctuary in the Afghanistan of the Taliban.[3] Jaish-e-Mohammad (Army of Mohammad, JeM), a Deobandi group created in February 2000 as a splinter group of Harakat-ul-Mujahidin, ostensibly to wage jihad in Kashmir,[4] was ideologically very close to the SSP. In fact, the SSP, JeM and LeJ appeared to be three wings of the same party: the members of the groups had the same profile and were mostly recruited from the rural and urban lower-middle classes of central and south Punjab, as well as from Deobandi madrasas. There was considerable overlap between the groups: many sectarian militants were part-time jihadis and vice versa. JeM, the jihadi façade of the SSP, became involved in sectarian warfare in Pakistan soon after its creation.[5]

Pakistani Sunni sectarian militants were natural allies of the Afghan Taliban, with whom they shared a radicalised interpretation of Deobandi Islam imparted in JUI madrasas. The entire leadership of these groups was made up of militants who had fought in Afghanistan, and the cadres were drawn from JUI madrasas. Although the SSP had foreign backers from the beginning, the coexistence after 1996 of al-Qaeda and sectarian militants in training camps inside Afghanistan reinforced the links between the SSP and international outfits. The SSP and LeJ leadership, notably Riaz Basra,[6] took refuge in Afghanistan when under pressure from Pakistani governments, particularly after the crackdown during Nawaz Sharif's second term as Prime Minister (1997–9).[7] Masood Azhar, the JeM chief, ran training camps in Taliban-ruled Afghanistan, and he spent much of his time in Kandahar.[8]

Rather than formal organisational links between the groups, connections were instead diffuse, being based on connections of the madrasas,[9] chance meetings in training camps, relationships between individuals and a community of interests. After the collapse of the Taliban regime in 2001, the militants, including those returned from Afghanistan, regrouped in Karachi. Previously friendly groups that worked more or less independently and with different goals merged operationally to fight the US and its allies, among them the Pakistani Army. According to Arif Jamal, 'the U.S. bombing and occupation of Afghanistan enraged the entire Deobandi movement in Pakistan. They turned their guns against General Musharraf when he decided to join the U.S.-led coalition against terror in order to save the Kashmir jihad'.[10] While some groups joined the fight, others became sleeper cells which were activated after 2007.

At the same time, there has been considerable fragmentation partly due to personal alliances born during the Taliban regime. Jihadi and sectarian groups have been replaced with more radical, small breakaway decentralised factions, which started operating as freelancers and hit-squads for foreign groups.[11]

New alignments after the 2002 ban

After the banning of the SSP and JeM in January 2002 (under Indian and American pressure), both groups kept a low profile, but this was only a camouflage in order to be able to provide logistical support for al-Qaeda activists. SSP and JeM cadres joined hands with various extremist elements in Karachi to provide safe houses to those militants. The restrictions were half-hearted as the government thought that it could control militant groups without eliminating them, since they might still be useful for both its regional and domestic policies.

The SSP was never dismantled: it was able to keep its organisational structure intact and function from April 2003 under a new name, Millat-e-Islamia Pakistan; the militants who had been detained were discreetly released and never stopped their activities. President

Musharraf went as far as legitimising the SSP by endorsing Azam Tariq, the SSP chief, who was allowed to contest elections[12] in October 2002 as an independent candidate from prison on the condition that he would support the regime, which he did. In exchange for playing the establishment's game and supporting the government, Azam Tariq obtained the release of many SSP militants and a lenient approach to the movement's activities. Tariq was assassinated in October 2003 and three factions emerged after his death due to disagreements about the control of madrasas and financial assets of the movement. The SSP was banned a second time in November 2003 and resurfaced in April 2004 under the name of the Sunni Action Committee; since 2006 it has been known as Ahle Sunnat wal Jama'at Pakistan (ASWJP).

The LeJ, which had been banned by Musharraf in August 2001, had established connections with al-Qaeda's leadership in Afghanistan in the 1990s and provided shelter in Pakistan to Arab militants after the fall of the Taliban. It mutated from a militant sectarian group focussed on Shia Muslims into suicide-attack squads carrying out operations for all groups, including being used by al-Qaeda to attack Western targets in Pakistan.[13] The level of coordination and organisation of the attacks and the new methods pointed to al-Qaeda being involved. It is thus not surprising that from May 2002—after Riaz–Basra's elimination in an alleged encounter[14]—the Pakistani government claimed that the LeJ was the Pakistani branch of al-Qaeda and started blaming every act of terrorism on that group. The LeJ was a very convenient scapegoat, and blaming it was a way to protect the real perpetrators in order to save the jihad in Kashmir.[15] Many attacks were in fact carried by other Deobandi groups, including some previously active in Kashmir and close to the military establishment, such as Harakat ul-Jihad ul-Islami (HUJI)[16] and JeM. From 2004, the changing policy on Kashmir had forced many groups to move their fighters to North Waziristan, where they set up training camps.

JeM, which adopted the name of Tehrik Khuddam ul Islam (Movement of the Servants of Islam), should have been the logical target of the Army after the attack on the Indian Parliament in December 2001, but it was not targeted until December 2003. JeM militants were hunted only after the two assassination attempts on President Musharraf that month, as the military establishment came to understand the change within its own proxies, which had previously had a mostly anti-India agenda. The complicity of lower-level military personnel and police officers in the activities of JeM became a major concern. Over one thousand people were rounded up and kept in prison without trial for months. Those who were not detained took shelter in Azad Kashmir, the FATA and the Kohat area of the NWFP (which had long been an SSP/JeM stronghold). Under American pressure, Pakistan had shut down camps in Azad Kashmir, but it was widely reported from early 2005 that new camps had been established around Balakot and Mansehra in the NWFP. After the earthquake of October 2005, militants relocated to the FATA (particularly North Waziristan, Lower Kurram and Orakzai), which became a sanctuary for members of banned sectarian groups. The arrival of 'Kashmiris' (in fact Punjabis) in the FATA in 2005 changed the dynamics of the training. The number of fighters increased, particularly when they were joined from 2006 by militants jailed in the crackdown of 2003–4 who moved to the FATA after their release. These Punjabi jihadis had no emotional ties with the local people, had benefited for a long time from state patronage, were better trained and were known to be more brutal than the Pashtuns.[17] Moreover, many of the Punjabi militants started their career as criminals and could be hired as mercenaries by different groups. This was the case in 2007 when Punjabi militants were used by Maulvi Nazir against Uzbeks in South Waziristan.[18]

Sectarian groups and the FATA

The SSP/JeM has a support base in the Kohat-Hangu area of the NWFP, gateway to the Kurram and Orakzai tribal agencies. Before September 2001 both groups had established madrasas and recruitment centres in that area, which has a long history of Sunni-Shia conflict.[19] After JeM/SSP militants regrouped in Kohat and in the FATA, there was an upsurge in sectarian attacks both in the FATA (notably in Kurram Agency from April 2007) and in the settled areas. Sectarian violence was not a new phenomenon in Kurram, which is the only tribal agency with a significant Shia population; approximately half of the region's 500,000 inhabitants are Shia. Upper Kurram is inhabited largely by the Turi (the only Pashtun tribe which is wholly Shia), while

Lower Kurram is inhabited by Sunnis, mostly from the Bangash tribe.[20] Turi occupy the most fertile area of Kurram Agency. There are long-standing disputes over ownership of forests, hills, land and water resources between Sunni and Shia tribes, and sporadic incidents of communal violence have taken place since the 1930s.[21] Many argue that there was not a Sunni-Shia problem in Kurram, rather tribal rivalries which were given a sectarian colour.

The massive influx of Afghan refugees in the 1980s caused a distortion in the demographic and sectarian balance of the area. One of the impacts of the Afghan crisis on the Tribal Areas was the increase in religious institutions, which translated inflammatory literature into Pashto and thereby reinforced sectarianism. Sectarian violence erupted in the 1980s into massacres of Shia Muslims, with Afghan refugees helping local tribes against their Shia rivals. Afghan refugees introduced a militant brand of Sunni ideology at a time when the Shias of Kurram under the leadership of Allama Arif Hussain al-Hussaini had been radicalised by the Iranian Revolution. Clashes grew in intensity and frequency, while the local administration was viewed as indifferent or seen as taking sides.[22]

The Shias did not offer shelter to al-Qaeda and the Afghan Taliban fleeing Tora Bora in 2001, and certain clans betrayed the Arabs to the authorities. Attempts by the Taliban from Waziristan to exploit the situation in Kurram were rebuffed with heavy losses. From April 2007, unabated sectarian strife threw the whole of Kurram into complete chaos. The Sunnis accused Iran of providing weapons to Shia fighters and warned in April 2007 that if the Pakistan Army did not take action, Sunnis would come from other parts of Pakistan to help the locals. This did not take long to happen. Madrasas in South Punjab, linked openly to banned sectarian-jihadi groups such as SSP/JeM (or supporting them covertly), began sending militants to the FATA.

Lal Masjid as a turning point

The storming of Islamabad's Lal Masjid (Red Mosque) in July 2007 was a turning point. It brought together Pashtun and Punjabi militants against a common enemy: the Pakistani government allied with the infidel forces of the US in the 'War on Terror'. The Lal Masjid had long been a SSP/JeM stronghold. Maulana Abdullah, the father of Abdul Rashid and Abdul Aziz, was involved in sectarian politics in the 1980s, supporting the SSP while motivating thousands of people for jihad in Afghanistan. He was assassinated in 1998 by suspected Shia militants because of his anti-Shia sermons. The Lal Masjid showed its street power for the first time after the assassination of Azam Tariq in October 2003, when the students of Jamia Faridia (the madrasa affiliated to the Lal Masjid) ransacked a cinema and restaurants, looted shops, smashed the windows of hundreds of cars and stole a trunk containing the gifts of worshippers from a nearby Shia shrine while the police made no attempt to intervene.[23]

The sectarian dimension of the Lal Masjid saga was overlooked in the West. JeM militants, and particularly Mufti Abdul Rauf, one of the JeM chief Masood Azhar's brothers, played an active role, as well as Javed Ibrahim Paracha. The militants entrenched in the mosque were made to believe that the soldiers who led the assault were all Shias. A pamphlet was circulated in Islamabad informing of the arrival of LeJ to attack government forces, which they claimed consisted largely of Shia Muslims.[24] After the assault, the militants proclaimed a jihad against the Army and the security forces, and the Army as an institution became a direct target, particularly its Shia members. From the summer of 2007 onward, sectarian killings in the FATA and the beheading of captured Shia members of the Army and the Frontier Corps were carried out as revenge for the assault on the Lal Masjid. JeM reorganised under Mufti Abdul Rauf, who established a training camp in Kohat, and there was an upsurge in sectarian attacks both in the FATA and in the settled areas (notably in Dera Ismail Khan and Hangu, two cities where sectarian tensions were endemic).

The TTP and sectarian groups

The emergence of the Tehrik-e-Taliban Pakistan (TTP) as an umbrella group in December 2007 was another turning point which brought to light the Punjabi-Pashtun nexus. Punjabi militants started providing manpower for attacks outside the FATA and the NWFP on behalf of other networks in addition to continuing, or rather expanding, their own jihad against Shias. Sectarian attacks have become an extension of the TTP war against cities. There is at the same time competition and cooperation between the TTP and the SSP/JeM/LeJ—the so-called Punjabi Taliban—who share common interests. Hassan Abbas has defined the Punjabi Taliban as

> a loose conglomeration of banned militant groups of Punjabi origin—sectarian as well as those focused on the conflict in Kashmir—that have developed strong connections with Tehrik-i-Taliban, Afghan Taliban and other militant groups based in FATA and NWFP.[25]

Given their knowledge of Punjabi cities and their security structures, they have proved to be valuable partners for the TTP as it started targeting cities in Punjab. The Punjabi-Pashtun nexus reportedly share each other's madrasas, training facilities, sanctuaries and jihadi cadres to carry out operations across Pakistan.[26] NWFP Governor Owais Ghani gave this warning in September 2008:

> Militants in the tribal areas of the NWFP have established firm networking [with jihadi groups] in Southern Punjab and most fresh recruits for suicide-attacks are coming from there. Militant leaders and commanders are also coming from Punjab. ... It will be ill-advised to think that the militancy will remain confined to the NWFP. Militants' activities have already shifted to the settled areas and Punjab and they have established strong links with south Punjab.

Tactical alliances are based on more than shared ideology: Pashtuns and Arabs in the FATA provide a sanctuary, money and training sites, while Punjabis provide manpower and logistical help in the cities of the Punjab. Attacks in the major cities are conducted by locally-based urban groups and not by Pashtuns from the FATA, even if the TTP claims responsibility. Punjabi militants have been linked to attacks claimed by the TTP, for instance the Marriott hotel bombing in Islamabad in September 2008 and the attacks on the Sri Lankan cricket team and the police academy in Lahore in March 2009. Some of the assailants were identified as Siraiki-speakers from south Punjab, which suggests that LeJ networks were facilitating attacks on behalf of the TTP.

Sectarian groups have exploited the Talibanisation of the FATA and the NWFP to expand their operational space while the state was ignoring the situation and tolerating a level of anti-Shia violence at the periphery. At the same time, the TTP has exploited the Sunni-

Shia divide in Kurram and Orakzai to expand its operational space by acquiring the cooperation of the Sunni locals who support the TTP for sectarian rather than ideological reasons. Taliban attacks in Kurram and Orakzai were meant to force Shia Muslims onto the defensive and displace them in order to gain access to Upper Kurram, which has strategic value as a route to Afghanistan. Under Hakimullah Mehsud's leadership, the TTP became more sectarian due to his association with anti-Shia militants and particularly his relative Qari Hussain Mehsud (known as Ustad-e-Fedayin, or trainer of suicide-bombers), who was a member of the SSP and LeJ before joining the TTP.[27] The government was regularly blamed for doing nothing to stop the influx of militant outsiders from North Waziristan. Instead of intervening to stop the violence, it kept claiming that there was no sectarian problem in Kurram, blaming a foreign hand for pitting the tribes against one another.[28]

The TTP-Punjabi nexus is nowhere more visible than in Darra Adam Khel,[29] a strategic location on the highway linking Peshawar to the south via the Kohat tunnel (opened in 2003) which is the main route for the NATO supply convoys that travel from Karachi to the border crossing into Afghanistan at Torkham. Here LeJ has become the most active group. The local commander of the TTP, Tariq Afridi, is a former member of the SSP and is affiliated to the LeJ as is the TTP central spokesman, who uses the pseudonym Azam Tariq. Militants seized the Kohat tunnel in early 2008 and paramilitary forces regained control after only three days of heavy fighting. However, the militants did not disappear from the area; on the contrary, they expanded their presence with the help of members of banned sectarian-jihadi groups who set up training camps in the region.[30] Moreover, local criminal networks have found common ground with the militant outfits and have been involved in high-profile targeted killings and abductions for ransom. In the FATA, the disintegration of the institutional structure has provided an open space to criminal gangs who have access to weapons and have borrowed Taliban rhetoric.

The road from Parachinar, the agency headquarters, to Peshawar has been blocked since April 2007.[31] Shia truck drivers were abducted and beheaded while passing through Darra Adam Khel on their way to Kurram, and Shias going to Peshawar were forced to travel via Paktia and Kabul. Those who took the risk of travelling through Kohat and Darra Adam Khel were often abducted: '[t]hey stop every vehicle, ask the passengers to remove their shirts [to identify Shias by the marks left on their back by Muharram flagellations] and also check their ID cards [to identify Shias by their name]'.[32] Ceasefires and peace *jirgas* (assemblies) failed; NATO forces and the Afghan government invited elders of rival factions to a military base in Paktia, but the talks concluded without any agreement.[33] Shias migrated to the cities due to the attacks and were forced into enclaves which made them easy targets. By blocking the road, the TTP has effectively put the Kurram Shias under siege and, at the same time, has expanded its control in Lower Kurram by backing sectarian fighting.

After taking control of Kurram, the TTP moved to the Orakzai Agency where 10 to 15 per cent of the Orakzai tribe is Shia. This agency, which does not share a border with Afghanistan, was at relative peace until October 2008.[34] Historically, the conflict was principally over the ownership of the Syed Mir Anwar Shah shrine in Kalaya, which originally belonged to the Shias and was given to the Sunnis during British rule.

Orakzai was the birthplace of the Pakistani Taliban. A Taliban force using the name of Tehrik-e-Taliban was raised in the area in 1999 by Akhundzada Aslam Farooqi, a tribal leader affiliated with the SSP; Shia villages were attacked and families displaced. Clashes erupted over the Kalaya shrine, which had been renovated in 1999: it was demolished by the Pakistani and Afghan Taliban and converted to a Sunni Idgah. Shias were branded as *kuffar*, expelled from fertile land and ordered to pay *jizya* (the poll-tax levied on non-Muslims) in 2000. In 2004 foreign militants displaced by military operations in Waziristan began moving into Upper Orakzai, where they found a safe haven.[35] They were joined from 2006 onward by members of the SSP/LeJ from Darra Adam Khel. After the creation of the TTP, Hakimullah Mehsud was appointed as its commander in Orakzai. He imposed *jiziya* on Hindus and Sikhs who had lived unharmed for centuries in the FATA: houses and businesses belonging to Sikhs have been occupied, and Sikhs who could not pay the *jizya* took shelter in Shia areas and in Peshawar. In February 2010, three Sikhs were abducted for ransom, one of whom was found beheaded a few days later. Attacks on shrines have become a regular occurrence in Orakzai, aimed at parting ways with established norms and values and constructing a new identity.

The re-emergence of sectarian groups in Punjab and Karachi

As Taliban influence grew in the FATA, sectarian groups reasserted themselves across the rest of Pakistan and helped the TTP to spread its influence in Punjab, Karachi and other cities. This has been facilitated by inaction and denial on the part of the state, which blamed every-thing on Pashtun groups and claimed for a long time that the Punjabi Taliban did not exist. It was only after a series of attacks in Lahore and the attack on Army General Headquarters (GHQ) in Rawalpindi in October 2009 that the possibility of collusion between the sectarian organisations based in Punjab and the TTP was finally raised. After a long period of denial and blaming the 'foreign hand' (India), Interior Minister Rehman Malik acknowledged in October 2009 that '[t]he banned Tehrik-e Taliban Pakistan, Jaish-e Mohammad, al-Qaeda and Lashkar-e-Jhangvi are operating jointly in Pakistan'.[36]

The SSP and JeM have re-emerged in Punjab, particularly in Jhang and in Bahawalpur, both safe-resting places away from drone attacks.[37] Madrasa-mosque networks and semi-retired veteran jihadis are the critical link for recruitment, and sectarian hatred is exploited to induce militancy in madrasa students who are sent to the FATA for training and return to the Punjab to carry out attacks. According to estimated figures, over five thousand students from Punjabi madrasas moved to Waziristan in the aftermath of the Lal Masjid operation. The SSP/LeJ has also reverted to violence against Hindus, Sikhs, Christians[38] and Barelvis,[39] who support military operations and have branded the Taliban as un-Islamic. Moreover, sectarian violence against Shias has become commonplace in Balochistan, which had been largely spared until 2004. Hazaras have been the victims of targeted killings generally attributed to LeJ. In 2010, LeJ Alami had claimed suicide-attacks against Shias in Quetta and the NWFP. Attacks on widely-dispersed locations are also a way for the TTP to open new fronts, demoralise the Army and take the pressure off the FATA. Military operations in the FATA, particularly in Waziristan in 2009, have also forced the militants to shift to areas further away from the Afghan border.

According to some sources,[40] the PunjabiTaliban are represented in the TTP's *shura* (council). Among others, this was the case for Aqeel (alias 'Dr Usman'), the Punjabi militant captured after the October 2009 attack on GHQ in Rawalpindi: a former army medical corps soldier from Kahuta (Punjab), he joined LeJ and later JeM before becoming a member of the TTP.

Militants fleeing drone strikes and military operations are increasingly moving to Karachi.[41] The city has long been a safe haven for jihadi and sectarian groups which have links with prominent Deobandi madrasas. After Azam Tariq's assassination, the SSP under Ali Sher Hyderi, a Sindhi assassinated in 2009, had expanded its presence in Sindh, which led to an upsurge in sectarian attacks. The SSP is active again in Karachi: it held a meeting in March 2008 against the Danish cartoons of the Prophet Muhammad and two other gatherings in June and August 2009 with displays of weapons under police protection. Such actions are ostensibly used to put pressure on the Muttahida Qaumi Movement (MQM), which the SSP perceives as supporting Shias.

Karachi is at the same time a place to hide, rest, work seasonal jobs, get medical treatment and source funds through banks and money-changers, robberies, kidnappings for ransom, and drugs- and arms-trafficking. The TTP and LeJ have joined hands in Karachi, where the suicide-attacks carried out since 2006, particularly against Shias, are attributed to the LeJ working in tandem with the TTP. Karachi is described as the hub of sectarian organisations.

Restrictions against banned sectarian groups have been relaxed in the Punjab since 2006. A rally was organised near the Lal Masjid in Islamabad in April 2006 by the SSP; the participants, under police protection, chanted anti-Shia slogans. Since the 2008 election campaign, the Punjab government has been willing to talk to sectarian groups. It was announced on several occasions that Malik (a founder of the LeJ who has been jailed since 1997 and charged in forty-four cases for the murder of seventy people, although he has never been convicted due to 'lack of evidence'), would be released. This was, in fact, part of a deal linked to a by-election that year in Bhakkar in which the Pakistan Muslim League (Nawaz)'s prospective Chief Minister Shahbaz Sharif intended to stand: the SSP withdrew its candidate in exchange for the release of Malik Ishaq, among other conditions. Sharif was

PASHTUN AND PUNJABI TALIBAN

elected unopposed, but Malik Ishaq was not released. It is widely alleged that the attack on the Sri Lankan cricket team in March 2009 was mounted originally to kidnap the cricket team in order to get LeJ militants released from prison.

It can be argued that the SSP is a new ally for the PML-N in the Punjab. Ahead of by-elections for the provincial assembly in Jhang in March 2010, two convicted SSP militants who had been jailed since the mid-90s were released and the administration was told to accommodate the SSP in the city. When Rana Sanaullah, Punjab's law minister, visited Jhang in February 2010, he took with him SSP leader Maulana Mohammad Ahmed Ludhianvi in an official vehicle of the Punjab government with police escort. In doing so he brought the SSP into mainstream politics and legitimised its ideology. Questioned about his contacts with the SSP, Rana Sanaullah answered that he had met Maulana Ludhianvi to secure votes for the by-elections; he added that the SSP had a vast following and vote-bank and that its support made political sense.[42] He even stated that during the next local government elections, the SSP would be a PML-N ally 'whenever and wherever required'.[43]

Conclusion

Sectarian violence makes strategic sense for Punjabi militant groups: its fallout plays into a larger mayhem the militants have planned to unleash on Pakistan. The aim of sectarian conflict is to alter the pluralistic nature of Islam in Punjab. A social Talibanisation in Punjab is not on the agenda of the SSP/LeJ, but attacking Shias is no longer the only goal of sectarian groups. The Punjabi militants, according to Imtiaz Ali, 'are more hard-line, more fundamentalist and more connected to a global agenda'[44] than the Pashtun Taliban.

Whatever the successes against the Taliban and al-Qaeda, a third threat—sectarianism—has emerged, and the state is not paying attention. The nexus between politicians and banned groups is still active. Punjabi militants are not seen as a threat, and much of the population believes that India is behind acts of terror in the Punjab. The attacks in Punjabi cities should in fact be seen as a watershed in Pakistan's relations with groups who have benefited from state patronage for decades:

while in the beginning they were facilitating the Taliban, they have joined with them to engage in attacks against the state. But the battle against sectarian terror is not coherent: links between the Punjab government and the SSP have been exposed in Jhang, and the open support that the Punjab government gave to the SSP for electoral purposes could widen the sectarian divide in the province. Shias and other minorities are waiting for the state to shake off its denial and come to their rescue. Pakistan is not Iraq: Muslim sects are not spatially segregated, and rural and urban areas are not stratified along sectarian lines. Nonetheless, the ideology of sectarian parties has already had a destructive effect on society. Sectarian strife cuts much deeper than is officially acknowledged: it is a much bigger problem than Talibanisation, and it has the potential to destabilise the region, posing an existential threat to the country and beyond.

PART FOUR

TRANSNATIONAL JIHADI-SUNNI SECTARIAN CONVERGENCES

9

'IT'S JUST A SUNNI-SHIA THING'

SECTARIANISM AND TALIBANISM IN THE FATA (FEDERALLY ADMINISTERED TRIBAL AREAS) OF PAKISTAN[1]

Shia Muslims make up 15 to 20 per cent of the population of Pakistan for a total of at least 25 million, making Pakistan's Shia community the second largest in the world after that of Iran. Sectarianism which is, in Pakistan, more a Deobandi[2]-Shia rather than a Sunni-Shia conflict,[3] comes from the belief that the sect which one professes is the only true one and that the followers of other sects should be converted to one's own sect or exterminated. Sectarianism is often seen as the consequence of Zia-ul Haq's Islamisation policy in the 1980s, which involved a state monopoly on religion and the dominance of a particular sect (i.e. Sunni Islam). Sectarian consciousness had always existed but it was mostly confined to theological debates and clashes during the month of Muharram, the month during which the Shias mourn the martyrdom of Hussain, the Prophet's grandson, at Karbala, but it never prevented co-existence. From the mid-1980s onwards, sectarianism has degenerated into violence and over 4,000 people have been killed.[4] Before 2001, sectarian violence mostly affected the Punjab and Karachi, although violent incidents also erupted in Kurram Agency in the mid-1980s. The federal government tolerated some degree of sectarian

147

violence in the FATA because the area was seen as peripheral and it did not affect Sunni-Shia relations in the rest of Pakistan.

A US drone missile attack on a Taliban training camp in February 2009[5] highlighted the growing importance of Pakistan's Kurram Tribal Agency in the war along the frontier with Afghanistan. Unlike Pakistan's other six tribal agencies, the conflict in Kurram is complicated because of its sectarian divisions, which have flared into violent encounters between the region's Sunni and Shia Muslim communities. Sectarian violence has added a new dimension to the conflict between the Tehrik-e Taliban Pakistan (TTP, the Pakistani Taliban)[6] and the state in the FATA. Although sectarian violence has only a loose association with the Taliban, the attacks are designed to create chaos in the region. Rising sectarianism in Khyber-Pakhtunkhwa (ex-NWFP)[7] and in the FATA is a direct offshoot of growing Talibanisation and of the arrival of Punjabi Sunni militants in the area in the recent years. Different strains of militancy have overlapped to the point where it is no longer relevant to treat sectarian violence as separate from al-Qaeda attacks and religious militancy in Punjab as different from FATA.

Communities in conflict

Sectarian violence is not a new phenomenon in Kurram, which is the only tribal agency with a significant Shia population. Around 40 per cent of the region's 500,000 inhabitants are Shia. Upper Kurram is inhabited largely by the Turi (the only Pashtun tribe which is wholly Shia) while Central and Lower Kurram are inhabited by Sunnis, mostly Bangash.[8] The Bangash are Ghurgusht Pathans, descendants of Ghurgusht, son of Qais Abdul Rashid, the legendary ancestor of the Pashtuns. Driven out from Gardez (Paktia) by the Ghilzai tribes, they moved to the Kurram Valley in the latter part of the fourteenth century. They claim to be of Arab origin.[9] All the Bangash of Upper Kurram are Shia. The Bangash clans living in Lower Kurram and Kohat are all Sunnis, while other Bangash clans are Shia, Sunni, or a mix of both. Historically the Turi were under Bangash domination until the eighteenth century when they attacked the Bangash—apparently in retaliation for an insult made to a Turi woman—which turned them into *hamsaya* (dependants) and pushed them into Lower Kurram.

The Turi are the largest tribe occupying the most fertile area of the Agency. They were considered by the British as 'alag', or different, from their neighbours because of their origin (Turks or Mongols who migrated from Persia) and their Shia faith. They are now considered to be Ghurgusht Pathans.

The Turi allowed General Roberts passage to Afghanistan during the Second Afghan War in 1877. The Afghans who had tried unsuccessfully to extend their influence in the area[10] renounced their claim over Kurram as a result of the Treaty of Gandamak in 1879.[11] The Turi requested the British take over the administration of the area because they feared aggression by the neighbouring Sunni tribes, and particularly the Mangal. This occurred with the establishment of the Kurram Agency in 1892, when the Turi found themselves on the British side of the Durand Line, established in 1893. The agency headquarters at Parachinar (about 70,000 inhabitants) is less than 100 km from Kabul (the so-called parrot's beak of Parachinar going deep into Afghan territory). Contrary to other parts of the FATA, Parachinar has had a very good education system since the colonial era. The next important town is Sadda, which is situated in Lower Kurram on the left bank of the River Kurram.

There are longstanding disputes over ownership of forests, hills, land and water resources between Sunni and Shia tribes and sporadic incidents of communal violence have taken place since the 1930s, particularly during Muharram or Nowruz (the Iranian new year as celebrated by the Shias). Sunnis have consistently demanded that Nowruz celebrations should be banned on the basis that they are un-Islamic. Many argue that historically there was no Sunni-Shia problem, and that tribal rivalries have only assumed a sectarian hue at specific moments. Clashes were often the result of petty disputes: for instance, the riots that erupted in 1973 in Parachinar were sparked by a row over the height of the minarets at the main Sunni mosque and the Shia imambargah.[12]

The massive influx of Afghan refugees in the 1980s caused a distortion in the demographic and sectarian balance of the area. Before the arrival of the refugees, Pashtuns took religion for granted. Religion was not a cause of conflict and it did not need to be emphasised and used for political aims. The strong Pashtun identity obviated the need for an alternative or sectarian identity. The Afghan jihad disturbed this balance and concentrated religious and temporal affairs in the hands of the mullahs. Religion became a cover for geopolitics, and sectarianism was fostered with the not so clandestine support of various states and of the Pakistani military establishment. One of the impacts of the Afghan crisis on the Tribal Areas was the increase in religious institutions that translated inflammatory literature into Pashto, which reinforced sectarianism in the area.

Sectarian violence erupted in 1982 with massacres of Shias in Sadda's bazaar.[13] Sixty-eight Shia families took refuge in Parachinar. A jirga[14] resolved the matter in 1990 and paved the way for the Shias to return to their homes, but its decision was never implemented. The Shias argued, not without reason, that Afghan refugees had helped local tribes against their Shia rivals. Indeed, the Turi were labelled as an impediment in the jihad, as pro-Iran or as pro-communist because they refused to allow Sunni Afghan refugees into their areas and often opposed the use of the Parachinar area as a launching pad for Afghan mujahidin.

Afghan refugees introduced a militant brand of Sunni ideology at a time when the Shias of Parachinar, under the leadership of cleric Allama Arif Hussain al-Hussaini (trained in the Shia theological centres of Najaf and Qom), were being radicalised by the Iranian Revolution. As modern weapons became available, clashes grew in frequency and intensity, while the local administration was viewed as indifferent or seen as taking sides.[15] The first large-scale attack took place in 1986 when the Turi prevented Sunni mujahidin from passing through their territory to Afghanistan. General Zia-ul Haq allowed a massacre of the Turi Shias at the hands of the Afghan mujahidin in conjunction with the local Sunni population.[16] Hundreds of Sunnis and Shias were killed, and Shias who were still in a majority in Sadda (Lower Kurram) before the riots were pushed into Upper Kurram.[17] Allama Hussaini was assassinated in 1988 and the Turi held General Zia responsible. There were major clashes again in 1996, in which over 200 Sunnis and Shias were killed after Shia activists murdered a college principal in Parachinar.[18] After 1996, a 'Parachinar paradigm' came into existence, characterised by the use of heavy weapons by both sides, support of the Afghan refugees and the Taliban for the Sunnis, and the deployment of the army to restore law and order.

150

'IT'S JUST A SUNNI-SHIA THING'

Impact of the collapse of the Taliban State

The Shias, staunchly opposed to the Sunni Taliban and Arabs, did not offer shelter to al-Qaeda and the Afghan Taliban fleeing Tora Bora in December 2001. One tribe agreed to shelter the Arabs but another turned 200 of them over to the authorities, which took them to jail in the NWFP city of Kohat. A gunfight on the way to Kohat left ten Arabs dead on 19 December 2001. The graves of the Arabs in Kurram (Arhawalai) have become a place of pilgrimage for locals.

The nature and the dimension of the sectarian conflict have changed since 2001. Kurram has once again become strategically important as it shares a border with the Afghan provinces of Khost, Paktia and Nangarhar, and has a relatively large Afghan refugee population. The conflict is not tribal or sectarian per se, but is instigated by the Taliban who want access to Afghanistan and are supported by local criminal elements. They use tribal and sectarian differences to fuel the conflict and keep the government out. Moreover, the FATA and the Kohat area have become a sanctuary for Punjabi members of Sunni extremist groups that were banned in 2002 and took shelter in the tribal areas, particularly in Lower Kurram and Orakzai Agency. These groups include the Sipah-e Sahaba Pakistan (SSP), the Lashkar-e Jhangvi (LJ) and the Jaish-e Mohammad (JeM), three branches of the same Punjabi Deobandi sectarian network.

In September 2005, the federal government ordered the expulsion of more than 100,000 Afghan refugees from Kurram. It is not clear whether the measure was successful or implemented, but it was seen by the Shias of the region as a return to the previous demographic balance of power which had been tilted in favour of Sunnis. Sunnis feared that the departure of the Afghans might prompt Shias to demand the repatriation of Shias displaced from Sadda after the 1982 clashes, which had been decided by the 1990 jirga. After the earthquake of October 2005, militants belonging to Lashkar-e Taiba (LeT), an Ahl-e Hadith group, and other Deobandi groups active in Kashmir relocated to FATA and the Kohat area, a Sunni stronghold.

Kurram has been in the grip sectarian of violence since April 2007—in the last four years, more than 1,500 persons have been killed and 5,000 others have been injured.[19] The violence started in April

2007 after Sunnis chanted anti-Shia slogans during a procession in Parachinar. Shia leaders complained to local political authorities, and on the following day a Shia religious procession was fired upon.[20] In the clashes that ensued, mortars and rocket-propelled grenades were used, resulting in heavy casualties that left 215 people dead and over 600 injured.[21] When soldiers attempted to intervene, they were attacked by both sides.[22] The Sunnis accused Iran of providing weapons to Shia fighters. Mast Gul of the Harakat-ul-Mujahidin (HuM), a jihadi group active in Kashmir, alleged in a 9 April press conference in Peshawar that Iran was providing money and weapons to the Shias, and that Sunnis would come from other parts of the country to help their local brethren if the Pakistani army did not take action. This did not take long to happen: after a period of closure, madrasas in South Punjab[23] openly linked to outlawed jihadi-sectarian groups—or giving them support covertly—resurfaced under new names and started sending militants to the FATA. After 9/11, these madrasas started receiving foreign students from Uzbekistan, Tajikistan and Afghanistan, and they continue to receive considerable foreign funding, particularly from Pakistani expatriates. In addition, the militants are increasingly dependent on criminal activities for the financing of their operations: kidnappings for ransom and bank robberies are commonplace.[24] These movements recruit their men from private security firms, notably in Karachi, and when they are assigned to guard banks, they rob them, and the money is brought to the FATA. People kidnapped for ransom, notably in Karachi, are also brought to the FATA.

The storming of Islamabad's Lal Masjid (Red Mosque) in July 2007 was a turning point for sectarian feelings in the country. The militants entrenched in the mosque were made to believe that the soldiers who led the assault were all Shias. A pamphlet circulating at the time in Islamabad announced the arrival of LJ militants to attack government forces whom they claimed consisted largely of Shias.[25] The army as an institution has become a direct target, and particularly the Shias in the army. Moreover, the present government is perceived as being pro-Shia. From the summer of 2007, sectarian killings in the FATA and the beheading of captured Shia members of the army and the frontier corps took place in revenge for the assault on Lal Masjid.

After the Red Mosque assault, JeM reorganized under Mufti Abdul Rauf, Masood Azhar's brother, who established a training camp in

Kohat, long a hotbed of sectarian violence and a stronghold of the SSP. Javed Ibrahim Paracha, a former member of the national assembly for Kohat, has openly declared that he is at war with the Shias and most of the sectarian violence in Kohat and Hangu has been blamed on him. After JeM and SSP militants regrouped in Kohat and in Lower Kurram (traditionally an SSP stronghold), there was an upsurge in sectarian attacks both in FATA and in the settled areas, notably Dera Ismaïl Khan and Hangu.

A new round of sectarian violence began in November 2007. Sunnis accused the Shias of hurling a hand grenade at the central mosque in Parachinar during Friday prayers, while the Shias accused Sunnis of firing rockets at homes and mosques. The army used helicopter gunships to control Parachinar and Sadda, but the fighting continued in the rural areas. Local Sunnis were joined by al-Qaeda fighters and Taliban from Waziristan who targeted the paramilitary forces.[26] Displaced Taliban from South Waziristan[27] bolstered the Taliban activities in Kurram. The first Waziristan laskhar (tribal army) was sent to Kurram in October 2007 under Qari Hussain who had strong links with the SSP.[28] They fought Shias for two months. Forty villages were destroyed and ninety-five places of worship attacked in 2007; 2,300 families were also displaced after their houses had been set ablaze.

According to the United Nations High Commissioner for Refugees (UNHCR), 6,000 Sunnis, mostly women and children, fled to Afghanistan in January 2008.[29] In the following month a suicide attack in front of the election office of the Pakistan Peoples Party candidate (a Shia) killed forty-seven people and wounded around one hundred.[30] The clashes intensified during the summer and the government was blamed for doing nothing to stop the influx of militant outsiders from Waziristan. Hakeemullah Mehsud sent more Sunnis from Waziristan into Kurram and Faqir Alam Mehsud, who had been appointed as the local commander in April 2008, boasted of having personally beheaded at least seventy Shias and 'Sunni collaborators'.[31]

In June 2008, people from Kurram staged a demonstration in front of the Parliament House in Islamabad seeking the intervention of the federal government, but to no avail. Instead of intervening to stop the violence, the government kept claiming that there was no sectarian problem in Kurram, blaming a foreign hand for pitting the tribes against each other.[32] Many Bangash decided to move into Afghanistan. In July 2008, thirty Sunni militants escaped from Sadda jail and attacked a convoy of relief goods sent to Parachinar, beheading fourteen Shia truckers.

As the violence continued, the road from Parachinar to Peshawar was blocked, resulting in a shortage of food and medicines. Shia truck drivers were abducted and beheaded while passing through Dara Adam Khel on their way to Kurram. Shia communities were besieged as Sunnis controlled the road from Parachinar to Thall. People going to Peshawar were forced to travel via Paktia and Kabul. Those who took the risk of travelling through Kohat and Dara Adam Khel—where the Taliban and members of SSP and LJ have been active since early 2007[33]—were often abducted: 'They stop every vehicle, ask the passengers to remove their shirts [to identify Shias by the marks left on their back by Muharram flagellations] and also check their ID cards'.[34] Paramilitary troops were frequently abducted—while Sunnis were generally released, Shia soldiers were often beheaded. In all around 400 people were killed during this round of violence.

In August 2008, Wali ur Rehman, a TTP leader, made an offer to the Turi: if they stopped blocking the TTP's access to Kurram into Afghanistan, the TTP would allow them to travel unimpeded and provide protection to Shia travellers. Turi elders refused as they suspected the TTP of wanting to take over the area.[35]

A unilateral ceasefire was declared by the Turi ahead of Ramadan (September 2008), but the bloodshed continued.[36] A peace jirga was later convened in Islamabad under the supervision of the Political Agent of Kurram; fifty members sent by each of the twelve tribes were joined by parliamentarians from both groups. An agreement was reached; the tribes were to vacate each other's territory, the road reopened (it had remained closed for two years), electricity restored (it had been cut for 118 days) and dozens of people who had been abducted by rival clans were to be released.[37] But the ceasefire was very fragile and the peace agreement was not implemented. The road was blocked again after twenty days owing to firing at travellers. There was a shortage of life saving drugs due to the road closure, patients had to be transported to Peshawar through Afghanistan and several, including children, died before reaching the hospital.[38] By blocking the road, the Taliban are effectively putting the Kurram Shias under siege, and at the same time they have expanded their control in Lower Kurram by backing sectarian fighting.[39]

A 5 December 2008 bomb blast targeting the Saray-e Alamdar-e Karbala (known as the Parachinar imambargah) in the Kucha Risaldar district of Peshawar killed as many as thirty-four people and wounded over 120 others, who mostly hailed from Parachinar. This crushed all hopes that the peace agreement would be implemented. In early 2009, a jirga spent two months in Kurram without finding a solution to the conflict. The government-sponsored jirga gave up its efforts. In May 2009, NATO forces and the Afghan government invited elders of rival factions to a military base in Paktia after Sunni elders had complained to Afghan and NATO forces that the Turi had blocked movement and transportation of food. The Turi denied these accusations and demanded safety and the reopening of the Thall-Parachinar road.[40] The talks concluded without any agreement.[41] Both communities accuse each other of drawing support from the outside—the Sunnis are alleged to be backed by the Taliban and the Shias by Iran, and the Afghan Hazaras as foreigners are blamed (the hidden external hand). A Bangash malik saw 'no Sunni-Shia tension rather a third hand involved in pitting the two tribes against each other'.[42]

New clashes erupted in June 2009 when militants opened fire on officials and jirga members in Lower Kurram: nearly 150 people were killed in two weeks.[43] The blockade of Upper Kurram was reinforced from August 2009 when Taliban militants were brought from Orakzai, Khyber and Dara Adam Khel under the leadership of Hakeemullah Mehsud, who took over as TTP leader after Baitullah Mehsud's death in a drone attack. The Thall-Parachinar road was briefly reopened in November 2009 and a relief convoy of twenty-five trucks reached Parachinar. But this was only a brief lull in the conflict. In March 2010, six truck drivers who had been kidnapped were found dead near Thall. A letter found in the pocket of one of the victims said that anyone supplying goods to the Parachinar Shia community would meet the same fate.[44] A few days earlier, a convoy of Shias travelling from Peshawar to Parachinar was attacked by a suicide-bomber near Thall, killing at least fourteen people, including women and children. Turi and Bangash elders sent an open letter to the government asking it to come to their rescue and claiming that the 'siege and economic blockade since April 2007 had converted the paradise-like valley into a Gaza strip'.[45]

A general perception that the Shias had emerged as the winners in the struggle led to retaliatory violence in other parts of the province. Due to the attacks many Shias have migrated to Upper Kurram or to the cities (Thall, Hangu, Kohat). They have been forced into enclaves, which makes them easy targets (for instance 'Shi'agarh' 10 miles from Kohat on the road to Hangu). Much of the Sunni population in Parachinar has migrated to Lower Kurram while Sunni Mangal tribesmen are trapped in Upper Kurram and can only reach Peshawar through Afghanistan.

The Pakistani military establishment, under pressure from the United States to launch an operation against the Haqqani network in North Waziristan, is attempting to relocate the militants in Upper Kurram and to use the Kurram Agency to provide transit or sanctuary to its Afghan Taliban allies.[46] The strategy has been to impose the Haqqani network as 'mediators' to help resolve the sectarian conflict.[47] Three Shia leaders and Sajid Turi, a member of the National Assembly (MNA), had been co-opted to meet two sons of Jalaluddin Haqqani, but they did not have the *wak* (customary designation) to conduct a jirga on behalf of Kurram's people, who had been resisting efforts to cede their territory to the Taliban.[48] At the end of October 2010, the government announced that it was closing the Parachinar-Gardez-Kabul route in order to clamp down on sectarian violence. The people of Kurram are again trapped and cut off from the rest of Pakistan. Meetings were held in Islamabad at the end of November 2010 between commanders of the Haqqani group and TTP with elders of Kurram Agency, but they failed to reach an agreement as the militants said that the Thall-Parachinar road would be reopened only if it could be used by the Taliban, and if Turi tribesmen made assurances that they would not hinder militants' movements to and from Afghanistan via Kurram Agency.[49] In the meantime, the media reported that Sirajuddin Haqqani and his fighters had relocated to Kurram Agency with the knowledge of the Pakistani military to escape the drone attacks in North Waziristan.[50]

Sectarianism spreads to the Orakzai Agency

The sectarian clashes spilled over to the Orakzai Agency (450,000 inhabitants)[51] where 10 per cent of the Orakzai tribe are Shia (Isakhel,

Akhel, Turikhel, Muhammadkhel, a portion of Alikhel). The Shiites live south of the Mastura River. The Orakzai are believed to be the descendants of Karlanr, a son of Gurgusht. When the Bangash were ousted by the Turi from Kurram, they ousted the Orakzai from the country around Kohat.[52] The agency does not share a border with Afghanistan, and was at relative peace until October 2008.[53] Historically, the conflict in Orakzai was mainly over the ownership of Syed Mir Anwar Shah Shrine at Kalaya. This shrine, which originally belonged to the Shias, was given to the Sunnis during British rule. The Shias were later allowed to visit and ensure its maintenance.

The Kalaya Syed, who were established pirs of the Orakzai Shiite clans, were settled on land extending from the border of Kohat to Kurram. In 1923 Mulla Mahmud Akhunzada led a lashkar of Sunni Orakzai and Shia Manikhel Orakzai to evict the Kalaya Syed who moved to Kohat.[54] In 1927 the Shia Bar Muhammadkhel brought the Syed back to the Tribal Areas. Mulla Mahmud mobilised a lashkar with Afridis and Sunni Orakzai who were promised shares of the lands of the Shias. Hundreds were killed on both sides and all Shias were evicted from Orakzai. The Sunnis submitted a petition to the chief commissioner in Peshawar claiming that Shias were committing crimes such as kidnapping Sunni women. The British supplied weapons to the Shias and Mulla Mahmud sought help from Afghanistan. The Afghan king refused to interfere because of the risk of a British intervention. In 1930 the Shias took back some land. A jirga decided that lands held before 1927 should be returned to Shias.[55] In 1936, the British colonial administration demarcated Sunni and Shia areas to minimise the chances of conflict. Orakzai was made into the separate tribal agency of Tirah, confirming the territorial holdings and regional presence of the Shia tribes.

In 1998, after clashes over flag raising on Nowruz, Taliban from Orakzai attacked the Shia village of Shahukhel and razed it to ground, killing scores of Shias, while numerous families were displaced and took refuge in Shia villages; the army intervened.

The shrine was renovated in 1999 (the opening ceremony was held on 20 June 1999). Shia residents wanted to organise processions and use musical instruments inside the shrine. A Taliban force was raised in the area in 1999 by Aslam Farooqi, a tribal chief affiliated with the

SSP. In 2000 the Taliban declared that the agreement—which allowed Shias access to the shrine—was un-Islamic and they warned the Shias not to return. The militants occupied a hilltop and fired RPGs and mortars on neighbouring Shia villages.[56] The Taliban demolished the half-built Shia mosque and converted it to a Sunni *Eidgah* (prayer ground for Eid festival). The Shias offered the Taliban a plot of land, but they insisted on occupying the land on which the Shia shrine was built. Shias were chased away because they were considered to be unbelievers (*kafirs*). The Taliban remained active in the area until the end of 2001.

In October 2006, the shrine was reduced to rubble after a seven-day battle over its ownership that killed at least eighteen people. People from both communities were banned from entering the disputed area,[57] which is in the custody of the frontier corps. After a ceasefire was accepted, the Shias moved back to their area across the Toi River (Sunnis occupy the north and Shias the south). Sunnis who were not ready to negotiate agreed because they had regained control of the whole Layra (Kalaya) area. Since the assault on the Red Mosque in 2007, attacks on shrines have become a regular occurrence in Orakzai.[58] They are aimed at parting ways with established norms and values and at establishing a new identity. These attacks are inscribed in the targeting of shrines and mosques all over Pakistan: between December 2007 and December 2010, thirty major attacks against shrines, mosques and other religious targets have killed 800 people. The aim is to create chaos and also to force the armed forces to divert their attention away from the war on terror.

In 2004, foreign militants displaced by military operations in Waziristan began moving into Upper Orakzai, where they found a safe haven.[59] They were joined from 2006 by members of the SSP and LJ from Dara Adam Khel and by militants from Khyber Agency. After the creation of the TTP in December 2007, Hakeemullah Mehsud was appointed as its commander in Orakzai, while Tariq Afridi, the commander of the TTP in Dara Adam Khel, found shelter in Orakzai.

Orakzai has become a new centre of gravity for the TTP's leadership, a safe haven for Punjabi militants and a launching pad for attacks targeting NATO logistics into Afghanistan and for suicide attacks in Peshawar and other cities of Khyber-Pakhtunkhwa.

There is an economic dimension to the conflict in Orakzai. Shias are relatively affluent compared to Sunnis in the Tribal Areas. They own property and control resources such as forests, mountains, and fertile agricultural land. As such, some Sunni militants prevent them from cutting their trees and selling them. The Taliban also expelled the Shias from fertile land and forced them to pay *jizya* (poll tax on non-Muslims).[60] Shias who had acquired contracts for developing coalmines were expelled from the area by the Taliban, who stated that infidels had no right to extract coal.

In one instance, Sunni Ali Khel tribesmen rejected the Taliban's banishment of Shias from some areas and raised a lashkar to fight the Taliban.[61] The grand jirga that took place in October 2008 was attacked by a suicide bomber, killing over one hundred Sunnis and Shias. Despite this, the Taliban did not succeed in dividing the Ali Khel along Sunni-Shia lines because the whole tribe had agreed to resist the Taliban. The Storikhel, also a mixed Sunni-Shia tribe, similarly stand united against the Taliban.

The trouble in Kalaya continued with a suicide car-bomb killing six people at a jirga called by the Shias to settle a dispute with the Sunnis in December 2008. Clashes erupted again in April 2009 when a Sunni girl eloped with a Shia boy and the couple took shelter in Kalaya.[62] The Sunni tribesmen refused to hand over the couple to the Taliban, who wanted to execute them. This ended with a clash between Baitullah's and Tariq Afridi's men. In October 2009, a bomb attack on a village near Kohat left thirty-five Shias dead and in April 2010 a double suicide-attack at a refugee camp in Kacha Pakha, a Shia area of Kohat, killed forty-one displaced Shias from Orakzai.[63] This was probably in retaliation for the uprising of the Storikhel Shias against the TTP at the end of 2009. In December 2010, a suicide-attack left eleven dead in a Shia-run hospital in Hangu district and another fifteen Shias—including women and children—were killed in Kohat when a suicide bomber blew himself up close to a minivan that was about to depart for Kalaya. A spokesman for the Taliban of Dara Adam Khel claimed responsibility and said that Shias were targeted.[64]

The Taliban based in Lower Orakzai have also been stirring sectarian violence in Kohat and Hangu (Shias are in a majority east of Hangu; there are Shia villages between Kohat and Hangu).[65] There were clashes in Hangu (NWFP) during Muharram in 2009, which left seventeen dead and thirty injured. Clashes erupted when people from Kohat who were protesting against the curfew imposed in Hangu on the eve of Ashura were attacked by Sunnis supported by the Taliban. It took three days to restore calm to the city.[66]

Sectarianism spreads to Dera Ismaïl Khan, Dera Ghazi Khan and Bhakkar

Besides Hangu, Dera Ismaïl Khan has emerged as another major sectarian flashpoint. The city, situated 250 km south of Peshawar, and which has always been tense during Muharram, is now among the most sensitive districts where sectarian clashes claim scores of lives. A large population from Waziristan migrated to the city after the start of the military operations, which exacerbated the ethnic and sectarian tensions. Over 800 people have died in targeted killings and suicide bombings directed at funeral processions[67] or the bazaar. Many families have left the city where sectarian violence continues in spite of a peace deal signed in early July 2009. Sectarian violence has spread to Bhakkar and Dera Ghazi Khan, cities of the Punjab with a history of sectarian tensions. Shia families fleeing sectarian violence in Dera Ismaïl Khan have begun to settle in Bhakkar, a district with a large Shia population. A suicide bombing in October 2008 targeting Rashid Akbar Niwani, a member of parliament belonging to a very influential Shia family, left twenty-two dead and over sixty injured.[68] Dera Ghazi Khan has also become a target. An attack on a Shia procession in February 2009 led to riots that lasted for several days.

Conclusion

There was an upsurge in sectarian violence throughout 2009 due to the increase of operational spaces for jihadi-sectarian groups as the consequence of the weakening of the state's presence in the region. The operation Rah-e Najat, launched at the end of 2009 in Waziristan, was described as a success by the Pakistani military, but as usual, the militants were only dispersed and many of them moved to Kurram and Orakzai. The army organised a media trip to Kurram in early July 2010 and presented the area as pacified,[69] claiming that ninety-six militants had been killed and 3,000 to 4,000 militants driven out, but, according to locals, the Taliban still control a good part of Central Kurram. A few days later, eleven Shiites travelling from Kurram to Peshawar via Afghanistan were ambushed and killed in Chamkani (Paktia).

The population wants peace and security, but traditional leaders from both communities have lost control over the situation as very young fighters fill the ranks on both sides of the conflict.[70] Jirgas are no longer effective in resolving issues, particularly in the rural areas of Kurram. Even as American drones target sites within the Kurram tribal agency, the continuing struggle between Sunnis and Shiites shows few signs of abating. Sectarian violence is likely to become endemic as the Taliban have, to some extent, succeeded in exploiting sectarian strife to expand their space, while the state remains in denial about the sectarian conflict in the FATA.

10

CONNECTIONS AND DYNAMICS

Although in the 1990s ex-Soviet Central Asia, Afghanistan and Pakistan were the scene of a spectacular multiplication of Islamic movements, these were not centrally coordinated. Personal rivalries, ethnic divisions between Uzbeks, Tajiks, Pashtuns, Punjabis and Sindhis, and caste divisions in Pakistan, in addition to differing strategies, often placed such movements in opposition to each other, or at least obstructed any real unity between them. However, networks of personal relationships often played a substantial role, especially among the former Islamic volunteers who fought in Afghanistan from 1984 to 1992, and in the context of relationships between masters and pupils or among contemporaries in the Pakistani madrasas, all based on ethnic connections.

The Central Asian movements are not coordinated among themselves, even if relationships between commanders do exist on the ground. Uzbeks and Tajiks fought shoulder to shoulder between 1992 and 1997, with the consequence that members of the Islamic Movement of Uzbekistan were able to find refuge and protection in the upper Gharm valley in Tajikistan between 1998 and 2000. The Taliban did not play a coordinating role; they were part of the general military agglomeration, but were not at its centre. Their particular function was to give refuge to fleeing militants and lay the groundwork for the construction of Islamic fighting formations in which ethnic origins would supposedly no longer be an issue. Afghanistan served as a melting-pot for a new generation of transnational combatants, but it was not the headquarters of radical Islamism.

The two truly international conglomerations were the Bin Laden network (al-Qaeda) and the Pakistani movements. They took parallel paths and remained institutionally distinct, even though they displayed affinity after the Gulf War of 1991.

The al-Qaeda movement and the Afghans

The radicalisation of al-Qaeda was to be fully realised from the time that Bin Laden returned to Afghanistan from Sudan and assumed direct control. Between 1992, when Kabul fell into the hands of Ahmed Shah Massoud, and 1996, when it was taken by the Taliban, the foreign volunteers present in Afghanistan did not appear to be centralised and lacked clear objectives. Some fought on the side of Gulbuddin Hekmatyar against Massoud, but the majority were attached to local commanders, who were nearly all Pashtuns. For example, in the Pashtun pocket around Kunduz in the north, there was a strong Arab presence attached to the Saudi-based International Islamic Relief Organisation; the latter concerned itself particularly with the Tajik refugee camps, which it barred Westerners from entering. Similarly, in the Kunar valley close to the Pakistani frontier, small Afghan emirates were set up which were practically the counterparts of the Pakistani Islamist movement Dawat wal Irshad, led by Muhammad Afzal in Upper Nuristan and Jamil al-Rahman among the Safi tribe of Pesh, also in that region. In 1992 Massoud's administration in Kabul had no Arab member, and he was not unduly concerned by the presence of Arabs on Afghan soil. There were regular clashes between the Afghan population and the Arabs, who for want of clear aims took to making periodical denunciations of what they regarded as popular superstitions, such as visits to the tombs of saints and the displaying of flags at the tombs of martyrs.

The encounter between Bin Laden and the Taliban changed the rules. The Taliban entrusted to Bin Laden control of the non-Pakistani militants, while the Pakistani organisations, especially the Harakat-ul-Mujahidin, took control of a number of training camps in the province of Paktia. In 1996 the Harakat ul-Ansar were given the task of managing the Salman ul-Farsi training camp in Paktia after the Hizb ul-Mujahidin militants, connected to Hekmatyar, were driven out by the Taliban. The camp was re-named Amir Muawiya (founder of the Umayyad dynasty in the Seventh century CE) and became a sanctuary for the anti-Shia militants of the Lashkar-i-Jhangvi. The Al-Badr 1 and 2 camps of the Jamaat-i-Islami were also given to Harakat ul-Ansar.

During this period Bin Laden brought the Arabs under his control and isolated them from the Afghan population. The leaders were installed in what amounted to residential complexes near Kandahar and Jalalabad, while the ordinary fighters were grouped together in cantonments in Kabul and Kunduz. At the same time a third echelon was established, made up of militants from Western countries who were being trained to return home and carry out terrorist activities. A select group functioned in Afghanistan under the leadership of Abu Zubayda; this Palestinian from Gaza, born in the Saudi capital Riyadh in 1971 and holding an Egyptian passport, was a former member of Islamic Jihad and resident in Afghanistan.

The leaders came almost entirely from the first generation of militants who had come to Afghanistan to fight the Russians, with the exception of Bin Laden's spokesman, a Kuwaiti named Suleiman Abu Gheith who became his close aide, and was seen sitting beside him in the post-11 September videos. This group included Bin Laden, Ayman al-Zawahiri and Mohammed Atef, *alias* Abdulaziz Abu Sitta, *alias* Tasir Abdullah, *alias* Abu Hafs al-Misri—a former Egyptian police officer who had been in Peshawar since 1983 and whose daughter had married Bin Laden's son.

However, a new generation of Bin Laden's militants arrived, who differed from the veterans of the 1980s. In general these new arrivals did not come directly from the Middle East, and were not distinguished for their political insight or for any preexisting religious commitment. Whatever their nationality, whether they were from Arab countries or from the West, they had been re-Islamised in the West, often through contact with Arab 'Afghans' (i.e. veterans of the fighting in Afghanistan) who were attached to the radical mosques. One of the best known of these mosques is at Finsbury Park in London, and is directed by Abu Hamza, an Egyptian political refugee in London since 1981, who had served his time in Afghanistan. Zacarias Moussaoui, Djamel Beghal, Kamel Daoudi and Ahmed Ressam, all of whom are on trial at the time of writing for involvement in the al-Qaeda network, passed through this mosque en route to Afghanistan.

The perpetrators of the attacks of 11 September 2001, or at least the leaders of the group, had similar profiles. They were educated and well assimilated in the West, where they were studying, and had left their family circles and emigrated from their countries of origin. They were the 'second generation' of Islamic extremists, who threw themselves abruptly into radicalisation without passing through the intermediate stages of religious or political militancy. Although their origins were similar to those of the first generation—they come from the Gulf countries, Algeria and Egypt—their profile was different in the sense that they routinely came by way of a period spent in the West and by way of a phase of activism, without a previous stage of piety and religious observance (Bin Laden had studied religion, and then become progressively radicalised over a long period). Within this category were the two assassins of Massoud, one of whom, Dahman Abd al-Fattah, was a Tunisian graduate in journalism who had attended three universities in Belgium. Another noteworthy case among the 'Afghans' was Abdelilah Zyad, a Moroccan resident in France, who was sentenced to eight years in prison for the Marrakesh incident of 24 August 1994.[1] To this second generation should be added, finally, a third category—that of the converts, who had not existed in the 1980s except for Black Americans.

The relationship between members of this second generation and Afghanistan was also different. They never mixed with the Afghan population, living apart with volunteers from other countries. They were hardly interested in their local surroundings and came to Afghanistan only to be trained there to take part in the global jihad against the United States, in which neo-fundamentalism and classic anti-imperialism were mingled. As rebellious youths, disaffected from their societies, they became the tools of al-Qaeda. They fought bravely, as their resistance to the joint attacks of the Americans and the Northern Alliance in 2001 proved, but their separation from the population and their ignorance of the language and of local society made them vulnerable and unfit for guerrilla warfare. However, their methods of combat, which were completely distinct from the Afghan tradition and included the suicide attack on Massoud on 9 September and the uprising of the prisoners of Qala-i-Jangi on 25 November 2001, demonstrated that they could overturn the traditional order.

A final significant element was that within the framework of al-Qaeda militants from different countries would find themselves operating side by side. Could this solidarity survive the disappearance of the organisation as such? There exists at least one example: the link between the brother of Yusuf Ramzi (Wali Khan) and the brother of Janjalani, who went together to the Philippines where they attempted to mount an attack on the Pope in December 1995.

In every case the leadership of al-Qaeda proves to be international, with a strong Arab representation. In 1998 Bin Laden announced the creation of an international Islamic Front for jihad against the 'Crusaders' and the Jews. This front included the Pakistani Lashkar-i-Taiba, the Egyptian Jihad and Gamaat, the Pakistani Harakat-ul-Mujahidin, and militants of other national origins. The dominant components were nevertheless Pakistani and Egyptian. The Majlis al-Shura, the movement's consultative council, comprised—in addition to Bin Laden himself—Zawahiri, Zubayda and Atta, who were Egyptian, and the Uzbeks Yoldashev and Namangani (according to the partial information which it has been possible to obtain).

The fusion between the Taliban and al-Qaeda

In the light of the chronology of events, it could have appeared that the Taliban movement became radicalised under the pressure of events but that it did not share the jihadist ideology of Osama Bin Laden. However, after the military campaign of October and November 2001 new factors indicated the extent to which the aims of al-Qaeda and those of the Taliban had come together. This process of convergence probably dates from the year 2000, when from the autumn onwards manifestations of radicalisation began to appear. These included the eradication of the opium poppy, which served only to undermine the Taliban's support in the society of the region. Another instance was the destruction of the statues of Buddha at Bamiyan, which had existed throughout the entire Islamic period; this was carried out in the teeth of Pakistani pressure and the unanimous advice of the Arab ulema. Further factors were the obligation on Hindus and Sikhs resident in

Kabul to wear distinctive symbols, and the arrest of Christian aid workers on charges of proselytisation. Finally, the declaration by Mullah Omar to the BBC on 15 November 2001 calling for the destruction of America indicated his ideological alignment with Bin Laden.

Without the role played by al-Qaeda, the Taliban, who have never been accused of playing an active part in the attacks of 11 September, would in all probability have continued in power. It is a paradox that foreign influence brought about the fall of the Taliban. By accentuating the ideological aspect of the Taliban phenomenon, al-Qaeda severed its linkage with traditional Afghan society. The political agenda was in fact dictated by Osama Bin Laden, but the local dynamics in the end tilted the balance in favour of the American intervention. It is certainly the case that the foreigners were only a reinforcement and not a decisive strategic element in the regional context, even though al-Qaeda succeeded in taking control of the Taliban, or at least of Mullah Omar's immediate circle.

The role of Pakistan

In Pakistan two concurrent phenomena have played a determining role in the evolution of the Islamic movements since the first Afghan war. These are the strategy of the Pakistani army and hence *a fortiori* of the military intelligence service (ISI); and the radicalisation of the traditional movements.

The Pakistani military intelligence services and the radical tendency

The Pakistani military intelligence services have always made use of, and supported, Islamic radical movements in the context of the regional policy of Pakistan in Afghanistan and Kashmir. This relationship was not only a matter of tactical exploitation. Some senior officials of the ISI became increasingly close to the Islamic radicals. These included Hamid Gul and Osman Khalid, as became clear from the positions they adopted after their retirement. However, religious convictions do not in themselves explain the relationship, which was essentially the result of a carefully thought-out regional policy that the Pakistani army and the ISI supported the Islamists, especially after

General Zia-ul Haq seized power in 1977. During the Afghan war the principal beneficiary of their aid was Hekmatyar's Hizb-i-Islami. Subsequently it was the Taliban.

There were clear links between the ISI and certain extremist movements active on the domestic front and in Kashmir. It was with the aid of the ISI that Dawat wal Irshad created Lashkar-i-Taiba (the Army of the Pure) in 1990. The ISI changed its tactics in Kashmir in 1993 following the attack on a group of Western tourists at Srinagar in 1992; from this date onwards the Pakistani secret services no longer operated openly in Kashmir but cloaked their activities behind intermediaries in what amounted to nothing less than a sub-contracting and privatisation of the jihad. They also halted financial support for movements aimed at the independence of Kashmir and only helped those that favoured its annexation to Pakistan. This meant that the Jammu and Kashmir Liberation Front lost much of its influence to the advantage of the Hizb ul-Mujahidin, who was active on the ground and linked to Jamaat-i-Islami. This faction in its turn was supplanted by more radical movements at the instigation of the Pakistani authorities. Indeed, after the destruction of the Babri mosque at Ayodhya in December 1992 the Pakistani secret services also aimed to profit from the radicalisation of Indian Muslims by recruiting motivated youths and training them, in Kashmir among other places, so that they would be able to attack Hindus throughout India. Finally, the ISI wanted movements active in Kashmir to attack the Hindus of Jammu and the Buddhists of Ladakh and so frighten them into leaving Kashmir. The Hizb ul-Mujahidin was reluctant to do this, since it wished to restrict its operations to Kashmir, but other movements, such as the Harakat-ul-Mujahidin and the Lashkar-i-Taiba, were prepared to extend their activities beyond Kashmir and therefore became, after 1994, the groups favoured by the ISI. General Pervez Musharraf, then chief of staff, called on the Lashkar-i-Taiba to reinforce his offensive in Kashmir in the spring of 1999 in the Kargil sector.[2]

A kind of escalation took place. For complex reasons the Pakistani secret services encourage splits in the radical movements. This was partly to be able to control them better, but was also in order to cover the tracks left by their operations. The Jaish-i-Mohammad was apparently set up with ISI support as a counterweight to the Lashkar-i-Taiba, which had become too powerful in Kashmir. This was a relative set-back, since far from reining in the tempo of terrorist action it caused the two movements to compete so that each would seek to carry out more spectacular operations than the other.[3] An additional reason for the ISI's encouragement of splits is its desire to separate the Afghan and Kashmiri jihads and to distance the Pashtuns from operations in Kashmir. The intention behind the establishment of the Jaish-i-Mohammad was to give a Kashmiri and Punjabi face to the jihad, and to localise the training camps in Kashmir.

The sacking of General Mahmud Ahmed, director of the ISI, after the 11 September attack because of his Islamist orientation was also precipitated by the attack on 1 October 2001 against the regional assembly in Srinagar, an especially symbolic target, in which thirty people were killed. Responsibility for this attack was claimed by the Jaish-i-Muhammad, and although this was almost immediately repudiated, India launched a campaign against Pakistan, which it accused of supporting the movement. The Jaish-i-Muhammad normally avoided contact with the press, but some individual members had contacted newspapers to claim responsibility for the attack. The question naturally arises: who asked them to do this, and why? No doubt it needed to be proved that official Pakistani approval of the American intervention in Pakistan did not mean a slackening of the country's interest in Kashmir.

The ISI also supported the Taliban at the time of their rise to power in 1994. General Naseerullah Babar, Pakistan's Minister of the Interior, paid a visit to the Taliban in October 1994, and Colonel Imam, its consul-general in Herat,[4] helped them to take that city in 1995. A pro-Taliban lobby thus came into being in Pakistan, run both by retired officers, including Hamid Gul and Aslam Beg, and by Deobandi circles, including Fazlur Rehman and Sami ul-Haq. At that time General Hamid Gul, as Defence Attaché at the Pakistani embassy in Kabul, supervised the training of commandos. A number of senior officers were seconded to the Taliban, and in 2000 these were General Said Safar and General Irshad—who was wounded and replaced by General Munir. In November 2001 the Pakistanis had to send several aircraft to rescue their officers who became trapped in Kunduz with the besieged Taliban and al-Qaeda militants during the Northern Alliance offensive. Sipah-i-Sahaba militias participated directly in the fighting against Massoud, and were probably responsible for the murder of Iranian diplomats at Mazar-i-Sherif in the north of Afghanistan in August 1998. Two other groups which took part were the Harakat-ul-Mujahidin and the Jaish-i-Muhammad, whose base was at Rishkor, south of Kabul.

This pro-Taliban policy certainly put Islamabad in direct contact with the activist Islamic networks. However, to avoid an overt clash with Washington, it has always handed over to the Americans activists who were explicitly identified as the perpetrators of terrorist actions. Aimal Kasi (who carried out an attack on CIA operatives at Langley, Virginia, in January 1993), Yusuf Ramzi (a nephew of Khalid Sheikh Muhammad and master-mind of the attack on the World Trade Center in February 1993) and Mohammed Sadiq Odeh (behind the attack on the US embassies in Nairobi and Dar es Salaam in August 1998) were arrested and extradited to the United States between 1994 and 1996, despite violent objections from General Hamid Gul. In addition, no suspect would ever be handed over without a specific request being made by the Americans.

The attack of 11 September 2001 certainly changed the situation. Washington then did what it had previously refused to do, namely exert strong pressure on Pakistan to sever its links with the Taliban and with Bin Laden's radicals. Hence, after the American bombing of Afghanistan in August 1998, the ISI found itself in a delicate position: it made a great effort, more or less successfully, to give the impression that the Afghan and Kashmiri jihads had been isolated from each other, especially by creating splits within the radical movements. The Pakistani military intelligence services still hoped for American support over Kashmir, even while they were arming and supporting anti-American, anti-Israeli and anti-Saudi groups with the sole intention of destabilising India. However, these groups were definitively declared by the United States to be terrorists, or had their sources of finance placed under close surveillance. After 11 September 2001 Britain put the Lashkar-i-Taiba on the list of prohibited terrorist movements, and this gave rise to a vicious campaign by Hafiz Saeed against Western culture and particularly against the Christian schools in Pakistan.

However, Washington clearly distinguished between Kashmir and Afghanistan, with the effect that Pakistani activist groups, even while they were being placed on terrorist registers, were not subjected to real repression and kept their capacity for militant action intact.

Pakistani Islamists at the heart of transnational links

The radicalisation of the conservative Islamic movements took place in the wake of the incident caused by the publication of Salman Rushdie's novel *The Satanic Verses* in 1988, and more especially after the Gulf War. It reached its peak with the American bombing campaign against the Taliban in 1998. The traditionalist movements at that time became explicitly anti-American and began to advocate jihad. This radicalisation took place alongside the growing use by the Pakistani army of its Islamic auxiliaries. Bin Laden became a popular hero, and two mass gatherings in Pakistan, with the participation of the retired generals, mobilised the Islamist tendency in Pakistan against the United States.

A breakdown of the foreign prisoners held by Massoud[5] shows that 39 per cent belonged to the Pakistani Harakat-ul-Mujahidin movement (*alias* Harakat ul-Ansar). Only thirty-three out of 110 Pakistanis identified themselves as Pashtuns, which indicates that the basis of Pakistani support went well beyond ethnic solidarity. Even more oddly, the other political affiliations were extremely varied. Members of Jamaat al-Tabligh were present, but so too were adherents of Nawaz Sharif's Muslim League, demonstrating that radicalisation had in fact penetrated to militants of all backgrounds, including political parties which rejected armed struggle. Only 43 per cent of the 110 were students of religion. The foreign presence in the Pakistani madrasas was less measurable and seemed to be proportionally less significant. In March 2002, the authorities counted 35,000 foreign students, of whom 16,000 were Afghans and 15,000 Arabs. It is certain that networks interpenetrate. Young Pakistanis living in Britain and captured in Afghanistan had often spent time in the Pakistani madrasas. The transnational links between the Pakistani Islamists and the Taliban and al-Qaeda do not appear to have an organisational base. In reality everything rests on personal connections, the connections of the madrasas, chance meetings in training camps and community of interest. An example of this fluidity is the case of Sheikh Omar Saeed, who was liberated along with Masood Azhar at the time of the hijacking of the Indian Airlines plane in December 1999 and was afterwards with the

Taliban and Bin Laden in Kandahar. A British citizen, born in 1973 into a wealthy Pakistani family in the textile business in London, he moved to Lahore and was imprisoned in India for the kidnapping of three Western tourists in Kashmir, an operation he organised in order to bring about Masood Azhar's release. He had been educated at Aitchison School at Lahore for two years, and afterwards studied at the London School of Economics. Then in 1993 he went to Bosnia on a humanitarian mission, where he came in contact with Pakistani militants belonging to Harakat ul Ansar. A few months later he was back in Pakistan where he underwent training in Miranshah (Waziristan) and then in the Khalid bin Waleed camp in Afghanistan, where he became an instructor, and where he reportedly met Masood Azhar who asked him to go to India. Sheikh Omar returned to Britain in 1994 and obtained an Indian visa on his British passport. After a short stay in the Harakat ul Ansar training camp near Jalalabad in Afghanistan, he was sent to India with the mission to capture Westerners in exchange for Masood Azhar. He is said to have transferred US$100,000 from Pakistan via Dubai to Muhammad Atta, one of the perpetrators of the 11 September attack. He is also said to have been linked to the Pakistani intelligence services, and in particular to Mahmud Ahmed, who was dismissed as ISI director by General Musharraf, and is also supposed to have been an agent for al-Qaeda in Lahore. Unlike Masood Azhar, he kept a low profile after his release and allegedly shuttled between Pakistan and Afghanistan. He apparently had connections with Abu Zubaida and with Ramzi Binalshibh and Khalid Sheikh Mohammad. In February 2002 he was arrested for the abduction of the *Wall Street Journal* journalist Daniel Pearl, who was murdered by his kidnappers. On 5 February Sheikh Omar Saeed is known to have gone to the house of Ejaz Shah, the provincial Minister of the Interior and a former official of the ISI. His arrest was announced on 12 February, at the end of a visit to the United States by General Musharraf. Sheikh Omar Saeed was sentenced to death on 15 July 2002 for his involvement in the kidnapping and murder of Daniel Pearl, and at the time of going to press his appeal is pending before the High Court. Although the United States asked for his extradition, President Musharraf has reiterated that as 'a principled stand' he would not extradite him or any Pakistani national suspected of helping the Taliban or al-Qaeda networks.

Another notable personality is Mufti Nizamuddin Shamzai, the spritual adviser of Mullah Omar, principal of the madrasa at Binori Town in Karachi and the teacher of Masood Azhar. He supported the Jaish-i-Mohammad in whose establishment he participated, was a member of the Zia-ul Haq's Majlis-i-Shura, and belonged to the Jami'at-i-Ulema-Islam. He travelled to South Africa, among other destinations, to persuade Muslim communities to support the Taliban, and in early October 2001 was a member of the delegation which went to Kandahar with General Mahmud Ahmed, officially to persuade Mullah Omar to abandon Bin Laden but in fact to encourage the Mullah not to give in. Mufti Shamzai, who was present at the marriage of Osama Bin Laden's eldest son in 2000, issued a fatwa in September 2001 calling on Muslims to wage jihad against the United States if they attacked Afghanistan. The fatwa also stated that according to the Sharia, citizens of Muslim countries which supported the United States or any other infidel force were no longer obliged to obey their governments. Mufti Shamzai developed a method of recruiting volunteers which ensured that no-one could be signed up without careful screening.

A third example of the Islamic connection between Taliban Afghanistan, al-Qaeda and Pakistan was the link between Abdullah Azzam, Osama Bin Laden and the Markaz Dawat wal Irshad, to whose establishment Bin Laden appears to have made a significant financial contribution. It should be remembered that Osama Bin Laden regularly spoke to the annual conventions of Lashkar-i-Taiba by telephone, from Sudan in 1995 and 1996 and from Afghanistan in 1997. The Markaz Dawat wal Irshad, which had been close to Saudi Arabia during the Gulf War, had afterwards distanced itself from the kingdom for the same reasons as Osama Bin Laden had done so. These were the stationing of American troops on Saudi soil, and allegations of corruption against Saudi society and the Saudi royal family. After the model of Harakat-ul-Mujahidin, the Lashkar-i-Taiba became part of the International Islamic Front for Jihad, created by Bin Laden in 1998, in opposition to the United States and Israel. This move gave concern to the Pakistani authorities.

The Pakistani Islamists in general expressed their support for the Taliban through mass meetings. For instance, a meeting was organised by Sami ul-Haq on 10 January 2001 at Akora Khattak to protest against

174

the adoption of UN Security Council resolution 1333 against the Taliban. This brought together the Jami'at-i-Ulema of Pakistan (JUP), from the more moderate wing; the Jamaat-i-Islami, through its leader Qazi Hussein Ahmed; the Jami'at-Ulema-i-Islam, also through its leader Maulana Fazlur Rehman; the Sipah-i-Sahaba with Maulana Azam Tariq; the leader of the Jami'at-i-Ahl-i-Hadith, Moheenuddin Lakhvi; the head of the Ikhwan, Muhammad Akram Awan; the head of the Tehrik-i-Islami, Dr Israr Muhammad; Maulana Sufi Muhammad of the Tehrik-i-Nifaz-i-Shari'at-i-Muhammadi; General Hamid Gul; General Aslam Beg; Ejaz-ul Haq, son of General Zia-ul Haq; Mufti Nizamuddin Shamzai; Maulana Masood Azhar of the Jaish-i-Muhammad; the head of the Harakat ul-Jihad, Muhammad Saeed; the head of the Harakat-ul-Mujahidin, Fazlur Rehman Khalil; Bakhat Zamin of the al-Badr Mujahidin; and the leader of the Jami'at ul-Mujahidin, Mufti Bashir Ahmed Kashmiri.

Following the announcement of the American campaign in 2001, the majority of these movements joined the Pak-Afghan Defence Council, founded in December 2000 by Maulana Sami ul-Haq in protest at the UN-supported international sanctions against the Taliban but there was no agreement on strategy. Shamzai and Fazlur Rehman wanted a confrontation with the Musharraf government, while factions like the Jami'at-i-Ulema-Pakistan were more cautions. Nevertheless at the moment of the anti-American demonstrations in the autumn of 2001, the protest movement against the American campaign took on a purely Pashtun ethnic aspect. Even in Karachi at least 80 per cent of the demonstrators were Pashtuns. The same applied to the Pakistani volunteers captured in Afghanistan during the campaign of 2001, in contrast to the variety among those taken prisoner earlier. These were Pashtuns, even though the Northern Alliance characterised them as 'Punjabis'. This ethnic connection explains why the demonstrations were concentrated in Peshawar, Quetta and Karachi, and did not touch Lahore and Rawalpindi.

Here one can observe the structural limitations of the Pakistani religious movements. Behind a façade of unanimity and the radicalisation of their language in favour of the Sharia and against the Americans and Musharraf, they were deeply divided along ethnic and caste lines. Support for the Taliban has been above all based on the Pashtun connection, which explains the role played by the small-scale movement of Maulana Sufi Muhammad, the Tehrik-i-Nifaz-i-Shari'a-i-Muhammadi (TSNM), which is based in tribal Pashtun areas. However, the Baluchis, the Sindhis and the Muhajirs, who are in any case less susceptible to the prevalent neo-fundamentalism, have remained aloof from mobilisation, while the Punjabis will only act if Musharraf gives up Kashmir, which the Americans have not asked him to do.

The Pakistanisation of al-Qaeda

After the fall of the Taliban, the militants, including those who had returned from Afghanistan, regrouped in Karachi with the support of some elements of the ISI, which had not been entirely purged. The militants were disillusioned with their leaders, who had not been able to unite against the government to prevent it from allying itself with the United States. Keen to show that their capacity to cause trouble was undiminished, they mounted spectacular operations against targets hitherto spared, including Westerners and women. This magnified the repercussions of their actions and further weakened Musharraf, who became a hostage to these movements, and was now perceived as incapable of defending either Pakistani citizens or foreigners. These operations, all carried out after 12 January, included the kidnapping of Daniel Pearl on 23 January 2002; the assassination of Shia doctors in Karachi; the attack in March 2002 on the Protestant church in the diplomatic quarter of Islamabad which caused the deaths of five people, including two Americans; the attack deliberately aimed at Shia women and children in a place of worship at Bhakkar in April; the attack in Karachi on 8 May which caused the deaths of eleven employees at the French Naval Construction Department at Cherbourg as well as three Pakistanis; the attack on the American consulate in Karachi on 14 June which caused twelve deaths; the attack on a missionary school in Murree on 5 August which killed six; and the attack on a missionary hospital in Taxila on 9 August which killed four. Musharraf evidently understood the message because, following the kidnapping and killing of Daniel Pearl, repression of the jihadists halted until attacks on Westerners began in earnest. Meanwhile the Pakistani secret services did nothing to hinder the regrouping of the Pakistani and Arab jihadists within Pakistan.

CONNECTIONS AND DYNAMICS

From May 2002 the government started blaming every act of terrorism on the Lashkar-e Jhangvi, which was described by the authorities as the Pakistani wing of al-Qaeda. Putting the blame on Lashkar-e Jhangvi had a dual purpose: it showed the United States that Pakistan was really cooperating in the war against al-Qaeda, while at the same time showing Pakistani public opinion that the government was serious in dealing with sectarian terrorism.

After the attacks on Westerners in 2002 the police arrested many activists, who were invariably described as belonging to the Lashkar-e Jhangvi. This raised a number of questions. To attribute responsibility for every terrorist act to a peripheral sectarian outfit which had been banned before 11 September seemed a very convenient way to protect the real perpetrators of the attacks and movements such as the Harakat al Jihad al Islami (HUJI) or the Harakat al Mujahidin al Alami (HUMA), especially because those arrested were never brought to trial but instead eliminated in false encounters. This modus operandi enabled the authorities to avoid bringing sensitive cases to trial and prevented the prisoners of making incriminating statements which would have put in doubt their alleged affiliation with al-Qaeda. On the other hand, it seems that the police had succeeded in infiltrating the Lashkar-e Jhangvi and to some extent dismantling it. This was confirmed by the arrest of its main activists in the following months, including Akram Lahori (whose real name is Muhammad Ajmal), who had been involved in thirty-eight cases of sectarian terrorism. This former bodyguard of Haq Nawaz Jhangvi, founder of the SSP, who had been active in terrorist activities since 1990, was arrested in June 2002. Ghulam Shabbir (alias Shabbir Fauji), who had trained the militants in Afghanistan for several years, was arrested in October 2002. The arrest of Qari Asadullah (alias Qari Abdul Hay, or Talha), chief of a breakaway faction of the Lashkar-e Jhangvi, was officially announced in May 2003. Described as the 'mastermind' of Pearl's murder, he had left Pakistan in 1997 to become the trainer at the Sarobi camp in Afghanistan. He was said to be an expert in explosives and chemicals, and had returned to Pakistan after the fall of the Taliban. His group enjoyed support in Karachi while Basra and his followers had a strong following in Punjab. As with most extremist outfits in Pakistan, ideology was never really a factor in the splits within the Lashkar-e Jhangvi, personality clashes among the leaders being the main cause.

The death of Asif Ramzi in December 2002 was a severe blow to the group. This member of the Gujarati Memon community, who belonged to Qari Asadullah's faction and claimed to have created the Muslim Unified Army (MUA), was the link with the Arabs who provided funds at a time when Lashkar-e Jhangvi was short of money. The official version of how he met his death was that he had been killed by the wrongly-timed explosion of a bomb, but he may have been eliminated by the agencies or by fellow activists. Nadeem Abbas, a member of the SSP and constable in the Sindh Anti-Corruption Establishment, was also killed in the blast.

Al-Qaeda militants who had initially found a safe haven in the tribal areas and later moved to Azad Kashmir, Punjab and Karachi would not have been able to do so without the connivance of the ISI. The authorities have confirmed that the militants who killed ten Pakistani soldiers and paramilitaries in Waziristan on 25 June 2002 were Uzbeks belonging to the IMU. In addition, several hundred members of al-Qaeda are said to have reached Azad Kashmir with the assistance of the Lashkar-i-Taiba among others. According to Pakistani intelligence agencies, at the beginning of 2003 between 200 and 300 al-Qaeda activists were hiding in Pakistan.

There seems to be disillusionment among al-Qaeda activists with the Pashtuns whom they often suspect of giving information to American intelligence officers. Actually they rely on the strong support networks which they have built among Pakistani Islamic parties during the Afghan war in the 1980s. Members of these groups give them shelter in the cities of Punjab and in Karachi, where they often hide in upmarket areas. So, even if weakened, al-Qaeda is very much alive in Pakistan and particularly in Karachi where jihad has been centralised, and which has become its new hub. It has been relatively easy for activists to merge into the population of Karachi, a megapolis of 15 million inhabitants where law enforcement is weak, where the ISI has kept its networks and which the security services do not control effectively— all the more so since as some of their operatives share the ideology of the activists. There have been several instances when al-Qaeda suspects escaped just before the American raids in Pakistan, apparently having been tipped off.

As al-Qaeda militants have fled to Pakistan, so have the local jihadi groups increasingly cooperated with them. The level of coordination and of organisation of the attacks launched in Pakistan from the spring of 2002—and the new methods, including suicide bombing—clearly point to al-Qaeda being implicated. Groups which were active in Kashmir (like Jaish-e Muhammad) or whose sole aim was to kill Shias (like the Laskhar-e Jhangvi) have merged operationally and started participating in anti-Western operations. However, the West is not the only target: in the message of Osama Bin Laden broadcast by Al-Jazeera on 11 February 2003, Pakistan was included in the list of so-called anti-Muslim apostate states (like Nigeria and Morocco) enslaved by the United States which have to be liberated through jihad.

The links between the Pakistani movements and al-Qaeda were exposed to the light of day at the time of the arrest of Abu Zubayda, who had been in the forefront of reorganising al-Qaeda in Pakistan, on 28 March 2002 in Faisalabad, the field of the radical Deobandi movements, and of some fifty al-Qaeda members, including twenty Arabs who were transferred to the US detention camp at Guantanamo Bay in Cuba. This arrest clearly put the spotlight on the links between the Lashkar-e Taiba and Arab militants—Abu Zubayda had been given shelter by local Lashkar-e Taiba office-holders. Two other top al-Qaeda leaders were arrested: Ramzi Binalshibh, a Yemeni national member of the Hamburg cell, on 11 September 2002 in Karachi, and Khalid Sheikh Mohammad, a Pakistani born in Kuwait, on 1 March 2003 in Rawalpindi. This was only a few days after the arrest in Quetta of Mohammad Abdul Rehman, son of Umar Abdul Rehman, the blind Egyptian religious leader now in prison in the United States. The links between the Arabs and Lashkar-e Taiba came to light once again after the arrest on 29 April 2003 in Karachi of Ali Abd al Aziz (also known as Ammar al Baluchi), another nephew of Khalid Sheikh Muhammad who reportedly financed the September 11 hijackers, and of Waleed Muhammad bin Attash, a Yemeni suspected of the attack on the USS *Cole* at Aden in October 2000. This man is reported to have stated that he was recruiting Pakistani volunteers for suicide missions against American targets and already had a dozen recruits from the Lashkar-e Taiba. Large quantities of explosives and weapons have been seized in Karachi. The Jaish-e Muhammad is also believed by many observers to be part of the al-Qaeda network and to have sent fighters to aid the Iraqi resistance against the United States.

In the absence of a centralised direction, makeshift aliiances—made of small groups decentralised and split into extremely compartmentalised cells of two or three members—are operating with increasing autonomy against targets of opportunity identified within the United States. They have in common the fact that their members have been in training camps in Afghanistan. They keep changing their names, and those they adopt—such as the Muslim United Army (MUA), Hizbullah al Alami, and Harakat ul Mujahidin ul Alami (HUMA)—tend to emphasise their transnational nature by using the terms *alami* (international) or united.

Asif Zaheer, who was arrested in December 2002 and sentenced to death for his involvement in the suicide-bomb attack against the French engineers in May 2002, was making bombs for different jihadi groups. He had been trained in Afghanistan and returned to Pakistan before the fall of the Taliban. He was heading his own faction of the Harakat ul Jihad ul Islami (HUJI), and formed Harakat al Mujahidin al Alami (HUMA). The Muslim United Army, which claims to be an alliance of jihadi groups (notably the Lashkar-e Jhangvi and the Harakat-ul-Mujahidin) and whose logo is a sword piercing the globe, came out in October 2002 when it claimed responsibility for a series of parcel-bomb attacks in Karachi targeting police officials. In an email message Asif Ramzi, chief of his own faction of the Lashkar-e Jhangvi, wrote: 'All the rightwing organisations have formed the Muslim United Army to organise groups against the United States. We are going to launch a war against anti-Islamic forces, police and other non-Muslims on the platform of the MUA.' ·Pakistani police did not take it seriously till 15 May 2003 when twenty-one petrol stations owned by Shell in Karachi were attacked with small bombs. The MUA claimed responsibility for the explosions and warned that major attacks would follow if the government did not stop its operations against the mujahidin.

The blurring of strategic and ideological alignments

The new radical Islamic tendency blurs the ideological and strategic lines of division which were so clearly laid down in the 1980s. Iran has the same enemy as the United States: the Taliban. The Pakistani army furthers the cause of the radical Islamists. The Taliban, which is a conservative and anti-communist movement, is radicalised against the Americans and finds an echo of sympathy within the Saudi ideological structure, dominated by Wahhabi ulema who are nevertheless in an alliance with the Americans. The Russians simultaneously fight the Islamists and make use of them, for example at the time of the aerial evacuation of Islamists trapped in Kyrgyzstan in the autumn of 2000. At a time when the struggle against Bin Laden's networks has increasingly taken on the nature of a security and police operation, the Islamic radicalisation of Pakistan, a state possessing nuclear capability, poses yet more difficult problems.

A new relationship exists between interests of state, viewed independently of ideological issues, and transnational networks of a kind which may operate even within the heartland of countries officially allied to the United States. However, the existence of these transnational networks does not itself constitute a novel strategic threat, since their operations are always conceived in the context of local considerations. The networks operate with two sets of criteria in view, the local and the global. One should not allow the resemblances between the language in which the two are set forth, with their appeal to the jihad and the ummah, to hide the essentially ethnic motivations that arise within the local context. The way in which the Taliban—which is essentially to say Mullah Omar—was willing to sacrifice governmental power for the sake of international solidarity was an entirely exceptional event, but it was precisely what brought about the regime's collapse. The American bombing revealed a popular discontent with the Taliban which Mullah Omar's strategy had not taken into account. The reasons for the decline and fall of the Taliban were tribal—and, paradoxically, nationalist. The treatment of prisoners and the evident half-heartedness of the fighting between Afghans, as distinct from that between the Afghans of the Northern Alliance and the Islamic volunteers, demonstrate that even after twenty years of war and ethnic polarisation, the sense of Afghan national identity had remained strong. In fact, the intensely ideo-logical nature of both the language and the practices of the Taliban served, because of their excesses, to alienate the people and thus exclude for the foreseeable future a role for radical Islam. Fundamentalism in its cultural and social forms will no doubt persist, especially in the tribal regions, but a long time will certainly elapse before it again takes political form. In a sense it was transnational Islamism carried to the extreme which destroyed both the Taliban regime and Afghan internationalism. The limit of the global movements has been reached: they come up against a barrier when local priorities begin once again to reassert themselves.

Other more material factors were also in play, but discreetly, since they were diametrically opposed to the values publicly espoused by the radical movements. These were ethnic, tribal and social considerations. Here again the triumph of the local over the global showed itself. The ethnic dimension, which in Central Asia adopts a nationalistic form, was particularly strong among the Pashtuns. Pashtun domination of the Islamic movements was to be seen among Qazi Hussein's Jamaat-i-Islami and the Jami'at-i-Ulema-i-Islam of Maulana Sami ul-Haq and Maulana Fazlur Rehman. However the dialectic between Pashtun identity and that of Islamic neo-fundamentalism operated in two directions. It gave a boost to fundamentalist Pashtun movements like the Taliban which, some time after the capture of Kabul by Massoud in 1992, reasserted Pashtun supremacy. Even royalists such as Hamid Karzai, at least for a period of some months, adhered at a particular moment to the Taliban, as did former Communists such as the Afghan General Tana'y. However, the tendency was reversible. In November 2001 tribal combatants of former Taliban allegiance rallied to Hamid Karzai. Finally, ethnic factors also served to set limits to the Taliban—which northern Afghanistan resisted not because it was more secularised but because it perceived the Taliban as an incarnation of Pashtun hegemonism.

At a less elevated level it was feasible for a fundamentalist movement to come into existence based on purely tribal considerations. This was the case with the TNSM led by Sufi Muhammad in the Malakand region, the emirates of Nuristan and the Pesh valley. Tribal issues were deeply embedded in the neo-fundamentalist movements, as became evident at the fall of Kandahar in December 2001 when the Taliban negotiated with a group of tribal chiefs each of whom was attempting to protect his own people. The dialectic between Islamism and tribalism was complex. The Taliban were both the protagonists of the phenomena of detribalisation, and its outcome, as was illustrated both in the crisis of the traditional élites and by the attacks mounted against customary law in the name of the Sharia.

The radical movements were therefore constantly under pressure from above—by means of internationalist influences which spoke the same language—and from below by local imperatives, which were often in practice disregarded but which continued nevertheless to conflict with the movements' formal ideology. This double reference made such movements vulnerable at times of serious crisis, since the resurgence of local motivations weakened them.

The question which therefore arises is: to what extent can real internationalism be identified? Although this study has identified certain focal points in Pakistan such as al-Qaeda, the coordination of the Pakistani religious movements, and the ISI, the relationship between these three is more arbitrary than structural. In fact Bin Laden's operative networks are more in Europe than in Pakistan. Volunteers are sent by European mosques, and the names of those involved in the process recur frequently. The list includes Abu Hamza, an Egyptian; Sheikh Bakri, a Syrian; Yasir al-Sirri, an Egyptian who is said to have provided credentials for Masood's assassins; Abu Qatada, (real name Omar Abu Omar), a Palestinian travelling on a Jordanian passport who is said also to be a member of Al-Muhajirun and of the fatwa committee of al-Qaeda;[6] and Abderraouf Hannashi, imam of a mosque in Montreal, who harboured Ahmed Ressam.[7] The persons specified have all denied being members of al-Qaeda, even though Bakri has openly supported it and Abu Qatada is said to have been a member of the al-Qaeda council for fatwas.[8] In fact these imams address an audience composed of second-generation Muslims of very varied ethnic and national origins. It is evident that the West is an important element in the construction of the networks which operate in Afghanistan.

True internationalism therefore relates to circles which are already globalised, which are in search of roots or new identities, and which mobilise around the issues of jihad and the ummah. However, the defeat suffered in 2001 with the fall of Kabul illustrates the limits of a mobilisation unable to reach beyond radical circles. The sole exception is where it links itself to local motivations: this is therefore both its strength and its weakness.

NOTES

INTRODUCTION: MARIAM ABOU ZAHAB'S MULTISCALAR APPROACH TO ISLAMISM: THE SOCIAL AND LOCAL ROOTS OF SECTARIANISM AND JIHADISM IN PAKISTAN

1. Her erudite knowledge of South Asian Shiism is also evident from texts which are not reproduced here, including her brief but enlightening analysis of the Muharram processions *julus* in Pakistani Punjab ('"Yeh matam kayse ruk jae?" (How could this matam ever cease?): Muharram processions in Pakistani Punjab', in Knut A. Jacobson (ed.), *South Asian religions on Display: Religious processions in South Asia and the Diaspora* (London: Routledge, 2008), p. 104–14. In this text she shows how this ritual has changed in the course of time, from the pluralistic celebrations of the past when Hindus took part in it and when, therefore, 'Processions were an important feature of a composite culture' ('"Yeh makan kayse ruk jae?"'), to and the rise of sectarianism because of both 'rationalist' reformist movements and foreign influences from the Gulf.

2. Mariam Abou Zahab's sense of transnational influences is also obvious in another text not reproduced here where she studies three women madrasas which are located at the interface not only of Shia traditions and Shia reformism, but also at the crossroad between South Asian Shiism and Iranian Shiism. 'Between Pakistan and Qom: Shi'i women's madrasas and new transnational networks' in Noor, Farish, Sikand, Yoginder, Van Bruinessen, Martin (eds), *The Madrasa in Asia: Political Activism and Transnational Linkages* (Amsterdam: Amsterdam University Press, 2008), p. 123–140.

3. O. Roy, *Holy Ignorance. When Religion and Culture Part Ways* (London: Hurst, 2010).

4. M. Abou Zahab and O. Roy, *Islamist Networks: The Afghan-Pakistan Connection* (London: Hurst, 2006).

5. 'Between Pakistan and Qom: Shi'i Women's Madrasas and New Transnational Networks', p. 137.

6. For instance, in some cases, the families of jihadi martyrs get additional prestige because of the sacrifice of one of them.

7. She even mentions the ISI in this respect, as she writes that 'the Inter-Services Intelligence (ISI) organized Sunni militant groups to contend with the "Shiite problem"' ('The Politicisation of the Shia Community in Pakistan').

8. 'The Regional Dimension of Sectarian Conflicts in Pakistan' in Christophe Jaffrelot (ed.), *Pakistan: Nationalism without a Nation?* (Delhi: Manohar, 2002), p. 115–128.

9. She emphasises this dimension in a text which is not reproduced here: '"I shall be waiting for you at the door of Paradise": The Pakistani Martyrs of the Lashkar-e Taiba (Army of the Pure) in Rao, Aparna', Bollig, Michael, Böck, Monika (eds), *The Practice of War. Production, reproduction and Communication of Armed Violence* (New York/Oxford: Berghahn, 2007), p. 133–158.

10. 'I Shall be Waiting at the Door of Paradise', p. 139.

11. Ibid., p. 141.

12. 'I Shall be Waiting at the Door of Paradise', p. 152.

1. PAKISTAN: FROM RELIGIOUS CONSERVATISM TO POLITICAL RADICALISM

1. Cf. S. V. R. Nasr, 'Islam, the State and the Rise of Sectarian Militancy in Pakistan' in C. Jaffrelot, (ed.), *Pakistan: Nationalism without a Nation?*, (London: Zed Books, 2002), pp. 85–114.

2. Nevertheless, a precursor to Pakistani jihadism was Massoud Alvi, who in 1973 founded the Jabha-Khalidia at Khair ul-Madaris in Multan, where he taught. Fazlur Rehman Khalil, founder of the Harakat ul-Ansar, was his student. This movement became the international Jami'at ul-Mujahidin during the Afghan jihad.

3. *Takbir*, August 1999.

4. In addition a reconstruction was organised on the occasion of the Id al-Adha (the Feast of the Sacrifice) in Lahore's largest sports stadium with no reaction from the authorities, though all political assemblies were banned.

5. For them martyrdom is the sole guarantee of entry to paradise: the observance of the pillars of Islam (the profession of faith, prayer, the pilgrimage, fasting, and the donation of alms) are not sufficient.

6. In 1998 Mushahid Hussain, the minister of information in the government of Nawaz Sharif, accompanied the governor of the Punjab to Muridke to enlist the LT's support against sectarian violence.

7. Yusuf Ramzi was abducted from Pakistan by the US authorities for his part in the World Trade Centre attack in 1993, and imprisoned.

8. Aimal Kasi killed two CIA employees in Virginia, escaped to Pakistan, and was also abducted at random to the US after a period of liberty, sentenced to death and executed in November 2002. His body was repatriated to Pakistan, where he enjoys martyr status.

2. THE POLITICIZATION OF THE SHIA COMMUNITY IN PAKISTAN IN THE 1970S AND 1980S

1. Pakistan has the second largest Shia community after that of Iran.

2. There were violent clashes in 1956 and 1957, and more than one hundred Shias were killed in 1963 during sectarian riots in Terl near Khairpur (Sind) and in Lahore.

3. On Shia activism during this period, see A. Rieck, 'The struggle for equal rights as a minority: Shiite communal organizations in Pakistan, 1948–1968' in R. Brunner and W, Ende (eds), *The Twelver Shia in Modern Times: Religious Culture & Political History* (Leiden: Brill, 2001), pp. 268.

4. On the Zia regime's Islamisation policies, see A. Iqbal, *Islamisation in Pakistan* (Lahore: Vanguard Books, 1986); Sh.J. Burki and C. Baxter, *Pakistan Under the Military: Eleven Years of Zia ul-Haq* (Boulder: Westview Press, 1991).

5. On these issues, see M.Q. Zaman, 'Sectarianism in Pakistan: The Radicalization of Shiite and Sunni Identities', *Modern Asian Studies* 32/3 (1998), pp. 687–716; S.V.R. Nasr, 'Islam, the State and the Rise of Sectarian Militancy in Pakistan' in Christophe Jaffrelot (ed.), *Pakistan: Nationalism without a Nation?* (Delhi: Manohar, 2002), pp. 85–114; M. Abou Zahab, 'The Regional Dimension of Sectarian Conflicts in Pakistan', in Jaffrelot, pp. 115–128; M. Abou Zahab, 'Sectarianism as a Substitute Identity: Sunnis and Shiites in Central and South Punjab' in S. Mumtaz, J.-L. Racine, Imran Anwar Ali (eds), *Pakistan: The Contours of State and Society* (Karachi: Oxford University Press, 2002), pp. 77–95.

6. The formation of the Pakistan Peoples Party by Zulfiqar Ali Bhutto in November 1967 was a blow for the Ayub regime as it channelled mounting labour and student unrest against Ayub Khan. Students played a major role in the disturbances, which spread in Punjab and Karachi in 1968. The movement led to the resignation of Ayub Khan in March 1969.

7. Mohammad Ali Naqvi, a medical doctor born in 1952, was the founder and most prominent leader of the ISO. He was assassinated in 1995 by Sunni extremists. For details, see his biography: T. R. Khan, *Safir-e*

Inqilab [The ambassador of revolution], (Lahore: A1 Arif Academy, 1996).

8. Shia militancy in Karachi is of a totally different nature, partly because of the social structure of the community and the emergence in 1984 of the Muhajir Qaumi Movement (MQM). Nevertheless, it needs to be considered why, both in Lahore and in Karachi, student activists are mostly recruited in the medical and engineering faculties.

9. Bhutto introduced a separate *Islamiyat* syllabus for Shias in 1975.

10. In Iraq, the arrests of prominent Shia ulama and the bans on religious processions culminated in the repression of the 'Safer intifada' in February 1977. Syed Mehdi al Hakim, the eldest son of Ayatollah Mohsin al Hakim, accused of being an Israeli spy, fled into exile in Pakistan in 1970. The Iraqi government also began restricting the visas of all non-Arab seminarians in 1971, so that Pakistani clerics were compelled to leave Najaf. For details, see J.N. Wiley, *The Islamic Movement of Iraqi Shias* (Boulder & London: Lynne Rienner Publishers, 1992), pp. 45–53.

11. There is no *marja-e taqlid* in the Indian subcontinent, and in the 1980s the great majority of the community recognised Ayatollah Khoi as their *marja*.

12. There is no madrasa in South Asia where students might follow the full course of religious instruction required to become a *mujtahid*. They have to complete their studies in Iraq or in Iran.

13. Followers of Sheikh Muhammad al Khalisi (1890–1963), a revered Iraqi scholar.

14. On *Shaikhiyya* beliefs and the refutation of them by M. H. Dhakko, see Syed H.A. Naqvi, 'The controversy about the Shaikhiyya tendency among Shiite "Ulama in Pakistan"', in R. Brunner and W. Ende (eds), op.cit, pp. 135–149.

15. See V.J. Schubel, *Religious Performance in Contemporary Islam: Shi'i Devotional Rituals in South Asia* (Columbia: University of South Carolina Press, 1993).

16. Shia leaders asked Ayatollah Khomeini to intervene. Khomeini warned Zia that, if he continued to persecute Pakistani Shias, he would meet the same fate as the Shah of Iran. For a detailed first-hand account of the Islamabad events, see Brigadier Syed A.I. Tirmazi, *Profiles of Intelligence* (Lahore: Fiction House, 1995), pp. 272–283.

17. Also called *imambarghs*, the name given to Shia mosques in South Asia.

18. He was assassinated in 1985 by a member of the ISO.

19. The *Ahl-e Hadith* deny the legitimacy of the classical schools of law, insisting on the Quran and the hadith as the exclusive sources of guidance.

20. Sunni sectarian literature describes Shiism as a creation of the Jews to destroy Islam.

21. See note 2.

22. Deobandis are followers of the reformist school of thought associated with the madrasa founded in 1867 at Deoband (North India) which aimed at purifying Indian Islam of 'un-Islamic' practices. Barelvis, who represent traditional Islam centred on the shrines, revere the Prophet and the saints as sources of guidance and vehicles of mediation between God and human beings.

23. The embassy of Iraq published an announcement in the daily *Jang* congratulating Musavi on his election.

24. The great majority of the Pashtuns are Sunnis, except for the Turi and sections of the Orakzai and Bangash, who are Shias.

25. For details of his biography, see T. R. Khan, *Safir-e Noor* [Ambassador of Light] (Lahore: Al Arif Academy, 1994).

26. According to his 'official' biography, he was the only Pakistani to protest against the festivities in Persepolis in 1971.

27. The Saudi regime.

28. The final portion of a *majlis* in which the *zakir* evokes the incidents of Karbala and induces tears of grief in the congregation.

29. Assassinated later by Sunni extremists.

30. *Yom al Quds* and *Yom marg bar Amerika* are still celebrated by the ISO in Karachi.

31. It should be recalled that Punjabi society is very hierarchical and caste-conscious, whereas Pashtun tribal society is much more egalitarian. The fact that Allama Husseini was a Pashtun (and Sajid Naqvi a Punjabi) should not be underestimated when analysing the evolution of the TNFJ, all the more as the same phenomenon may be observed in other parties.

32. Sajid Naqvi is often blamed for favouring the naqvis. This caste bias is not limited to the Shias; it is also prevalent in the Deobandi and Wahabi jihadi movements operating in Kashmir.

33. A dozen Iranian diplomats and military officers have been killed in Pakistan by Sunni extremists.

3. SECTARIANISM AS A SUBSTITUTE IDENTITY: SUNNIS AND SHIAS IN CENTRAL AND SOUTH PUNJAB

1. Shehzad Amjad. 'Nation, State and Terrorism. Sectarian War vs Operation Cleanup', *The News on Sunday*, 11 May 1997. Most of the references in this chapter are taken from the press as few scholars have so far done academic research in the field of sectarianism in Pakistan.

2. Patrilineal descent group which is also, at least ideally, the main unit of endogamy. This notion, which has a 'sliding semantic structure' is sometimes used to denote caste (*zat* or *qaum*) (see Hamza Alavi, 'Kinship in West Punjab Villages' in *Contributions to Indian Sociology*, New Series, 6 (1972), pp. 1–27).

3. Mumtaz Ahmad, 'Revivalism, Islamization, Sectarianism, and Violence in Pakistan' in Craig Baxter and Charles Kennedy (eds), *Pakistan: 1997* (Boulder: Westview Press, 1997), pp. 101–123.

4. Till 1998, the conflict was between Deobandis and Twelver Shias (no Bohra or Ismaili was ever targeted), and it was often analysed as a proxy war between Saudi Arabia and Iran on Pakistani soil. An Ismaili scholar was assassinated in Karachi in September 1998 and the Urdu daily *Khabrain* published in December 1993 a statement attributed to the Sipah-e Sahaba Karachi which claimed that an Aga Khani state was being created in Gilgit and that Muslims would not tolerate it.

5. *Dawn*, 23 January 1998.

6. Khaled Ahmed, 'The Sunni-Shia conflict in Pakistan', *The Friday Times*, 30 January–5 February 1997.

7. *The Nation*, 26 May 1997.

8. Azmat Abbas, 'Punjab's worst year of sectarian violence', *Dawn*, 1 January 1998; Gul Rukh Rahman, 'Sectarian violence: where will it all end?' *The News*, 19 January 1998.

9. Zaigham Khan, 'The tragedy of Mominpura', *The Herald*, February 1998. According to *Dawn* (26 December 1998) 78 people were killed and over 80 injured in 36 incidents of sectarian violence in 1998 in the Punjab province alone.

10. Awais Ibrahim, 'Hostage to terrorism', *The Nation*. 18 January 1998.

11. S. H. Rahman, 'Sectarianism must be fought', *The Frontier Post*, 23 January 1998.

12. Mumtaz Ahmad. 'Sectarianism and Zia', *The News*, 15 April 1998, 'Revivalism, Islamization,' op.cit. (3).

13. Afak Haydar, 'The Politicization of the Shias and the Development of the Tehrik-e-Nifaz-e-Fiqh-e-Jafaria in Pakistan' in Charles H. Kennedy (ed.), *Pakistan: 1992* (Boulder: Westview Press, 1993); Saleem Qureshi, 'The Politics of the Shia Minority in Pakistan: Context and Developments,' in D. Vajpeyi and Y. K. Malik (eds), *Religious and Ethnic Minority Politics in South Asia* (Delhi: Manohar, 1989); Munir Ahmed, 'The Shi'is of Pakistan' in M. Kramer (ed.), *Shiism, Resistance and Revolution* (Boulder: Westview Press, 1987).

14. Mohamed Hanif, 'The Anatomy of Sects Appeal', *Newsline*, August 1990.

15. Sunni militant organisations received huge funding from Saudi Arabia and Iraq in the early 1980s to counter Shia militancy.
16. I am thankful to Nasim Zehra for this suggestion.
17. The Sunni-Shia conflict is sometimes depicted as 'the fourth India-Pakistan war'.
18. Mohammad Rauf Klasra, 'Poverty fanning sectarian tensions in S. Punjab,' *Dawn*, 26 September 1996.
19. Sharif al Mujahid, 'Sectarian Strife: The economic dimension', *The News*, 5 June 1997.
20. From 1880, through an extensive irrigation programme, the British government converted vast tracts of wasteland in the Punjab and Sindh into rich agricultural land known as 'canal colonies'. The large landholders of Central and South Punjab were the main recipients of land in recognition of their services to the British Raj. See Imran Ali, The *Punjab under Imperialism 1885–1947* (Princeton: Princeton University Press, 1988) and Imran Ali, 'The Punjab and the Retardation of Nationalism' in D. A. Low (ed.), *The Political Inheritance of Pakistan* (New York: St. Martin's Press, 1991), pp. 29–52.
21. Swadesh R. Bose and Edwin H. Clark II, 'Some Basic Considerations on Agricultural Mechanization in West Pakistan', *The Pakistan Development Review*, 1969.
22. Shahid Javed Burki, 'The Development of Pakistan's Agriculture: An Interdisciplinary Explanation' in R. D. Stevens, H. Alavi and P. J. Bertocci (eds), *Rural Development in Bangladesh and Pakistan* (Honolulu: University of Hawaii, 1976), pp. 290–315; Shahid Javed Burki, 'Development of towns: The Pakistan Experience', *Asian Survey*, vol 14 no. 8, 1974.
23. Moazam Mahmood, 'Change in Land Distribution in the Punjab', The *Pakistan Development Review*, 28: 4 Part II 1989.
24. Hamza Alavi, 'The Rural Elite and Agricultural Development in Pakistan' in *Rural Development*, op. cit. pp. 317–387.
25. *Poverty fanning*, op. cit (18).
26. Mahbub ul Haq and Khadija Haq, *Human Development in South Asia, 1998* (Oxford: Oxford University Press, 1998).
27. The Gulf States expelled thousands of illegal South Asian workers in 1996 and 1997 and Saudi Arabia, faced with a financial crisis and rising unemployment among its nationals, has embarked on a 'Saudisation' policy both in the public and private sectors.
28. Members of the lowest castes assigned menial works in rural Punjab where the main divide is between *zamindar* (landowning castes) and *kammi*.

29. Kaiser Bengali, *Why Unemployment?* (Karachi: Pakistan Publishing House, 1991); Syed Javed Burki, 'Migration, Urbanization and Politics in Pakistan' in W. Howard Wriggings and James F. Guyot (eds), *Population, Politics and the Future of Southern Asia* (New York: Columbia University Press, 1973).

30. The Punjab accommodated 5.3 million refugees which accounted for 25.6 per cent of its population in 1951. They influenced the local population and enhanced consciousness about Islam. See Mohammad Waseem, 'Partition, Migration and Assimilation: A Comparative Study of Pakistani Punjab', *International Journal of Punjab Studies* 4, 1 (1997) Sage Publications.

31. At the time of Partition, the areas which form Pakistan had a low level of urbanisation and middle-class occupations were largely dominated by Hindus and Sikhs (about 75 per cent of urban immovable property in the Pakistan areas belonged to Hindus before Partition). Immigrants from East Punjab constituted more than half the population of major cities in 1951. Sargodha had 67.9 per cent refugees, Jhang 37.9 per cent, Sahrwal 40 per cent, Lyalpur (Faisalabad) 70.4 per cent, Multan 43.7 per cent. Asad Sayeed, 'Growth and Mobilisation of the Middle Classes in West Punjab: 1980–1970,' in P. Singh and S. S. Thandi (eds), *Globalisation and the Region: Explorations in Punjabi Identity* (Coventry: The Association for Punjab Studies, 1996), pp. 259–288.

32. Ameneh Azam Ali, Zahid Hussain and Talat Aslam, 'Punjab: The Silent Majority?' *The Herald*, May 1987.

33. The land reforms and their consequences for the rural population explain partly why the PPP had such a large vote bank in rural Punjab in 1970.

34. *Dawn*, 26 September 1996.

35. *The Rural Elite*, op. cit. (24).

36. Extended residential site of a landlord.

37. Ahmad Bashir, 'Sectarian violence will grow,' *The Frontier Post*, 15 January 1998.

38. Jhang city, which had 8 madrasas in 1947, had 47 in 1998.

39. Nasir Jamal, 'Religious schools: who controls what they teach?', *Dawn*, 28 October 1996; '746 Punjab madrasas involved in sectarian activities,' *The News*, 7 March 1995.

40. Iqbal Ahmed, 'Roots of violence in Pakistan'; 'Feudal culture and violence', *Dawn*, 2 February 1993.

41. Shahid Ibrahim, 'Pakistan's Achille's heel—sectarian terrorism', *The Pakistan Times*, 8 April 1998.

42. A saying of the Prophet Muhammad (PBUH).

43. Someone who has learnt the Quran by heart and is thus entitled to add Hafiz to his name.
44. 649 madrasas were functioning in Lahore in 1998. 'Pakistan's Achille's Heel', op. cit. (41).
45. Memorisation of the Quran by heart. It is the first level of madrasa education and usually lasts three to four years.
46. Traditional curriculum of religious schools introduced in the middle mid-eighteenth century in India by Maulana Nizamuddin.
47. Imrana Khawaja, 'The making of an Islamic militant', *The Friday Times*, 12–18 January 1995. See also the annual reports of the Human Rights Commission of Pakistan (HRCP).
48. See Mark Juergensmeyer, 'The logic of religious violence: The case of the Punjab', *Contributions to Indian sociology* 22, 1 (1988) on the empowering of marginal groups through the use of violence.
49. Talat Aslam, 'The Madrasah Factor', *The Herald*, September 1992.
50. Ahson Saeed Hasan, 'Sectarianism: roots and possible solutions', *The News*, 11 February 1998.
51. Barelvis are the followers of Ahmad Raza Khan (d. 1921) a native of Bareilly who led a reaction against the import of Wahabism into Indian Islam. Barelvis believe in the special powers of *pirs* (spiritual guides) and they worship the graves of saints. They believe that the Prophet Muhammad (pbuh) has unique knowledge of the unknown and is composed of God's light and they hold major celebrations for his birthday (*Milad un Nabi*).
52. Mohamed Hanif, 'In the Name of Religion', *Newsline*, September 1994.
53. Umbrella organisation of religious schools.
54. 'A white-collar job at a desk in an important office with some elements of power and patronage is the only goal of the majority of young [urban] persons.' Government of *Pakistan, Report of the National Manpower Commission, 1989* (Islamabad: Ministry of Labour and Manpower and Overseas Pakistanis, 1989), p. 82.
55. Aamer Ahmed Khan, 'Blind Faith', *The Herald*, June 1994.
56. Tariq Rahman, 'The Making of a Mominpura', *The News*, 18 February 1998.
57. Spiritual guide.
58. Hasan Mujtaba and Mazhar Zaidi, 'A Tale of Two Cities', *Newsline*, September 1994.
59. Ayesha Jalal, 'Partition', *The News*, 25 May 1998.
60. Talat Aslam, 'The New Sectarianism', *The Herald*, August 1991; 'The Lady and the Maulana', *The Herald*, Election Special 88; 'The Jang in Jhang', *The Herald*, Election Special 90.
61. For example, a poster widely circulated in Karnal District during the

campaign for the 1937 election quoted fatwas from leading *ulema* suggesting that a vote for a Shia candidate was a vote for a kafir and that Sunnis should not sit with Shias or assist them, they should not follow their funerals nor bury them in their graveyards, (See David Gilmartin, '"Divine Displeasure" and Muslim Elections: The Shaping of Community in Twentieth Century Punjab,' in *The Political Inheritance of Pakistan*, op. cit. (20). pp. 106–130.) Such fatwas are often quoted in SSP literature.

62. The lower class in the urban areas is also mainly Sunni.
63. About 65 per cent of the land in Jhang belongs to the Shias (*Newsline*, September 1994).
64. 'Revivalism, Islamization', op. cit. (3).
65. Abdus Sattar Qamar, 'Jhang: High Tension?' *The Herald*, August 1990; Abdus Sattar Qamar, 'Sects and Violence', *The Herald*, August 1990; Sohail Akbar Warraich, 'Jhang: A City Divided', *The Herald*, February 1991.
66. Khalid Hussain, 'The Jehad Within', *Newsline*, August 1990; Sharif al Mujahid, 'The rise of sectarianism', *Dawn*, 3 May 1997.
67. Adnan Adil, 'Sectarian violence threatens Bahawalnagar and Bahawalpur', *The Friday Times*, 21–27 November 1996.
68. Muhammad Qasim Zaman, 'Sectarianism in Pakistan: The Radicalization of Shi'i and Sunni Identities', *Modern Asian Studies* 32, 3 (1998) pp. 689–716.
69. Ibid.
70. Adnan Adil, 'Who will untie the sectarian knot?' *The Friday Times*, 28 July–3 August 1994; Adnan Adil, 'Among the Believers', *The Friday Times*, 2–8 March 1995.
71. Monthly *Al Haq*. vol. 14, n. 3, December 1978, pp. 26–27. 'The Shias are also controlling the key positions in the (civil and military) services and are in majority (in these services). This is despite the fact that they are hardly two percent of the total population of Pakistan [...] We must also remember that the Shias consider it their religious duty to harm and eliminate the Ahl-e Sunna.' (Quoted in *Sectarianism in Pakistan* [op. cit. 68]). Such statements are commonplace in the publications of sectarian Sunni parties.
72. *The News*, 14 January 1998.
73. *Roots of violence*, op. cit. (27).
74. An extremist anti-Shia movement created in the early 1990s in Central Punjab for the accession of Kashmir to Pakistan.
75. 'Revivalism, Islamization', op. cit. (3).
76. Aamer Ahmed Khan, 'The Rise of Sectarian mafias,' *The Herald*, 1994.
77. 'Unemployed youths are recruited by the sectarian parties in the far-

flung villages in the name of jihad and with the promise of lucrative financial reward', Asma Jahangir, *The News*, 8 February 1998.
78. Meaning here the ordinary people.
79. Personal communication, Lahore, May 1998.
80. Adnan Adil, 'Siege of Niaz Beg', *The Friday Times*, 21–27 July 1994; Adnan Adil, 'Intra-SMP battle leads to peace at Niaz Beg', *The Friday Times*, 28 November–4 December 1998.
81. Azmat Abbas, 'Who controls terrorist organizations?' *Dawn*, 3 February 1998.
82. Rauf Klasra, 'Exploiting sectarian differences to get concessions', *Dawn*, 27 January 1998.
83. Rauf Klasra, 'Reasons for court's failure to decide sectarian cases', *Dawn*, 19 January 1998. Judge Nayyar Iqbal Ghauri who awarded death sentences to 14 culprits—Sunnis—involved in the Iranian Cultural Centre case and to 8 culprits—Shias—involved in the Masjid ul Khair (Multan) case has reportedly decided to stay permanently in the USA as he was terrified for his life since he declared the judgment on 16 December 1998 (*Dawn*, 15 January 1999).
84. The PPP entered into an alliance with the SSP in 1995. Two SSP leaders became provincial ministers in the Punjab government and since Maulana Azam Tariq, leader of the SSP and member of the National Assembly from Jhang, was an enemy of Syeda Abida Hussain, a Shia leader despised by Benazir Bhutto, he enjoyed complete immunity during the Bhutto government ('Revivalism, Islamization', op. cit. (3)).
85. 'Revivalism, Islamization', op. cit. (3).

4. THE SUNNI-SHIA CONFLICT IN JHANG (PAKISTAN)

1. In the Pakistani context, sectarianism refers to the conflict between Sunnis and Shias.
2. The SSP was banned by President Musharraf on 12 January 2002, along with 4 other jihadi outfits but its militants were not really targeted in the crackdown on extremist groups which followed the ban.
3. Among others, Maulana Tahir ui Qadri, a prominent Barelvi leader.
4. In true Punjabi fashion, this prominent political family is divided into two rival factions. The first one was led by the late Colonel Abid Hussain and now by his daughter Abida Hussain (former federal minister in Nawaz Sharif's government and ambassador to the USA), her husband Fakhr Imam and their daughter Sughra Imam who started her political career in December 1998 as Chairman of the district council. The other faction is led by Makhdoom Faisal Saleh Hayat who is the *sajjada nashin* of Shah Jewna. A central leader of the PPP, he defected

in 2002 to join the PML (QA), he is the current federal minister of Interior. Leaders of both factions contested elections against one another at the local and at the national level in 2001 and 2002.

5. According to the 1951 census, Muhajirs formed 49 per cent of the population of the district and 65 per cent of the population of the municipal area of Jhang.

6. Bilal Zubeiri. *Tarikh-e Jhang*. nd, np.

7. The local Shias blame, for instance, the Muhajirs for having introduced Hindu customs in the Muharram processions while many Muhajirs consider the local Shias as uneducated and ignorant of 'true Shiism'.

8. The Jats of Rohtak were the target of a Shuddi movement launched by the Arya Samaj in the 1920s and was aimed at reconverting them to Hinduism.

9. One of them was Sahibzada Nazir Sultan linked to Sultan Balm shrine who defeated Arif Khan Sial.

10. Two of the three Sunnis elected in 1970 had joined the ruling PPP and they contested the election in 1977 on PPP tickets (PPP was very much seen as pro-Shia). The number of National Assembly seats in Jhang was increased from 1 in 1965 to 3 in 1970, 5 in 1977 and 6 in 2002.

11. For more details about the politicisation of the Shia community, see Mariam Abou Zahab, 'The politicisation of the Shia community in Pakistan in the 1970s and the 1980s' (paper presented at the Conference on Images, Representations and Perceptions in the Shia world, Geneva, October 2002).

12. This does not mean that the traditional zakirs who often have no formal religious education and who have always been economically dependent on the feudals were marginalised. Both styles of *majlis* coexist in Punjab and attract crowds.

13. There have also been recent allegations about links between the SSP and al-Qaeda networks.

14. Haq Nawaz's militancy against Shias annoyed Maulana Fazlur Rehman who did not want to antagonize his sizeable Shia constituency in Dera Ismail Khan and who opposed his election as amir of the JUI for Punjab.

15. *Dastur-e Asasi*, Sipah-e Sahaba, nd.

16. He graduated in 1971 from Khair ul Madaris in Multan, joined the JUI and started teaching in a madrasa of Toba Tek Singh in 1972.

17. See for more details Maulana Mohammad Ilyas Balakoti, *Amir-e Azimat* (Jhang Saddar: Jamia Usmaniya, nd). This tendentious book is the 'official' biography of Haq Nawaz Jhangvi.

18. Mukhtar Ahmad AH, 1999.

19. The Punjab Land Alienation Act of 1900.

20. It is often said that the best *zakirs* of Jhang were Hindus.

21. These two professions are often described as powerful mafias.

22. Sheikh Iqbal's personality is very controversial. In the 1970s, Sheikh Iqbal owned a petrol pump, a hotel, a cinema hall and dozens of buses.

23. A case was falsely registered against Shias who became martyrs in the eyes of the Shia community.

24. Sheikh Iqbal was himself assassinated in March 1995 by the SSP. The only son of Sheikh Iqbal, who is a high civil servant, was designated in the FIR registered after the assassination in January 1991 of Isar ul Qasmi, the successor of Haq Nawaz, in which Sheikh Iqbal's family was in fact not involved. Sheikh Iqbal's brother, Sheikh Akram, was elected *tehsil nazim* in 2001, defeating the SSP candidate, Zahoor Sajid Janjua, brother of late MPA Riaz Hashmat Janjua.

25. The importance of caste in Jhang can be judged from the fact that our informers always refer to Ibbetson's book 'Punjab Castes' published in Lahore in 1916 and based on the Census Report of 1881. This book is regularly reprinted both in Pakistan and in India and has recently been translated into Urdu.

26. Mukhtar Ahmad Ali, op. cit. Muhajirs, both Sunnis and Shias, are said to be more assertive and to resort quickly to violence because they do not have the same values and family networks than the locals who have many other ways of resolving conflicts before resorting to violence.

27. Isar ul Qasmi was from Samundri and Azam Tariq settled in Karachi was born in a village near Chichawatni.

28. The Punjab government did not move against the SSP between 1988 and 1993 because the Islami Jamhoori Ittihad (IJI) saw it as a potential ally and because the targets of the SSP, namely Ahmadis and Shias, were seen as supporters of the PPP. Benazir Bhutto sought the alliance of the SSP against the PML; Azam Tariq enjoyed a quasi-immunity when the PPP was in power because he was an arch enemy of Abida Hussain who was despised by Benazir Bhutto.

29. Saleem Fauji was killed in a police encounter in 1992. Azam Tariq attended his funeral and pronounced a very provocative speech describing him as a martyr. His death provoked the attack of a police APC with a 17 mm anti-aircraft gun which caused the death of 4 policemen and provoked a police operation against the SSP.

30. Drug and alcohol trafficking witnessed an increase of 250 to 300 per cent after the outset of sectarian violence. Khalid Hussain, 'Live and Let Die', *The Friday Times*, 3–9 September 1992.

31. Abida Hussain, her husband Fakhar Imam, and Amanullah Sial were defeated in the elections.

5. THE SSP: HERALD OF MILITANT SUNNI ISLAM IN PAKISTAN

1. The first month of the Islamic calendar, during which Shias commemorate the martyrdom of Hussain (grandson of the Prophet Mohammed) and his companions at Karbala in the year 680.
2. There is little statistical evidence regarding adherence to religious groups, but it is estimated that Shia Muslims make up 15–20 per cent of the population. In 2007, this amounted to between 25 and 30 million people, making Pakistan's Shia community the second largest in the world, Iran having the largest.
3. Afzal Iqbal (1986); Charles Kennedy (1990).
4. The reformist school of thought associated with the madrasa founded in Deoband (northern India) in 1867. The original aim of the Deobandi school was to purify Indian Islam by discarding 'non-Islamic' practices such as the cult of saints and the rites and practices adapted from Hinduism.
5. S. Vali Reza Nasr (2002), pp. 85–114; Mohammed Qasim Zaman (1998); Mariam Abou Zahab (2007), pp. 97–112.
6. International Crisis Group (2005).
7. Mariam Abou Zahab (2004), pp. 135–48.
8. Founded in Punjab in the late nineteenth century by Mirza Ghulam Ahmad who claimed that he had received a revelation and that he was the promised Messiah and a prophet without a book. The Ahmadi movement advocates a defensive jihad; its members also engage in peaceful proselytising. Most Muslims consider the Ahmadis as outside orthodox Islam. The Ahmadiyya have been subjected to persecution throughout the Indian subcontinent. See Yohanan Friedman (1989).
9. In Pakistan, the term 'feudal' denotes the owners of large landed estates who consolidated their power under colonial rule and continue to dominate the political life of the country.
10. Also known as Ahl-e-Sunnat, disciple of Ahmed Raza Khan (died in 1921), originally from Bareilly. The Barelvi movement embodies the Sufi traditions of the subcontinent. Barelvis are particularly devoted to the Prophet Mohammed and believe in the intercession of saints and martyrs.
11. Muslims who left India in 1947 and settled in Pakistan.
12. The Sheikh caste is composed of alleged descendents of the Qureshi Arab clans, and therefore occupies a high position in the subcontinent's Muslim caste hierarchy. In reality, most of its members are Hindu converts.

13. For details on Jhang and the SSP's exploitation of local rivalries, see Mariam Abou Zahab (2004).
14. A relatively high turnout for elections in Pakistan.
15. All assassinated SSP leaders are buried within the walls of this seminary.
16. Mohammad Amir Rana (2004).
17. The non-irrigated areas from which the army has been drawing recruits since the colonial era.
18. A dissident faction of the MQM created in 1992 with the support of the intelligence agencies.
19. The Iranian consul in Lahore assassinated in December 1990.
20. Hassan Abbas (2005), p. 207.
21. Maulana Fazlur Rehman was appointed president of the Parliamentary Foreign Affairs Commission by Benazir Bhutto.
22. S. Vali Reza Nasr (2002).
23. Police officers who were also SSP members participated in attacks against Shias in Karachi. One of them was killed in May 2004 in a suicide attack on a Shia mosque.
24. The fact that the SSP has never called for a detailed investigation or the conviction of those responsible tends to support this theory.

6. SALAFISM IN PAKISTAN: THE AHL-E HADITH MOVEMENT

1. Bernard Haykel, *Revival and Reform in Islam: The Legacy of Muhammad al-Shawkani* (Cambridge: Cambridge University Press, 2003).
2. The family was originally Sunni and converted to Shiism like many at the Awadh court.
3. Dietrich Reetz, *Islam in the Public Sphere: Religious Groups in India 1900–1947* (Delhi: Oxford University Press, 2006), p. 88.
4. For details on the Ahl-e Hadith, see Barbara D. Metcalf, *Islamic Revival in British India: Deoband, 1860–1900* (Princeton: Princeton University Press, 1982/Karachi: Royal Book Company, 1989), pp. 268–96.
5. See Reetz, *Islam in the Public Sphere*, Appendix 1 'Articles of Faith of the Ahl-e Hadith', pp. 323–6.
6. Ibid., p. 92.
7. Ibid., See also Yoginder Sikand, 'Islamist Militancy in Kashmir: the Case of Lashkar-i Tayyeba', *Qalandar*, webmagazine October 2005, www.islaminterfaith.org
8. Reetz, *Islam in the Public Sphere*, p. 100.
9. Some of them call Pakistan *Shirkistan*!
10. Abdul Qadir Gilani is commemorated on 11 Rabi' al-Thani and food is prepared in his name. *Giyarwin sharif* literally means the 'Sacred

Eleventh' [of the lunar month], the celebration of the urs (death anniversary) of Abdul Qadir Gilani on 11 Rabi'ul Thani. In Punjab it is celebrated not only once a year but food is distributed in Abdul Qadir's name on the eleventh of every month.

11. Metcalf, *Islamic Revival in British India*, p. 275.
12. Reetz, *Islam in the Public Sphere*, p. 92.
13. The first sura of the Qur'an recited at every religious occasion and particularly for the benefit of a deceased person.
14. Reetz, *Islam in the Public Sphere*, p. 73.
15. Ibid.
16. Ibid., p. 74.
17. The Jamaat-e Islami supported Saddam Hussain.
18. Khaled Ahmed, 'The power of the Ahl-e Hadith', *The Friday Times*, Lahore, 12–18 July 2002.
19. Born in 1945 in Sialkot in the Sheikh Sethi trading community, Ehsan Elahi Zaheer studied in Salafi madrasas in Gujranwala and Faisalabad before leaving to study from 1963 to 1965 at the University of Medina. After graduating, he returned to Pakistan and received MAs in Arabic, Islamic studies, Urdu and Persian. While in Saudi Arabia, he was taught by Shaykh al-Albani and Shaykh Ibn Baz, among others. He travelled extensively around the world for *da'wa* purposes and wrote many books, most of them refutations of Shias, Sufis, Barelwis, Ahmadis, Isma'ilis and Baha'is. In 1980 he wrote a book entitled *Shias and Shiism*, which denounces Shia Islam as heresy and accuses the Shias of being Zionist agents in Islamic countries. This book, translated into Arabic and English, was widely distributed by the Saudi Government. Ehsan Elahi Zaheer died in March 1987 after a bomb explosion inside a mosque in Lahore perpetrated by Shia militants. Wounded, he was taken to Saudi Arabia on the order of King Fahd, who sent his private plane. He died in Medina and Shaykh Ibn Baz led his funeral prayers. The assassination of Ehsan Elahi Zaheer marked the start of sectarian violence in Pakistan.
20. For details, see Muhammad Amir Rana, *Jihad-e Kashmir-o-Afghanistan: Jihadi Tanzimon aur Mazhabi Jamaaton ka ek Jaiza* (Lahore: Mashaal Books, 2002), pp. 222–31.
21. The Markaz Jamiat Ahl-e Hadith UK, whose headquarters is at the Green Lane mosque in Birmingham, has been a registered charity since 1976. It controls 41 mosques and madrasas in the UK.
22. Abdul Sattar Khan, '88 seminaries teaching more than 16,000 students', *The News*, 6 July 2007. In 2007, Islamabad had two Ahl-e Hadith madrasas with about 200 students.
23. The number of students in Deobandi madrasas is estimated at 200,000; around 190,000 students are studying in Barelvi madrasas.

24. They share this emphasis on Hadith with the Deobandi madrasas.

25. For the Ahl-e Hadith, there is no harm in learning English as long as one does not adopt Western culture and decadence.

26. See Muhammad Amir Rana, *Jihad-e Kashmir-o-Afghanistan*, pp. 213–68.

27. For details, see Mariam Abou Zahab "'I Shall Be Waiting for You at the Door of Paradise": the Pakistani Martyrs of the Lashkar-e Taiba (Army of the Pure)', in *The Practice of War: The Production, Reproduction and Communication of Armed Violence*, Aparna Rao, Monika Böck, Michael Bolling (eds), (Oxford/NewYork: Berghahn Books, 2007). See also Mariam Abou Zahab & Olivier Roy, *Islamist Networks: The Afghan-Pakistan Connection* (London: Hurst, 2004), pp. 32–46.

28. Hafiz Saeed, who migrated with his family to Pakistani Punjab in 1947, studied at the King Saud University in Saudi Arabia from 1978 to 1980. After returning from Saudi Arabia, he joined the Abdul Rasul Sayyaf Salafi group and participated in the Afghan jihad.

29. See Muhammad Amir Rana, *Jihad-e Kashmir-o-Afghanistan*, pp. 235–58.

30. Hafiz Saeed. Interview in *Takbir* (Karachi), 12 August 1999, pp. 37 ff.

31. 'Today is the era of jihad [...] Only jihad can teach a lesson to *kufr*,' is a sermon of Amir Hamza in Masjid al Aqsa, Rawalpindi, given on 11 August 2006. 'The best way to protect the honour of the Holy Prophet is jihad [...] If the Muslims did not wage jihad against the West today, they will regret it tomorrow' is a quote from a speech of Hafiz Saeed addressing a rally in Rawalpindi, *Ghazwa*, 29 June 2006.

32. This is a recurrent theme in Lashkar-e Taiba literature and in the martyrs' testaments. The Lashkar-e Taiba justified jihad against the Americans in Iraq because Iraqi Muslim women were raped in Abu Ghraib, adding 'the Americans are dishonouring our mothers and sisters. Therefore, *jihad* against them has now become mandatory'. Quoted by Daniel Benjamin and Gabriel Weimann, 'What the Terrorists Have in Mind', *The New York Times*, 27 October 2004.

33. Sermon in Masjid-e Qudsia, Lahore, quoted by Praveen Swami, 'From Faith to Hate', *Frontline*, 14–27 July 2007.

34. See Muhammad Amir Rana, *Jihad-e Kashmir-o-Afghanistan*, p. 242.

35. *Ghazwa*, 7 April 2005.

36. For details, see Abou Zahab, "'I Shall Be Waiting for You at the Door of Paradis": The Pakistani Martyrs of the Lashkar-e Taiba (Army of the Pure)'.

37. The Kunar province of Afghanistan, bordering the Bajaur Agency in Pakistan, had for a long time been a stronghold of the Ahl-e Hadith school of thought. In 1985 Maulana Jamil ul Rahman, educated in the Panjpir madrasa in Swabi, formed a strict Salafi party, the Jamaat ul Da'wa ilal Quran wa Ahl-e Hadith, and increasing numbers of Arabs

came to fight in its ranks. See Maulana Amir Hamza, *Qafilat da'wat-o jihad* (Lahore: Dar ul-Andalus, 2004); David Edwards, *Before Taliban: Genealogies of the Afghan Jihad* (Berkeley: University of California Press, 2002), pp. 153–6.

38. The LeT considers the MJAH no longer Salafi because it associates with non-Salafis.
39. See Mohammad Amir Rana, *Jihad-e Kashmir-o-Afghanistan*, pp. 214–16.
40. All courses are taught in Arabic and about ten students get admission in Medina every year.
41. NBC News, September 2007.
42. For details on the training, see Abou Zahab, '"I Shall Be Waiting for You at the Door of Paradise": The Pakistani Martyrs of the Lashkar-e Taiba (Army of the Pure)'.
43. Mohammad Amir Rana, 'Jammatud Dawa has no Global Network or Ambitions: Mujahid', *The Daily Times*, 25 May 2004.
44. Mian Muhammad 'Asif, in charge of public relations for the Jamaat ul Da'wa Peshawar zone, in *The Daily Times*, 18 November 2003.
45. 'It helps to negate the negative propaganda against us', Amir Hamza, Arif Jamal, 'Invitation of Another Kind', *The News*, 2005 (exact date unknown).
46. Interview with Hafiz Saeed, 24 October 2005. http://in.rediff.com/news/2005/oct/24inter1.htm
47. 'Foreign NGOs Weakening People's Faith: Hafiz Saeed', *Daily Times*, 2 May 2004.
48. Arif Jamal, 'The Message Spreads', *The News*, 10 August 2003.
49. Zafar Iqbal, an Arain, accused Hafiz Saeed, a Gujjar, of promoting Gujjars. It is ironic to see a Salafi organisation succumb to the virus of the Hindu caste system! In July 2004 Zafar Iqbal created Khair un Nas, a breakaway faction for which he tried to get support from Saudi ulama.
50. 'The Lal Masjid talks about Shari'a, therefore we support it', in a sermon of Hafiz Saeed, Rawalpindi, 27 April 2007.
51. 'Dawa Distances Itself from Lal Masjid Management', *Dawn*, 17 July 2007.
52. Sermon in Masjid-e Qudsia, Lahore, 17 August 2007.

7. *KASHARS* AGAINST *MASHARS*: JIHAD AND SOCIAL CHANGE IN THE FATA

1. I am indebted to the editors and to Hugh Beattie for their comments and advice on an earlier draft of this chapter.
2. 'There is evidence that junior, or depressed, lineages saw employment abroad and the economic opportunities at home as an avenue of escape

from their positions in society': Akbar S. Ahmad, *Resistance and Control in Pakistan* (Cambridge: Cambridge University Press, 1991), p. 97.

3. For instance, in 2010 there were about 350,000 Pakistani Pashtuns in Dubai alone, more than half of them from the FATA.

4. For an analysis of social change among Pashtuns, see Inam ur Rahim and Alain Viaro, *Swat: An Afghan Society in Pakistan: Urbanisation and Change in a Tribal Environment* (Karachi: City Press, 2002). Although the local dynamics in Swat and Waziristan are very different, similar trends can be observed in the transformation of society since the mid-1970s.

5. 'From the regime of General Zia ul Haq onward, the state started to fund the mullas directly, giving them financial independence. Over the years the mullas took on an enhanced political role in the tribal community and gradually became more powerful than the malik. With new resources and status, the local religious figures were able to emerge.' Marvin G. Weinbaum, 'Counterterrorism, Regional Security, and Pakistan's Afghan Frontier', Testimony to the U.S. House of Representatives Armed Services Committee, Washington DC, 10 October 2007.

6. This paper draws from my research in the region since the 1980s, from interviews with residents from Waziristan and from written material on the FATA. Owing to the inaccessibility of the field since the start of military operations, interviews took place in other parts of Pakistan as well as in Europe and the USA.

7. In South Waziristan this refers to Suleimankhel and Dotani.

8. A *mashar* has influence and command over the tribe and is member of the *jirga*. Although generally speaking *mashar* connotes *spin giray* (white beard), a *mashar* may be young.

9. *Traditional Structures in Local Governance for Local Development: A Case Study of Pakhtuns Residing in NWFP & FATA, Pakistan* (World Bank, 2004).

10. The misuse of the Afghanistan Transit Trade (ATT) by the tribals and Afghan traders created a new class of businessmen in the FATA. Moreover, from the 1980s transport became a major source of income for the tribals.

11. The Wazir resisted the demarcation of the Durand Line in 1893, which brought Waziristan, with the exception of Birmal, under the British sphere of influence. A *lashkar* led by the famous Mulla Powindah, a Shabikhel Mehsud who assumed the title of Badshah-e Taliban, attacked the British army camp in Wana. A punitive operation was launched and in 1895 Political Agents were posted to Miranshah and Wana; North Waziristan and South Waziristan were thus constituted.

12. J.M. Ewart, *Story of the North West Frontier Province* (Lahore: Sang-e-Meel, 2000) [reprint of the 1929 edition], p. 53.

13. For details about the FATA reform plan and the role of the Political Agent and the law enforcement system, see Pervaiz Iqbal Cheema and Maqsudul Hasan Nuri (eds), *Tribal Areas of Pakistan: Challenges and Responses* (Islamabad: Policy Research Institute/Hanns Seidel Foundation, 2005).

14. The beneficiaries were mostly the children of the *maliks* who are settled in cities outside the FATA.

15. Pashtuns started migrating in great numbers to the Gulf from the mid-1970s.

16. Before 1996, a college of about 35,000 *maliks* and other tribal elders would cast their votes on behalf of the population.

17. Cheema and Noori, *Tribal Areas of Pakistan*.

18. See, 'Pakistan: Countering Militancy in the FATA', International Crisis Group, 21 October 2009.

19. The Frontier Crimes Regulation was promulgated in 1901 by the colonial administration. For a detailed study of the FCR, see Khalid Aziz, *The Reform of the Frontier Crimes Regulations (FCR) and Administration of the Tribal Areas of Pakistan*, 22 November 2005, http://www.khalidaziz. com/art_detail.php?aid=51

20. For detailed statistics on the FATA, see http://www.nwfpbos.sdnpk. org/fds/2000/6.htm; Official estimations for 2002 gave a figure of 401,000 for North Waziristan and 467,000 for South Waziristan.

21. 'Over 100, 000 uprooted by military operations in Waziristan: UN', *The News*, 12 September 2009.

22. Apart from the conflicts with the local population (particularly in Karachi and Dera Ismail Khan), urbanisation is a disorienting process. Many tribals who took shelter in the settled areas or in Karachi will probably never go back to South Waziristan, particularly because there is no compensation process for the people who suffered 'collateral damage'. They risk lapsing into chronic poverty and their sense of deprivation is likely to increase.

23. Kaniguram suffered large-scale destruction during the military operations in 2009. There is a real risk that the language (Urmuri) and the culture of the displaced Burki will disappear as their children will speak only Pashto.

24. The Wazir and Mehsud claim to have originated from a common ancestor: Wazir son of Suleiman who had three sons, Musa, Mubarik and Mahmud. Musa, known as Darwesh because of his religious piety, is the ancestor of the Wazir and Mahmud of the Mehsud. For years, the Mehsud were a Wazir sub-tribe and they were sometimes referred to as the Wazir Mehsud in colonial literature.

25. Just like the Mehsud, the Zalikhel are famous for their resistance

against the British. They were instrumental in Nadir Shah's success in capturing Kabul in 1929, they were used to crush a rebellion in Kohistan in 1930, and they laid siege to Khost in 1933 when the partisans of Amanullah wanted to use them to get rid of Nadir. The monthly stipends they received from Kabul government were stopped after 1992 and restored by President Karzai in 2006. Iqbal Khattak, 'Karzai restores monthly stipend to FATA elders', *Daily Times*, 26 September 2006. Wazir and Mehsud were part of a tribal *laskhar* which entered Kashmir in 1948; the memory of jihad in Kashmir is very strong among them, and they are also proud of their support to the Pakistan military in the 1965 war with India.

26. According to the 1981 census, the Mehsud numbered 234,000 and the Wazir 61,000.

27. Mehsud are settled in East and Central Waziristan and Wazir in West and South. Wana has a Wazir majority.

28. When the Hindu traders left Tank after Partition in 1947, most of their shops were taken over by Mehsud.

29. F.W. Johnston, 'Notes on Wana (Recorded in 1903' in Robert Nichols (ed.), *Colonial Reports on Pakistan's Frontier Tribal Areas* (Karachi: Oxford University Press, 2005).

30. *Report on Waziristan and its Tribes* (Lahore: Sang-e Meel Publications, 2005) [reprint of the 1901 edition].

31. *Nikat* derives from *nika* (grandfather). It takes the meaning of hereditary rights and obligations. The *nikat*, which is not based on current population figures, appears unfair to the Wazir. *Nikat* had been in existence for quite a long time and the colonial administration had to take it into account. Akbar Ahmed refers to it as 'an inviolable law of tribal division' (*Resistance and Control in Pakistan*, p. 18).

32. Iqbal Khattak, 'Wazir tribesmen want independent agency', *The Friday Times*, 17–23 October 2003.

33. Iqbal Khattak, 'Wazir elder demands proportionate council seats', *Daily Times*, 5 December 2004.

34. Akbar S. Ahmed, *Pakistan Society: Islam, Ethnicity and Leadership in South Asia* (Karachi: Oxford University Press, 1986), p. 77.

35. He also opened a private school for girls in Wana bazaar.

36. Hafizullah Wazir, 'Ex-MNA among 26 killed in Wana blast', *Daily Times*, 24 August 2010; Iqbal Khattak, 'South Waziristan tense after cleric's killing', *Daily Times*, 25 August 2010.

37. Irfan Ghauri, 'Adult franchise system in FATA put clerics in Parliament: ISPR DG', *Daily Times*, 27 July 2006. Eight MNAs were elected, seven of them for the first time. Maulana Noor Mohammad was elected in South Waziristan.

38. In the 1973 Constitution, about 37,000 *maliks* were entitled to vote and elected members of the National Assembly.

39. For details about the JUI-F connection in Waziristan, see Khalid Aziz, *Causes of Rebellion in Waziristan* (Peshawar: RIPORT, 22 February 2007).

40. For an interesting profile of Nek Mohammad, see Tanvir Qaisar Shahid and Naim Mustafa, 'Nek Mohammad kaun tha? [Who was Nek Muhammad?],' *Pakistan*, 19 June 2004, and Mohammad Ilyas Khan, 'Nek Muhammad Wazir', *The Herald Monthly*, June 2004.

41. Local conflicts were played out in the context of army operations. The tribes made alliances of opportunity with the government or with the militants in order to gain advantage in local conflicts. In Pashtun society, 'duality structures all relationships. Betrayal is always a threat and alliances can shift, one is never defeated, except by death. While allied, Pashtuns are reliable until the point at which it is in their advantage in local disputes to no longer be reliable'. Haroon Akram Lodhi, 'Attacking the Pakhtuns', *The Global Site*, October 2001.

42. Maqbool Wazir, *Waziristan Chronology*. www.waziristanhills.com

43. It was perceived as a war against the Wazir. The Mehsud stayed neutral.

44. Nek Mohammad, Baitullah Mehsud and Maulvi Nazir are the archetype of *kashars* challenging the tribal system of power from below.

45. The army presence in Waziristan was described as a violation of the *purdah* of Pashtun territory. Invading tribal space is considered as penetrating private space and is an affront to tribal honour.

46. A third peace deal was signed in September 2006 in North Waziristan.

47. In June 2006, Sirajuddin Haqqani issued a decree that it was no longer Taliban policy to fight the Pakistan army. This marked the end of significant fighting in South Waziristan. Maqbool Wazir, *Waziristan Chronology*.

48. Ahmedzai Wazir, belonging to the Zalikhel clan, was born in Birmal (Paktika) in 1975; Mullah Nazir studied in a madrasa in Wana and joined the Afghan Taliban from 1996. He came back to Pakistan after the fall of the Taliban and fought the Pakistani military until he surrendered in 2004. He was appointed emir of the Taliban's Wazir faction in South Waziristan in 2006, and joined forces with the Pakistani military in March 2007 to defeat the Uzbeks. He refused to join the TTP and has been maintaining an ambiguous position playing both sides since 2008. Chris Harnisch, 'Question Mark of South Waziristan: Biography and Analysis of Maulvi Nazir Ahmad', *Critical Threats*, 17 July 2009.

49. Iqbal Khattak, 'Maulvi Nazir decides to stay neutral', *Daily Times*, 19 October 2009.

50. Iqbal Khattak, 'Mehsud unhappy over construction of Wana-Tank road',

Daily Times, 2 March 2010. There are two roads going from Wana to Jandola: one through Mehsud territory which was paved a long time ago, and the other going through the Gomal Zam dam area and bypassing Mehsud territory. Construction work is also underway on a Tank-Makeen road in Mehsud area.

51. 'Army close to winding up first phase of operation', *Dawn*, 5 November 2009.

52. Personal communication, October 2009. See also 'Army working towards development of S.Waziristan', AFP, 8 July 2010.

53. Weapons were not surrendered but 'offered'. The militants presented gifts—an old sword, Waziri daggers, prayer mats, *miswak* (toothbrush made of wood) and *tasbeeh* (prayer beads)—to the Corps commander and the civil and military officials accompanying him.

54. Iqbal Khattak, 'I did not surrender to the military, says Nek Mohammad', *The Friday Times*, 30 April—6 May 2004.

55. Nek Muhammad promised not to fight the army or harbour foreigners, in return for amnesty. He claimed later that no promise to deliver the foreigners to the government had been made (which is consistent with Pashtun values). The deal broke down and Nek Muhammad was killed in a drone attack in June 2004.

56. *Riwaj* is a body of social customs which has over time become the prevailing law. While Pashtunwali is universal, practices dictated by *riwaj* vary from tribe to tribe and from place to place. Abiding by *riwaj* is considered obligatory. There is a clash between *riwaj* and sharia in many matters, particularly concerning women; the sharia gives more rights to women than *riwaj*, Pashtuns generally give precedence to *riwaj* over the sharia which is more an ideal of social justice.

57. Some even claim that the 'most aggressive sons of *malik*s who have been killed' can be trained to take over and restore the old system.

58. For example, the aim of the Report of the President's Task Force on Tribal Reform submitted in April 2006 was the revival of the authority of the Political Agent.

59. Sartaj Khan, 'Changing Pashtun society', *The News*, 14 January 2010.

60. This is a reinvention of the *lashkar* which traditionally was not backed and armed by the state.

61. Good examples are the Salarzai *lashkar* in Bajaur and the Shinwari and Mullagori *lashkar*s in Khyber.

62. Repatriation of displaced Mehsud families was announced from July 2010, but many tribals were reluctant to go back to Waziristan owing to the destruction of infrastructure and the lack of security.

63. J.M. Ewart, *Story of the North West Frontier Province*, p. 66.

8. PASHTUN AND PUNJABI TALIBAN: THE JIHADI-SECTARIAN NEXUS

1. The NWFP was renamed Khyber-Pakhtunkhwa in April 2010.
2. See Mariam Abou Zahab, 'The SSP, Herald of Sunni Militancy in Pakistan', in Laurent Gayer and Christophe Jaffrelot (eds.), *Armed Militias of South Asia: Fundamentalists, Maoists and Separatists* (London: Hurst, 2009).
3. The LeJ had a training camp at Sarobi.
4. Masood Azhar was released from an Indian jail in December 1999 after the hijacking of an Indian Airlines aircraft which landed at Kandahar.
5. The first sign that JeM was sectarian was the assassination in May 2000 of a Shia doctor by bodyguards of Masood Azhar.
6. One of the founders of the LeJ, responsible for most anti-Shia attacks, Riaz Basra joined the SSP in 1986 and was a very active member: he was even a candidate for the 1988 general elections in Lahore. Jailed for the assassination of the Iranian diplomat Sadiq Ganji in 1990, he escaped from a court in Lahore in 1994. He was critical of SSP leaders and advocated violence, eventually creating the LeJ with Akram Lahori and Malik Ishaq. Basra spent several years in Afghanistan during Taliban rule and was detained in December 2001 when re-entering Pakistan.
7. The LeJ had tried to assassinate Nawaz Sharif on 3 January 1999 by planting a bomb under a bridge on the Lahore-Raiwind road.
8. Imtiaz Gul, *The Al Qaeda Connection: The Taliban and Terror in Pakistan's Tribal Areas* (India: Penguin Books, 2009), pp. 158–62.
9. Particularly Deobandi madrasas in Karachi.
10. 'The Growth of the Deobandi Jihad in Afghanistan', *Terrorism Monitor*, vol. 8 no. 2 (14 January 2010).
11. According to some sources, apart from the two main factions of the LeJ led by Basra and Qari Abdul Hay, there are at least seven small groups linked to LeJ operating in the Tribal Areas and in Karachi. One of them, the Hilal Group or Ghazi force, is focussed on revenge for Lal Masjid; another, based in Waziristan and led by Qari Hussain Mehsud, is closely linked to al-Qaeda and has been accused of providing manpower for bomb attacks in Punjab.
12. Ironically, Chief Justice Iftikhar Chaudhry played a role in validating his election, see 'Disqualification of Azam Tariq Sought', *Dawn*, 19 November 2002.
13. Mohammad Amir Rana, 'Enemy of the State—Lashkar-e-Jhangvi and Militancy in Pakistan', *Jane's Intelligence Review*, 31 July 2009.

14. Riaz Basra was killed two days before the recovery of Daniel Pearl's body. His death coincided with a new version of events issued by the Karachi police about the involvement of LeJ in Pearl's murder, which was actually a case of cooperation among members of several Deobandi groups.
15. Arif Jamal, 'A Profile of Pakistan's Lashkar-i-Jhangvi', *CTC Sentinel*, vol. 2 no. 9 (September 2009).
16. General Musharraf did not ban HUJI, which had supporters in the Armed Forces, notably in the Air Force.
17. Ayesha Siddiqa, 'The Two Faces of Jihad', *Newsline Monthly*, September 2009.
18. Mushtaq Yusufzai, 'Letter Explains Drive Against Foreign Militants in Waziristan', *The News*, 5 April 2007.
19. Kohat and lower Kurram have long been strongholds of the SSP and JeM. Javed Ibrahim Paracha, a former PML-N member of the National Assembly for Kohat who is known for his contacts with the Taliban, has declared openly that he is at war with the Shias.
20. The Bangash clans living in lower Kurram and Kohat are all Sunnis. All the Bangash of upper Kurram are Shias, while other Bangash clans are Shias, Sunnis or a mix of both.
21. For details, see Mariam Abou Zahab, 'Sectarianism in Pakistan's Kurram Tribal Agency' and Imtiaz Ali, 'Shiite-Sunni Strife Paralyzes Life in Pakistan's Kurram Tribal Agency', in Hassan Abbas (ed.), *Pakistan's Troubled Frontier* (The Jamestown Foundation, 2009).
22. Karachi, *Dawn*, 19 November 2007; *The Frontier Post*, Peshawar, 31 December 2007.
23. Abou Zahab, 'The SSP', note 1.
24. *Pak Tribune*, 20 May 2007.
25. 'Defining the Punjabi Taliban Network', *CTC Sentinel*, vol. 2 no. 4 (April 2009).
26. Amir Mir, 'Punjabis Here, Pushtuns There, Taliban Everywhere', *Middle East Transparent*, 25 October 2009.
27. Mukhtar A. Khan, 'A Profile of the TTP's New Leader: Hakimullah Mehsud', *CTC Sentinel*, vol. 2 no. 10 (October 2009).
28. *Dawn*, 26 September 2008.
29. Darra Adam Khel has long been considered a hub of criminals and is the largest illegal arms and munitions market of the region.
30. *Daily Times*, 29 January 2008.
31. The road was re-opened a couple of times for a few weeks, but it was closed again due to attacks on travellers. For instance, in March 2010 a convoy of civilians escorted by security forces was attacked in Kurram, with fourteen people killed and twenty-five injured; six Shia

truck drivers returning from delivering food items in upper Kurram were also kidnapped and killed.

32. *Dawn*, 6 September 2008.
33. *Dawn*, 24 May 2009.
34. *Herald Monthly*, October 2008.
35. *The News*, 13 June 2009.
36. Matt Wade, 'An unholy trinity', *The Age* (Australia), 21 October 2009.
37. Siddiqa, 'The Two Faces of Jihad'.
38. The attack perpetrated in August 2009 against Christians in Gojra (Punjab) was attributed to the SSP.
39. In March 2010 SSP militants attacked an Id Milad procession in Faisalabad. Although notice had been given of the planned attack, the police did nothing to prevent it. A mob subsequently burned the house of Zahid Qasmi, an SSP leader, and attacked a police station.
40. Baqir Sajjad Syed, 'Top Guns of Punjabi Taliban Captured', *Dawn*, 23 October 2009.
41. Imtiaz Ali, 'Karachi Becoming a Taliban Safe Haven?', *CTC Sentinel*, vol. 3 no. 1 (January 2010).
42. The PML-N candidate, Azam Chela, was elected with the support of the SSP.
43. Shafiq Awan, 'The Cost of Jhang By-Poll', *Daily Times*, 10 March 2010.
44. 'Punjabi Taliban Threat Growing', *The Washington Times*, 21 October 2009.

9. 'IT'S JUST A SUNNI-SHIA THING': SECTARIANISM AND TALIBANISM IN THE FATA (FEDERALLY ADMINISTERED TRIBAL AREAS) OF PAKISTAN

1. The seven tribal agencies which constitute FATA cover some 27,500 square kilometers on the border between Pakistan and Afghanistan and are home to over 3.5 million Pashtun tribesmen and at least 1 million Afghan refugees. After 1947, the Pakistani government continued to follow the policy of the colonial rulers towards the tribal areas and maintained the autonomous status of the FATA. The tribal areas fall under the control of the federal government through the Political Agent. Universal adult franchise was introduced in 1996 but political parties are not allowed to function. This means that elections do not involve political parties and that candidates run as independents even if everyone knows which party they support. For details see Pervaiz Iqbal Cheema and Maqsudul Hasan Nuri (eds), *Tribal Areas of Pakistan: Challenges and Responses* (Islamabad: Islamabad Policy Research Institute/ Hanss Seidel Foundation, 2005).

2. The reformist school of thought associated with the madrasa founded in Deoband in 1867.

3. Ismailis and Barelvis (the Barelvi movement embodies the Sufi tradition of the subcontinent) were not targeted until recently.

4. See Mariam Abou Zahab, 'Sectarianism as a Substitute Identity: Sunnis and Shias in Central and South Punjab' in S. Mumtaz, J-L. Racine, I. Ali (eds), *Pakistan. The Contours of State and Society* (Karachi: Oxford University Press, 2002), pp. 77–95; Mohammad Qasim Zaman, 'Sectarianism in Pakistan', *Modern Asian Studies*, 32/3, 1998, pp. 687–716.

5. This was the first drone attack in Kurram. It targeted the former Afghan refugee camp of Surkh Pul, 18 km south of Sadda, which had become a Taliban base after the refugees left for Afghanistan.

6. An umbrella group of around forty Pakistani Taliban groups active in the FATA created in December 2007 under the leadership of Baitullah Mehsud.

7. The name of the North West Frontier Province was changed into Khyber-Pakhtunkhwa in April 2010.

8. The six main Sunnite tribes in Kurram are Bangash, Mangal, Para Chamkani, Zaidashat, Alisherzai and Maqbal.

9. Teepu Mahabat Khan, *The Tribal Areas of Pakistan: A Contemporary Profile* (Lahore: Sang-e Meel Publications, 2008).

10. The Turi of Kurram began paying revenues to the Afghan state in 1850 when a governor was appointed by Kabul. Christine Noelle, *State and Tribe in Nineteenth-Century Afghanistan* (London: Curzon, 1997).

11. 'The district of Kurram, from Thall to the crest of the Shutargardan Pass, [...] will remain under the protection and control of the British government.'

12. Shia places of worship are called *imambargah* (or *imambarah*) in South Asia.

13. A training camp (Muaskar Sadda) run by Abdul Rab Rasul Sayyaf and the Ittihad-e Islami (a Salafi group) was established in Sadda in the 1980s next to a large Afghan refugee camp.

14. Council of elders.

15. *Dawn*, Karachi, 19 November 2007.

16. *Daily Times*, Lahore, 11 November 2007.

17. *The News*, Islamabad, 30 July 2000.

18. *Gulf Times*, 7 September 2005.

19. *The News*, 19 September 2008.

20. *Dawn*, 9 April 2007.

21. *The News*, 6 April 2008.

22. Mansur Khan Mahsud, *The Battle for Pakistan. Militancy and Conflict in Kurram* (New America Foundation, 2010); *Dawn*, 7 April 2007.

23. Particularly Bahawalpur: Dar ul Ulum Madania (the director is Sohaib Ahmed, Rashid Rauf's brother-in-law, graduated from Deoband), Jamia Siddiqia, Jamia Farooq-e Azam.

24. Criminal groups use the Taliban name or label to carry out their activities in total impunity.

25. *Pak Tribune*, 20 May 2007.

26. *Frontier Post*, 27 December 2007.

27. After the peace agreements between the Pakistani government and the Waziristani Taliban in 2005 and 2006, the militants wanted to use routes through Kurram for cross-border infiltration into Afghanistan, which the Shias of Kurram refused.

28. Qari Hussain Mehsud, the trainer of suicide bombers, claimed to be born in South Waziristan around 1988, joined the SSP/Lashkar-e Jhangvi when he was studying in a Deobandi madrasa in Karachi. He was killed in a drone attack in October 2010.

29. *Daily Times*, 2 January 2008.

30. *Daily Times*, 18 February 2008.

31. Mansur Khan Mahsud, op. cit.

32. *Dawn*, 26 September 2008.

33. *The News*, 15 February 2009. Afridis from Kohat and Dara Adam Khel migrated to Kurram to engage in anti-Shia violence, under the command of Tariq Afridi, the head of the TTP in Dara Adam Khel, who has close links with the SSP.

34. *Dawn*, 6 September 2008.

35. Mansur Khan Mahsud, op. cit.

36. *Dawn*, 2 September 2008.

37. *The News*, 7 December 2008; 17 December 2008.

38. *The News*, 9 April 2009.

39. Jane Perlez and Pir Zubair Shah, 'Power Rising: Taliban Besiege Pakistani Shiites', *The New York Times*, 26 July 2008.

40. This 89 km stretch of road is the only link between Parachinar and Kohat. Zulfiqar Ali, 'NATO starts mediation between rival Kurram factions', *Dawn*, 27 May 2009.

41. *Dawn*, 24 May 2009.

42. *Dawn*, 26 September 2008.

43. *Dawn*, 1 July 2009.

44. *Dawn*, 27 March 2010.

45. *Dawn*, 23 March 2010.

46. *Daily Times*, 4 November 2010.

47. *The News*, 29 October 2010; *Dawn*, 21 October 2010.

48. *Daily Times*, 4 November 2010. *BBC South Asia*, 'The Pakistani tribe that is taking on the Taliban', 21 October 2010.

49. *Dawn*, 30 November 2010.

50. *The Nation*, 10 November 2010; *The Long War Journal*, 22 October 2010.

51. Orakzai Agency was created in 1973. Previously it was a part of Frontier Region (FR) Kohat. The headquarter is located on Kohat-Thall road near Hangu since 1989, it was originally built in Kalaya but could not be occupied.

52. Teepu Muhabat Khan, *The Tribal Areas of Pakistan*, op. cit.

53. *Herald Monthly*, October 2008.

54. For details, see Abida Azim Afridi, *Syeds of Tirah* (Peshawar: Pakistan Study Centre, University of Peshawar, 1999).

55. Sana Haroon, *Frontier of Faith: Islam in the Indo-Afghan Borderland* (London: Hurst, 2007).

56. *Afghan News Center*, 18 January 2001.

57. *Daily Times*, 4 October 2006; *Pak Tribune*, 6 October 2006; *Dawn*, 7 October 2006.

58. *The News*, 10 March 2009; *Dawn*, 6 January 2010, 'Militants blow up six shrines in Orakzai'.

59. *The News*, 13 June 2009.

60. Sikhs and Hindus who had been living in Orakzai as *hamsaya* for a long time and never faced harassment have also been forced to pay *jizya* or to convert. Many of them have moved to Peshawar to save their lives; at least one Sikh was beheaded in 2009 after he had been kidnapped for ransom. *Dawn*, 3 May 2009.

61. *The News*, 11 February 2009.

62. *Dawn*, 21 April 2009.

63. At least 23,000 people had been displaced from Orakzai Agency in early 2010.

64. *Daily Times*, 9 December 2010.

65. *Reuters*, 5 December 2008.

66. Hangu has long been a very sensitive area. In 2005, a suicide bomber attacked an Ashura procession in Hangu. Forty people were killed, a curfew was imposed for four months and Hangu bazaar was torched.

67. *The News*, 21 February 2009.

68. *Dawn*, 8 October 2008.

69. The commander of the troops in Kurram said: 'I am 200 per cent sure we cleared the militants'. 'Fear belies Pakistan's boasts of becalmed borderlands', *Reuters*, 8 July 2010.

70. *The News*, 2 September, 2008.

10. CONNECTIONS AND DYNAMICS

1. Youths of Algerian and Moroccan origin settled in France murdered Spanish tourists in the reception area of a hotel in Marrakesh.

2. For further details see J.-L. Racine, *Cachemire: Au péril de la guerre* (Paris: Autrement, 2002).

3. Cf. the responsibility claimed by the two movements for attacks after 11 September.

4. A post he had held since 1994 and still occupied in 2001.

5. Julie Stirrs (formerly of the Intelligence and Research Department of the US State Department), 'The Taliban's International Ambitions', *Middle East Quarterly*, summer 2001.

6. According to a renegade, Al Fadl, see the *New York Times*, 21 February 2001.

7. Josh Meyer, 'Terrorist says plans didn't end …', *Los Angeles Times*, 4 July 2001.

8. There is often strong criticism of Bakri even in Islamist circles, accusing him of revealing the names of combatants who have gone to Afghanistan.

SELECT BIBLIOGRAPHY

Abbas, Hassan, *Pakistan's Drift into Extremism* (New York: Sharpe, 2005).

Abou Zahab, Mariam, 'The Politicization of the Shia Community in Pakistan in the 1970s and 1980s' in Silvia Naef and Farian Sahabi (eds), *The Other Shiites, From the Mediterranean to Central Asia* (Berne/New York: Peter Lang, 2007), pp. 97–112.

————, 'The Sunni-Shia Conflict in Jhang (Pakistan)' in Imtiaz Ahmed and Helmut Reifeld (eds.), *Lived Islam in South Asia* (Delhi: Social Science Press, 2004), pp. 135–48.

————, '"I Shall Be Waiting for You at the Door of Paradise": the Pakistani Martyrs of the Lashkar-e Taiba (Army of the Pure)', in *The Practice of War: The Production, Reproduction and Communication of Armed Violence*, Aparna Rao, Monika Böck, Michael Bolling (eds), (Oxford/New York: Berghahn Books, 2007).

Abou Zahab, Mariam & Olivier Roy, *Islamist Networks: The Afghan-Pakistan Connection* (London: Hurst, 2004).

————. 'The Regional Dimension of Sectarian Conflicts in Pakistan' in Christophe Jaffrelot (Ed.), *Pakistan: Nationalism without a Nation?* (Delhi: Manohar, 2002), pp. 115–28.

————. 'Sectarianism as a Substitute Identity: Sunnis and Shias in Central and South Punjab in Pakistan' in Sofia Mumtaz, Jean-Luc Racine and Imran Anwar Ali (Eds), *Pakistan: The Contours of State and Society* (Karachi: Oxford University Press, 2002), pp. 77–95.

Ali, Mukhtar Ahmad, 'Sectarian Conflict in Pakistan: A Case Study of Jhang', Regional Centre for Strategic Studies, Colombo, June 1999.

Amir Rana, Mohammad, *Jihad Kashmir wa Afghanistan. Jihadi Tanzimon aur Mazhabi Jamaaton ka ek Jaiza* (Urdu) [An A to Z of Jihadi Organisations in Pakistan] (Lahore: Mashal, 2004).

Benjamin, Daniel, and Weimann, Gabriel, 'What the Terrorists Have in Mind', *The New York Times*, 27 October 2004.

Edwards, David, *Before Taliban: Genealogies of the Afghan Jihad* (Berkeley: University of California Press, 2002).

Friedman, Yohanan, *Prophecy Continuous. Aspects of Ahmadi Religious Thoughts and its Medieval Background* (Berkeley: University of California Press, 1989).

Hamza, Maulana Amir, *Qafilat da'wat-o jihad* (Lahore: Dar al-Andalus, 2004).

Hamza, Amir, and Jamal, Arif, 'Invitation of Another Kind', *The News*, 2005.

Haykel, Bernard, *Revival and Reform in Islam: The Legacy of Muhammad al-Shawkani* (Cambridge: Cambridge University Press, 2003).

International Crisis Group, 'The State of Sectarianism in Pakistan', *Asia Report*, 95, 18 April 2005.

Iqbal, Afzal, *Islamisation in Pakistan* (Lahore: Vanguard Books, 1986).

Jamal, Arif, 'The Message Spreads', *The News*, 10 August 2003.

Kennedy, Charles, 'Islamization and Legal Reform in Pakistan, 1978–1989', *Pacific Affairs*, 63 (1), 1990, pp. 62–77.

Khan, Abdul Sattar, '88 seminaries teaching more than 16,000 students', *The News*, 6 July 2007.

Metcalf, Barbara D., *Islamic Revival in British India: Deoband, 1860–1900* (Princeton: Princeton University Press, 1982/Karachi: Royal Book Company, 1989).

Nasr, Syyed Vali Reza, 'Islam, the State and the Rise of Sectarian Militancy," in Christophe Jaffrelot (ed.), *Pakistan: Nationalism without a Nation?* (Delhi: Manohar, 2002), pp. 85–114.

Qasim Zaman, Mohammed, 'Sectarianism in Pakistan: The Radicalization of Shi'i and Sunni Identities', *Modern Asian Studies*, 32 (3), 1998, pp. 689–716.

Rana, Muhammad Amir, *Jihad-e Kashmir-o-Afghanistan: Jihadi Tanzimon aur Mazhabi Jamaaton ka ek Jaiza* (Lahore: Mashaal Books, 2002).

————, 'Jammatud Dawa has no Global Network or Ambitions: Mujahid', *The Daily Times*, 25 May 2004

Reetz, Dietrich, *Islam in the Public Sphere: Religious Groups in India 1900–1947* (Delhi: Oxford University Press, 2006).

Sikand, Yoginder, 'Islamist Militancy in Kashmir: the Case of Lashkar-i Tayyeba', *Qalandar*, webmagazine October 2005, www.islaminterfaith.org

Swami, Praveen, 'From Faith to Hate', *Frontline*, 14–27 July 2007.

Zaman, Muhammad Qasim, 'Sectarianism in Pakistan: The Radicalization of Shii and Sunni Identities', *Modern Asian Studies* 32 (3), pp. 689–716.

SELECT BIBLIOGRAPHY OF MARIAM ABOU ZAHAB'S THESIS (ENGLISH TRANSLATION)

The Jhang paradigm:

a) Le Sipah-e Sahaba Pakistan (SSP) dans le Penjab, 'Islamisation de la société ou conflit de classe?' *Cahiers d'études sur la Méditerranée orientale et le monde turco-iranien (CEMOTI)*, January–June 1999, no. 27, pp. 143–157.

b) 'The Regional Dimension of Sectarian Conflicts in Pakistan' in Christophe Jaffrelot (ed.), *Pakistan: Nationalism without a Nation?* (Delhi: Manohar, 2002), pp. 115–128.

c) 'Sectarianism as a Substitute Identity: Sunnis and Shias in Central and South Punjab' in Soofia Mumtaz, Jean-Luc Racine & Imran Ali (eds), *Pakistan:The Contours of State and Society* (Karachi: Oxford University Press, 2002), pp. 77–95.

d) 'The Sunni-Shia Conflict in Jhang (Pakistan)' in Imtiaz Ahmad & Helmut Reifeld (eds), *Lived Islam in South Asia: Adaptation, Accommodation and Conflict* (Delhi: Social Science Press, 2004), pp. 135–148.

e) 'The SSP: Herald of Militant Sunni Islam in Pakistan' in L. Gayer and C. Jaffrelot (eds), *Armed Militias of South Asia* (London: Hurst, 2009), pp. 159–175.

How the Jhang paradigm applies to other cases:

The politicisation of the Shias

a) 'The politicization of the Shia Community in Pakistan in the 1970s and 1980s' in Alessandro Monsutti, Silvia Naef & Farian Sabahi (eds), *The Other Shiites: From the Mediterranean to Central Asia*), Berne / New York: Peter Lang, 2007) pp. 97–112.

b) 'Yeh matam kayse ruk jae? (How could this matam ever cease?): Muharram processions in Pakistani Punjab' in Knut A. Jacobsen (ed.), *South Asian religions on Display: Religious processions in South Asia and the Diaspora* (London: Routledge, 2008), pp. 104–114.

c) 'Between Pakistan and Qom: Shi'i women's madrasas and new transnational networks' in Farish Noor, Yoginder Sikand & Martin van Bruinessen (eds), *The Madrasa in Asia: Political Activism and Transnational Linkages* (Amsterdam: Amsterdam University Press, 2008), pp. 123–140.

The tribal areas

a) Nawaz, Shuja, Abou Zahab, Mariam & Hussain, Azhar, et al. *FATA—A Most Dangerous Place* (Washington DC: CSIS, 2009), pp. 90–146.

b) '"It's Just a Sunni-Shia Thing": Sectarianism and Talibanism in the FATA (Federally Administered Tribal Areas) of Pakistan.' Communication à la conférence Sunni-Shia Contemporary Relations, Brussels, 30 September–2nd October 2009. 10 pp. 159–168.

c) 'Kashars against mashars: Jihad and Social Change in the FATA'. Communication à la conférence Rethinking the Swat Pathan, London, SOAS, 11–12 June 2010. 15 pp. 169–183.

SELECT BIBLIOGRAPHY

Variations on the Jhang paradigm: Ahl-e Hadith and Lashkar-e Taiba:

a) '"I shall be waiting for you at the door of Paradise": The Pakistani Martyrs of the Lashkar-e Taiba (Army of the Pure)' in Aparna Rao, Michael Bollig, Monika Böck (eds), *The Practice of War: Production, reproduction and Communication of Armed Violence* (New York/Oxford: Berghahn, 2007), pp. 133–158.

b) 'Salafism in Pakistan: The Ahl-e Hadith Movement' in Roel Meijer (ed.), *Global Salafism: Islam's New Religious Movement* (London: Hurst, 2009), pp. 126–142.

c) 'Deobandi Groups and Ahl-e Hadith', *Islamic Affairs Analyst*, Jane's Publications, July 2009, pp. 2–4.

Afghanistan:

a) With Olivier Roy, *Islamist Networks: The Afghan-Pakistan Connection* (London: Hurst, 2004).

b) 'The Social Roots of War in Afghanistan', Communication à la conférence Civilians and Citizenship: Ethnographic and Political Economy Perspectives on Civil War in South Asia, Delhi School of Economics, February 2010.

INDEX

Note: Page numbers followed by "*n*" refer to notes.

INDEX

Ghazwa (magazine), 109
Gheith, Suleiman Abu, 165
ghost schools, survey of, 60
Gilani, Abdul Qadir, 103,
  199–200n10
Giyarwin sharif, 199–200n10
Gondalavi, Hafiz Mohammad, 104
Green Revolution, 5, 58–9
guerrilla warfare, 38
Gujarati Memon community, 178
Gul, Hamid, 168, 170, 171
Gulf War (1991), 105, 164, 172,
  174

hadith, 102
Hafas, Umar bin, 70
hafiz-e Quran, 60
al Hakim, Syed Mehdi, 193–4n10
Hamza, Abu, 165
Haqqani, Jalaluddin, 7, 24, 156
Haqqani, Sirajuddin, 156, 206n47
Harkat-i-Inqilab-e-Islami, 24
Harkat-ul-Ansar (HUA), 25, 64,
  164, 165, 173, 186n2
Harkat-ul-Jihad-i-Islami (HJI),
  24–5
Harkat-ul-Jihad-al-Islami (HUJI),
  177, 180
Harkat-ul-Mujahidin (HUM), 24,
  25, 106, 132, 152, 164, 171,
  174
Harkat-ul-Mujahidin movement,
  172
Harkat-ul-Mujahidin-al-Alami
  (HUMA), 177, 180
Hasnain Construction Company,
  76, 90
Hassan, Sheikh Abdul Ghaffar, 104
Hayat, Asad (brother of Hayat,
  Faisal Saleh), 78
Hayat, Makhdoom Faisal Saleh, 78,
  195n4

Hazaras, 141
  massacre of, 22
Hekmatyar, Gulbuddin, 18
  against Massoud, 164
  Hizb-i-Islami, 169
hifz (course), 61
Hindu nationalist movements, 97
Hindu-Muslim riots (India), 65
Hir-Ranjha (epic), 69
Hizb ul-Mujahidin (HM), 30, 38,
  169
Hizb ul-Mujahidin militants, 164–5
Hizb-i-Islami, 18, 24
Hizbullah al Alami, 180
HJI. *See* Harakat ul-Jihad-i-Islami
  (HJI)
HM. *See* Hizb-ul-Mujahidin (HM)
Hobsbawm, 6
Hood, Robin, 9
HUA. *See* Harkat-ul-Ansar (HUA)
al Huda, Bint (sister of ul Sadr,
  Ayatollah Baqr), 45
HUJI. *See* Harkat-ul-Jihad-al-Islami
  (HUJI)
HUM. *See* Harakat-ul-Mujahidin
  (HUM)
HUMA. *See* Harkat-ul-Mujahidin-
  al-Alami (HUMA)
Hureira, Abu, 34
Husain, Nazir, 104
Hussain, Abida, 83, 84, 195n4,
  197n31
Hussain, Maulana Ghulam, 71
Hussain, Maulana Syed Nazir, 102
Hussain, Mufti Jaafar, 44, 45, 46
Hussain, Mushahid, 186n6 (ch.1)
Hussain, Syed Abid, 71, 195n4
Hussain, Syeda Abida, 192n84
al-Hussaini, Allama Arif Hussain,
  46, 72, 136, 150
  assassination of, 92
Huzaifa, Abi, 34

223

INDEX

INDEX